William Garratt

Loreto, the New Nazareth and its Centenary Jubilee

With the Apostolic Letter of Pope Leo XIII. Felix Domus Nazarena

William Garratt

Loreto, the New Nazareth and its Centenary Jubilee
With the Apostolic Letter of Pope Leo XIII. Felix Domus Nazarena

ISBN/EAN: 9783743388703

Manufactured in Europe, USA, Canada, Australia, Japa

Cover: Foto ©Lupo / pixelio.de

Manufactured and distributed by brebook publishing software (www.brebook.com)

William Garratt

Loreto, the New Nazareth and its Centenary Jubilee

Loreto the New Nazareth and its Centenary Jubilee

BY

WILLIAM GARRATT M.A.

Chamberlain of the Holy House

With the Apostolic Letter of Pope Leo XIII. " Felix Domus Nazaretana "

— ✠ —

Its glorious name fills the Catholic Universe. (Pius IX.)

— ✠ —

ILLUSTRATED BY MORE THAN FIFTY ENGRAVINGS

Fifty-fifth Thousand in Five Languages

— ✿ —

LONDON AND LEAMINGTON

ART AND BOOK COMPANY

NEW YORK, CINCINNATI, CHICAGO: BENZIGER BROS.

1895

LETTER ADDRESSED TO THE AUTHOR BY
MONSIGNOR THOMAS GALLUCCI, BISHOP OF LORETO.

DOMINE COLENDISSIME,

Legenti historiam Almæ Virginis Lauretanæ Domus a te perscriptam, facile mihi patuit confertam esse rebus, decoram sententiis, et validis documentis scitissime distinctam, ut nesciam utrum in ea pulcri e sus, an doctrinæ eis, an veri intelligentia magis probanda videatur. Amplectitur enim, et ordine digerit, et sanæ critices lance perpendit documenta, quæ amplissima exstant, tum de ejus origine et conditione dum Nazareth adhuc manebat, tum de mira in Dalmaticas oras, et deinde in agrum Picenum Translatione, ubi nunc Laureti incredibili populorum frequentia colitur. Insuper eruditione haud mediocri, et accuratissima temporum et locorum descriptione, factorum veritatem ab incredulorum mendaciis et procacitate vindicat, nec silentio præterit innumeras gentium peregrinationes et gratias, quarum in summis rerum angustiis ipsæ non semel compotes fiunt, et, data occasione, illas admonet de Sodalitate Universali sub Virginis Lauretanæ nomine eo consilio rite erecta, ut non dubitent honore et veneratione prosequi prodigium his documentis innixum, quæ omnem credibilitatem sibi a Christianis repetunt, quos non deficiat, ut optime dicunt, pietas fidei. Ad hoc, ne qua huic historiæ deesset laus, accedit quædam inaffectata et perpolita dicendi ratio, quæ lectorem summopere delectat.

Quum hæc ita sint, perlibenti animo tibi gratulor, et omnia fausta felicia a Domino adprecor.

✠ THOMAS,

Episcopus Lauretanus et Recinetensis.

LAURETI,
7 Kal. Octobris, an. MDCCCLXXXIX.

(THE SAME TRANSLATED.)

MUCH ESTEEMED FRIEND,

On reading your history of the Holy House of Loreto, I saw at once that it was full of matter, abounding in good feeling, and learnedly illustrated by weighty documents, so that I hardly know whether more to admire the excellent sentiments or the learning displayed in it.

Your book brings in, arranges in order, and weighs in a spirit of sound criticism the numerous existing authorities which treat of the origin and condition of the Holy House whilst still at Nazareth, and of its wonderful translation, first to Dalmatia, and afterwards to Loreto, where it is now visited by such crowds of devout people.

Moreover, your book defends the truth against the falsehoods and sneers of unbelievers with much learning, and with very accurate historical and local knowledge. It treats also of the numerous pilgrimages which come to Loreto from various nations, and of the signal favours which have so frequently been bestowed on them under the most trying circumstances.

You take occasion to speak of the General Confraternity of Our Lady of Loreto, erected for the purpose of promoting the honour and veneration due to this great wonder of God's power—which is vouched for by proofs entirely convincing to all Christians who have anything of what is aptly called the "piety of faith."

To complete the excellence of your book, it is written in an unaffected and polished style which is very pleasing to the reader.

Allow me, therefore, to congratulate you most sincerely, and to wish you every blessing from Almighty God.

✠ *THOMAS,*
Bishop of Loreto and Recanati.

[The above translation is by a Canon of St. George's Cathedral, Southwark.]

DEDICATION

BLESSED, O "Full of Grace," is the hallowed Chamber of thy Immaculate Conception, where God infused into thy body thy spotless soul. Blessed, O "Virgin, free, through grace, from every taint of sin,"*—blessed is the Place where, at the first instant of thy being, God poured into thy soul His grace, preserving thee, by virtue of thy Son and Saviour's merits foreseen, from every stain, and giving thee a "nature" ever "beautiful and inaccessible to all pollution."† "Thou art all fair, O Mary, and there is no original stain in thee. Alleluia."

Blessed, O thou who, as Aurora, camest forth to usher in the dawn,—blessed is the Holy House of thy auspicious Birth, the august Room where holy Ann, thy mother, brought thee forth. "Thy Nativity, O Virgin Mother of God, has filled the whole world with joy. Alleluia."

Blessed, O thou at whose consent heaven rang with jubilee —blessed is the Place of that life-giving consent. Ah! blessed, O "Advocate of Eve," who "didst loose the knot of her disobedience,"‡—thrice blessed is that better Eden where "to thyself and all mankind thou didst become the cause of salvation."§ "Thou didst believe the words of Gabriel, the Archangel," and "He Whom the whole world is unable to contain, being made Man, enclosed Himself in thy Womb. Alleluia, alleluia."

O Thou who art "more glorious than the Seraphim and more honourable than the Cherubim,"‖ how can we adequately venerate

* S. Epiphanius. † S. Ephrem. ‡ St. Irenæus. § *Ibid.* ‖ Liturgy of St. James.

thy Sacred Chamber, wherein thou wast conceived* and born †
Immaculate? How can we worthily revere that hallowed
Room in which "the Holy Ghost came upon thee ‡ and the
power of the Most High overshadowed thee," and "without
any violation of thy purity thou wast found the Mother of the
Saviour"?

Deign, O immaculate and ever-Virgin Mother of God, to accept
and prosper all that is done to make wider known the glories of
thy Sacred Dwelling. Guide and bless the hand that writes
and the zelators who labour. May the family of the Church
on earth, of which Jesus from His Cross made thee the Mother,
and Christ's Vicar has made thy holy Spouse the Patron—
may this whole family rejoice to be enrolled in the "Universal
Congregation of the Holy House." May the names of all
its members be written on the tablets of thy heart, and,
by thy intercession, *dwell in the House of the Lord unto
length of days,* and, hereafter, in that *house not made with
hands, eternal in heaven.* Amen.

Zelus Domus tuæ comedit me.

Dignare me laudare te, Virgo Sacrata.

*Nisi Dominus ædificaverit Domum; in vanum laboraverunt
qui ædificant eam.*

Virgo Lauretana, ora pro nobis.

* Julius II., Paul III., Pius IV., Pius IX.
† Pius IV., Sixtus V., Clement VIII., Innocent XII., Pius IX.
‡ Julius II., Paul III., Pius IV., Sixtus V., Clement IX., Clement X., Innocent
XII., Benedict XIV., Pius IX., Leo XIII.

Ave Maria.

CONTENTS

PART I.

Visit to Loreto and Nazareth—Description of the Holy House—Its Origin confirmed by its Dimensions, the Materials of which it is constructed, and the remains of the Paintings in Fresco with which it was decorated by Pilgrims to Nazareth—Testimony of the Sovereign Pontiffs and Saints—Honour rendered by the whole Catholic World.

PART II.

Honour rendered to the Holy House when it was at Nazareth—Detailed Account of its Translations.

PART III.

Sanctity of the Holy House of Loreto shewn by the Testimony of God.

* The author has visited the former site of the Holy House at Nazareth.

PART IV.

Monuments of the Various Translations of the Holy House.

PART V.

Testimony of Pilgrims before and after the Translation.

PART VI.

Historians of Loreto—Opinions of Theologians—Narrations, Poems, Discourses, Letters —Miracles similar to the Translation of the Holy House.

PART VII.

Guide to Loreto and its Environs.

PART VIII.

Sixth Centenary of the Translation into Italy.

PART IX.

The House of Mary the Seat of Wisdom.

* *Prov.* ix. 4.   † *Prov.* viii. 21.   ‡ *Prov.* viii. 19.   § *Prov.* viii. 35.   ‖ *Prov.* ix. 1.

Note.

This work is also published in the following sizes :

Super-royal 32mo, wrapper

Ditto,   cloth

Foolscap 8vo, wrapper

Ditto   cloth

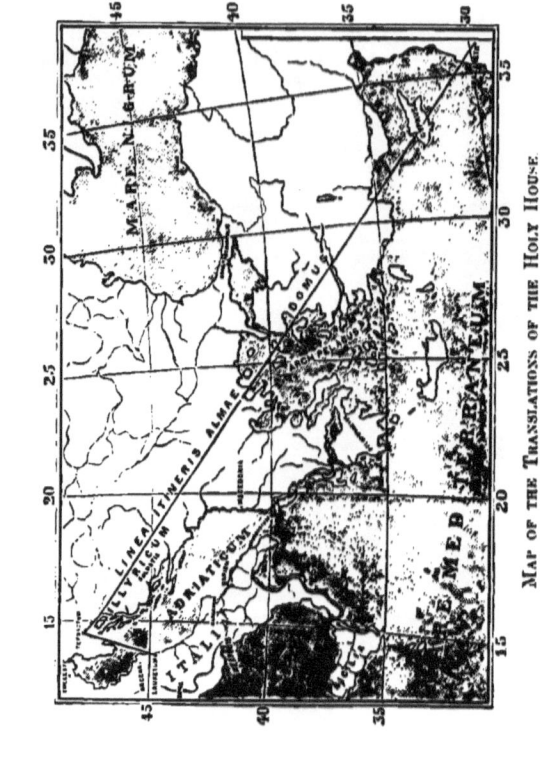

MAP OF THE TRANSLATIONS OF THE HOLY HOUSE.

" I have loved, O Lord, the beauty of Thy House."—Ps. xxv. 8.

PART I.

Visit to Loreto and Nazareth—Description of the Holy House—Its Origin confirmed by its Dimensions, the Materials of which it is constructed, and the remains of the Paintings in Fresco with which it was decorated by the Pilgrims to Nazareth—Testimony of the Sovereign Pontiffs and Saints—Honour rendered by the whole Catholic World.

No. 1.—THE BASILICA CONTAINING THE HOLY HOUSE.

CHAPTER I

The Sacred Hill, the Basilica, and the Exterior of the Holy House.

LORETO is situated upon a commanding eminence. On the east, the Adriatic spreads its blue expanse, with many a sail that comes from Ancona, Venice, Trieste and Fiume, and with many a flag lowered to pay homage to the glorious Virgin in her ancient home. In the distant West the lovely Apennines lift up their lofty heads veiled in virgin snow, as if grouped there to salute, with fittest emblem of unsullied purity, the House in which was wrought the Immaculate Conception, and where the very God of holiness became incarnate, and passed His earthly Life with His Virgin Mother, spotless as the virgin snow.

The view strikes a traveller returning from the Holy Land as remarkably similar to that from the heights above Nazareth, where Jesus, Mary and Joseph so often stood. The resemblance summons up memories of Carmel, Hermon and the Bay of Acre. Near the sea is Monte Conero, the Cumerian promontory, which, with an abbey of St. Romuald on its summit and Humana near its base, reminds one of Mount Carmel and of Caiffa; while Porto-Recanati stands in the place of Ptolomais, the Musone flows like the rapid Cison, and, inland, the Apennines rise up white as snowy Hermon. These points of resemblance increase the feeling of the sacredness of the spot that the Holy Family have chosen for the new site of their dear home. As Nazareth was fortified by the Crusaders, so has this new Nazareth been begirt with walls by the Sovereign Pontiffs. And it is thus that the saints represent to us the great Virgin of Nazareth, as a *strong City set on the heights, guarding those who come to her for refuge;* as the *Fortress built by God, the bulwark of the Church and of the Christian Faith.*

Above the city of Mary towers the grand cathedral, fortified as if by the bastions of a huge castle, and surmounted by the Virgin of Loreto resplendent in raiment of gold.

A vast square, adorned with the arcades of the Apostolical Palace, gives access to this magnificent Basilica, erected as a just tribute to the divine power that wrought the glorious Translation of the Holy House of Nazareth. On the façade is written in letters of gold :—THE HOUSE OF THE MOTHER OF GOD WHEREIN THE WORD WAS MADE FLESH.

The bronze gates by which we enter the Basilica are of singular beauty ; the bas-reliefs representing, among other subjects, Eve's transgression, that was repaired in this Holy House by the consent of Mary, who is the second Eve ; the creation of Adam out of the blessed ground of Eden, that prefigured the formation of the second Adam out of the immaculate substance of the Holy Mother of God, whom *the power of the Most High over-shadowed* in this sacred Dwelling ; the exaltation of the patriarch Joseph, whose position at the head of the government of Egypt was a type of the greatness of S. Joseph raised to be head of the Holy Family and patron of the Universal Church ; the removal of the *Ark of the Lord* containing the heavenly Manna, preceded by King David, the royal Psalmist, dancing for joy and striking on his harp harmonious chords of praise, an expressive figure of the rejoicing of the Holy Angels, while accompanying with their songs the translation of this new *Ark of the Covenant*, in which had dwelt *the Living Bread come down from Heaven.**

Twelve chapels, enriched with mosaics, form, as it were, a triumphal avenue leading to the Holy House ; eight more chapels encircle it, and it is crowned with a majestic dome, in which are seen patriarchs, prophets, apostles, martyrs, confessors, virgins, and, above them all, their Queen, whose praises the nine choirs of angels sing, while bearing in their hands her glorious titles set forth in the Litany of Loreto.

It is beneath this dome that rests that humble abode, rendered so heavenly by the dwelling within its walls of God Incarnate, *the desire of all nations.* This is that blessed House that so many millions of pilgrims have venerated, and in presence of which kings, princes, nobles and ambassadors from all parts of the world have bowed their foreheads in the dust.

On the marble of the eastern façade are read these words : "Christian Pilgrim, come hither in fulfilment of a pious vow, you have before your eyes the Holy House of Loreto, venerable throughout all the world on account of the divine mysteries accomplished in it and the glorious miracles herein wrought. It is here that most holy Mary,

* St. John vi. 51.

No. II.—THE HOLY HOUSE ENCASED IN MARBLE.

Mother of God, was born; here that she was saluted by the Angel; here that the eternal Word of God was made Flesh. Angels conveyed this House from Palestine to the town of Tersatto, in Illyria, in the year of salvation 1291, in the pontificate of Nicholas IV. Three years later, in the beginning of the pontificate of Boniface VIII., it was carried again by the ministry of angels and placed in a wood near this hill, in the vicinity of Recanati, in the March of Ancona; where, having changed its station thrice in the course of a year, at length, by the will of God, it took up its permanent position on this spot three hundred years ago. Ever since that time, both the extraordinary nature of the event having called forth the admiring wonder of the neighbouring people, and the fame of the miracles wrought in this Sanctuary having spread far and wide, this Holy House, whose walls do not rest on any foundation and yet remain solid and uninjured after so many centuries, has been held in reverence by all nations. Do thou, Pilgrim, pay religious homage in this place to the Queen of Angels and the Mother of grace, that, by her merits and by her intercessions with her most gracious Son, the Author of life, thou mayest obtain the pardon of thy sins, health of body and eternal bliss."

The pilgrims have so often made the circuit of the Holy House upon their knees that they have worn a furrow all around it, which has been aptly styled the Way of Faith and Love.

The sacred Dwelling is encased in the finest marble from Carrara; but, were it white as driven snow, it would not be pure enough to touch the hallowed Walls that it encloses. Beauty here enshrines holiness, but stands off from it, in token of unworthiness, and as if to show that this House, carried by the hands of angels, has no need of supports erected by the hand of man.

Over the *Window of the Angel* is represented the Annunciation, while all around the sacred Dwelling are other memorable events in the life of Mary, and statues of the prophets and sibyls who foretold the glories of the Virgin-Mother.

In size the Holy House is small, but its greatness is not to be measured by the space it occupies. It is great by reason of the saving mysteries fulfilled within its walls, the sublime memories of the Holy Family that lived in it, the love and veneration that all the faithful and the Sovereign Pontiffs have bestowed upon it, as the Sanctuary *the most august and the most sacred.* *

With still stronger reason we must place this building far above every surviving remnant of pagan antiquity. Doubtless the pyramids

* Pius IX.

of Egypt are imposing by their colossal proportions and by their great age ; doubtless the temples of Athens and of Rome call forth our admiration for the splendour and elegance of their architecture, which bears the stamp of genius ; but what is all this when compared with the House of the Holy Family ? Here we have the habitation of the divine Architect of our salvation, the Author of all genius, of all greatness, and of all perfection,—Jesus the ideal type and most perfect pattern of humanity, which He came to redeem and with which He did not disdain to dwell.

CHAPTER II

The Impression produced on entering the Holy House.

ON approaching to enter the Holy House, one reads over the bronze doorways : " Let the impure tremble to enter into this Sanctuary : the entire world has nothing holier. This edifice is holier than even the Basilica of S. Peter, Prince of the Apostles ; it is here that the Word was conceived and that the Virgin Mother was born. From the west, where the sun goes down, to the east, where he rises out of the waters, no place is more holy than this Place. In other places the fathers have set temples, but here troops of angels—the Virgin—God Himself has set this, which is so much more hallowed ! "

More than fifty silver lamps, ever burning night and day, impart a certain grandeur to the lowly Dwelling ; and at the altar we read in large letters of gold : *The Word was made Flesh and dwelt among us.* Nothing conceals the sacred stones inside ; and it is thrilling to look upon the actual walls that held Incarnate God, and to touch those stones thrice blest that sheltered Jesus from the cold in winter and the heat in summer. One recalls those words of Christ, *If these shall hold their peace, the stones shall cry out ;* *—if no human lips should sing Hosanna here, where I have come down for love of man, the stones would sound My praises !

Those sacred Walls, which trembled at the consummation of the mystery of the Incarnation, have a voice to tell us too to tremble with holy awe when we set foot where God has dwelt, and where the heavenly host in adoring wonder worshipped the Majesty Divine Incarnate. Here

* St. Luke xix. 40.

No. III.—The East End of the Holy House.

No. IV.— Interior of the Holy House with the new Reredos to be erected in commemoration of the Sixth Centenary.

the stoical heart feels a religious tremour come over it, the marble heart is warmed, and the most ungodly fall upon their knees impelled by an irresistible force ! *Behold he prayeth*, whisper angel voices. The soul so long frozen beneath the ice of irreligion is fired with a sacred flame of divine fervour ; it grieves for sin ; it aspires after God and holiness !

When we realise that we are kneeling in that very room where the Sacred Heart of Jesus throbbed with love for us, the union of our hearts with His seems almost palpable, and acquires an intensity till then unknown. Everything around us combines to inspire us with a boundless confidence in our dear Lord. It was the scene for many years of the Redeemer's supplications for the salvation of our fallen race. Here was His Sacred Heart ever cherishing in His love the thought of our redemption ; here, while His precious Mother was weaving the seamless robe of His Passion, and bedewing it with silent tears, He was preparing His sacred Body a sacrifice for immolation. No tongue of man or angel could express all that passed within the Heart of Jesus in this hallowed Chamber. Oh, how many sighs and tears came forth from His Sacred Heart while He offered to His Father the labours of His life and the anguish of His death ! At one time this room was to Him Gethsemane ; at another, the Pretorium ; at another, Calvary. He foreknew it all ; He foresaw it all ; He endured it all to draw our hearts to Him ! His life in this little Chamber was one of love to us. He was living here, not for Himself, but entirely for us ; and now He descends here again in His adorable Sacrament and asks us to give Him our heart in return for His love.

At the thought of Jesus of Nazareth living in this Holy House, our souls are greatly moved to devotion towards His Sacred Humanity. Who does not know the manifestations of faith at the feet of the Virgin of Loreto ?—how even men, coming to visit the Holy House in a spirit of mere worldly curiosity, and who on entering the sacred Dwelling were only half-christians with a wavering faith and an extinguished love, have gone forth from it full of conviction and ardour, enkindled by the Holy Spirit, ready to consecrate their powers and to give their very life in defence of the cause of Christ ?

Men who have not been to confession for forty years, on crossing the threshold of the hallowed Dwelling of her who is *the channel of all grace*, have not been able to resist the constraining power which urged them to seek the minister of God, whom they had so long avoided. As Mary of Egypt found herself repulsed by invisible hands from the door of the church of the Holy Sepulchre at Jerusalem, so sinners and heretics on attempting to enter the Holy House have been obliged to draw back before an irresistible force, until they had made a vow to become Catholic or to confess their sins. The Blessed Baptist of Mantua considered the Holy House of Loreto as more sacred than the Holy Sepulchre of Jerusalem; and Tursellini says, "No one enters this sacred place without feeling the presence of God and of the blessed Mother of God."

CHAPTER III

The Holy House stands without foundations, and its Stones, Mortar, Timber, and Frescoes bear testimony to its sacred origin.

THE Holy House is its own silent witness: it bears within itself the evidences of what it is and whence it came. It begins its testimony by asking us to look for its foundations. It discloses the fact that it has been separated from them, and tells us to go and find them in the holy ground at Nazareth, on which it was built.

When they were digging round the Holy House of Loreto, in November, 1531, with a view to surrounding it with marble, it was clear to everyone that its walls stood on the bare earth without foundations. There was present, during these excavations, Jerome Angelita, chancellor of the town of Recanati, and he bears his testimony as to what he saw. And at a later date, when a new pavement was being laid down, in 1672, many people passed their hands and sticks freely under portions of the sacred walls, the ground on which they rest being uneven.

When the pavement was being renewed again in 1751, in the pontificate of Benedict XIV., it was examined once more from the interior, excavations being made at the foot of the walls. This was done in the presence of the Archbishop of Fermo and the Bishops of Jesi, Ascoli, Macerata, and Loreto, and of three architects from other parts of Italy, and three master-builders, besides the architect of the works and many other people. An architect obtained permission to dig down to the depth of some six feet till he came to hard earth, such as foundations are always made to rest on to insure their firmness. It was manifest then that the Holy House was standing, contrary to all rules of building, without foundations on the uneven surface of the earth.

An official report of this was placed in the archives of Loreto, and it runs as follows: "We, the undersigned architects and superintendents, in accordance with our art, knowledge and conscience, certify that the sacred Walls of this Holy House, by us well known, from the first step

B

No. V.—The Church of the Annunciation and Franciscan Monastery at Nazareth, which stand on the site of the Holy House.

No. VI.—Interior of the Church of the Annunciation at Nazareth.

of the Altar to all the part containing the external Altar of the Annunciation, have not any sort of foundation : there is found under the sacred walls made ground, and in some parts dust, &c."

The Holy House of Nazareth is placed at Loreto on what was originally a public road. Jerome Angelita, who, as we have seen, was present at the time of the excavations made in 1531, writes in his *Relation of the Translations :*—"Wonderful to be said, more wonderful to be seen, it was found by all who wished to examine it, and they were many, that the *cubiculum* (that is, the chamber of the Blessed Virgin) stood without foundations ; *the dust that was on the surface of the road, when the cubiculum first lighted on it, being seen to remain there to this day.*"

There were discovered also in 1751, directly beneath the walls and on the surface of the ground, broken stones, such as are found on roads. A prickly bush planted at the side of the road was seen to have been crushed beneath the weight of the sacred building, that came down suddenly upon it ; some acorn shells, a snail-shell and a dried nut were picked up, and the earth that was taken out by the hand from under the walls was dusty like that of a roadway.

The identity of the *Santa Casa* of Loreto with the Holy House of Nazareth is confirmed by the stones of which it is built. The stone of Nazareth is limestone, and we find that there are two kinds of it :— *hard* limestone, called by the natives *Jabes*, and *soft* limestone, called *Nahari*. Two stones were brought back from Nazareth about the middle of the sixteenth century by John of Siena, one of three delegates who measured, for the third time, the foundations remaining at Nazareth. These trustworthy knights confirmed on oath the exact conformity of the measurements at Nazareth with those at Loreto, and, by producing the stones, proved the perfect similarity between the stones of the *Santa Casa* and those used in buildings at Nazareth.

Having often visited Nazareth between the years 1690 and 1714, a retired Archbishop of Eden, George Benjamin, visited Loreto and volunteered to sign a declaration as to the nature of the stones. After a careful examination of the stones at Nazareth, in 1732, a confessor of Santa Maria Maggiore, Rome, Joachim Ferrarese, declared on oath that he was convinced that the stones of which the Chapel of the Angel at Nazareth (which covers a portion of the original site of the chamber of the Annunciation now at Loreto) is composed, are in every way similar to those of which the *Santa Casa* of Loreto is constructed. A celebrated painter, Dominic Anthony Muradori, of the Academy of St. Luke at Rome, also declared on oath, in a document dated September 24, 1733, that he had observed with scrupulous attention the nature of the materials employed in the construction of the *Santa Casa* of Loreto, and that he was certain that they are natural stones of such a quality as he had never seen in any country he had passed through.

Although we quote these testimonies, the quality of the stones is not a matter that rests upon the evidence of past ages: the sciences of mineralogy and chemistry suffice to tell us what is the nature of the stones.

In 1857, Monsignor Bartolini sent to Professor Ratti, of the Sapienza, Rome, two specimens of stone that he had brought from Nazareth, and two taken from the walls of the *Santa Casa* of Loreto. The professor was not told anything about these specimens, and they were enclosed in four separate papers. In reply Dr. Ratti wrote as follows :—*

"Having taken a portion of each of the four specimens, and submitted it to a chemical analysis, it turns out that they are *all of the same nature*, being all formed of carbonate of magnesia and of ferruginous clay."

* "Ricorderà la Signoria Vostra Illma e Ilma di avermi inviato qualche tempo in addietro quattro piccoli saggi di minerali, perchè fossero sottoposti ad analisi chimica. Due di questi saggi sebbene involti in carte separate, erano distinti colle lett.re B. M. V., mentre gli altri due, sebbene separatamente incartati, non avevano alcun segno che li distinguesse.

"Esaminati da prima i caratteri fisici di ciascuno dei quattro saggi, mi sembra che vi sia una rassomiglianza, non già fra i due distinti con le medesime lettere B. M. V., ma invece fra uno di questi, ed altro senza indicazione, e che ora ho contrasegnato con la lettera X, come l'altro distinto con le medesime lettere iniziali B. M. V., più la lettera T, che ora vi ho aggiunto per riconoscerlo, somiglia il quarto saggio, l'altro cioè senza indicazione, e che troverà distinto con la lettera Y. I due primi difatti sonoassai più duri, e di color palombino, mentre gli altri due sono invece non solo assai poco duri, ma hanno di più un color biancastro. Egli è vero che ove si considerino attentamente i caratteri fisici di ciascuno de' quattro saggi, si trova in ciascuno alcunchè di proprio, e che perciò lo fa differenziare da tutti gli altri. Quello per esempio, de'due di color palombino e più duri, contrasegnato colle lettere B. M. V., ha un colore un poco più cupo, una compattezza un poco maggiore dell'altro, contrasegnato ora con la lettera X, al quale, come ho detto, d'altronde somiglia : e relativamente agli altri due, il color bianco, in quello distinto colle lettere B. M. V., tende un poco al rosso, le molecole sono piccolissime, e molto ravvicinate, la durezza è pressochè nulla, quasi fosse un precipitato chimico, polverulento raccolto in filtro e seccato : mentre in quello distinto colla lettera Y, non solo il colore tende un poco al giallo, ma le molecole sono più grosse, è più poroso e un poco più duro. Siccome pur queste differenze nella durezza, nella compatezza, nel colorito sono fra i saggi, che si somigliano, piccolissime ed a mio credere accidentali, ecco perchè ho detto che i quattro saggi inviatimi fisicamente considerati potevano dirsi due a due simili.

"Saggiata quindi chimicamente porzione di ciascuno de'quattro saggi, è risultato esser tutti della medesima natura, essendo tutti costituiti da carbonato di calce, da carbonato di magnesia, e da argilla ferruginosa. Che se v'è in alcuno dei saggi qualche differenza nelle quantità decomponenti, come per esempio, in quello più compatto e di color palombino, contrasegnato colle lettere B. M. V., si trova un poco più di argilla e di ferro, questa differenza non ne cambia la natura, e dipende da condizioni assolutamente secondarie, dall'aggregazione in ispecie fortuita di diverse dosi dei materiali medesimi.

"Soddisfatto così per quanto era in me, l'incarico ricevuto da Vostra Signoria Illma

Before submitting them to this chemical analysis, the Professor examined the physical characters of each of the four specimens; and he found a resemblance between all the four, all being limestone.

Let us call them for simplicity A, B, C, D,—A and B being stones from the walls of the Holy House, and C and D being from Nazareth. Professor Ratti found a special resemblance of physical character between A and C, both being rather hard, and of the colour *gorge de pigeon* (in Italian *palombino*), and only differing in A being slightly more compact and rather darker in colour. He found also a special resemblance of physical character between B and D, both being soft and of a whitish colour, and only differing in B slightly tending to a reddish colour, and D towards a yellow colour; the grains also in B were smaller and closer together, and it was softer than D. Of these differences he says: "These differences of hardness and colour are very slight, and, as it seems to me, accidental." Then, passing from the examination of their physical characters to the results of chemical analysis, he says: "If it happens that there is in any of the specimens a difference in the component parts— as, for example, where in the one which is the most compact and of the colour *palombino*, there is found a little more clay and iron, this difference does not alter the nature of the stone, and depends on the fortuitous aggregation of different quantities of the same materials."

Nothing could better prove the identity of the Holy House than the result of this analysis: the chemical composition of the stones taken from the walls of the *Santa Casa* is shown to be entirely identical with that of stones brought from Nazareth, of which one was of the kind called *Jabes* and the other of the kind called *Nahari*. *

We may further be certain that these stones, quarried out of the hill of Nazareth, were also put together on the spot; the mortar that unites them adds its testimony to the witness of the stones. At the same time that the valuable investigations were made by Monsignor Bartolini about the stones, some of the original cement of the Holy House was removed

e Rma, e ritornandole la porzione dei minerali, sopravanzata all'analisi chimica, ho l'onore di rassegnarmi con profonda stima e rispetto,

Di V. S. Illma e Rma
Umo e Dmo Servitore
FRANCESCO DR. RATTI."

See *Sopra la Santa Casa di Loreto*, di Monsignor Domenico Bartolini. Roma, De Propaganda Fide, 1861.

* *Jabes* often becomes of a dark red colour. Monsignor Bartolini, when reading his discourse before the Archæological Society at Rome, produced a specimen that he had taken from the Mountain of the Precipitation at Nazareth; and the colour of this stone was such that at first sight one would have mistaken it for brick. The walls of the Holy House are mostly composed of *jabes*; *nahari* is found in small quantities in the interior of the cupboard in the north wall.

and analysed.* Mortar, also, that had been extracted from the sacred Cave at Nazareth, from the workshop of St. Joseph, from the Synagogue at Nazareth, from Jacob's Well, and from the house of St. Elizabeth, was submitted to chemical analysis, and found to be formed of lime or chalk worked up with small pieces of vegetable charcoal. The cement of the Holy House of Loreto was proved to be composed of the same chemical constituents.

Monsignor Bartolini asks in conclusion : "Has anyone in Italy ever made use of a mortar composed of chalk, cinders or charcoal, when the soil abounds with volcanic substances that make the best mortar in the world ?" †

To the testimony of the stones and mortar we may add the witness of the frescoes.

S. Catharine, S. George, S. Anthony, saints greatly honoured in the East, and S. Louis of France, royal pilgrim of Nazareth, whose forms have been traced upon the sacred walls, *being dead yet speak*,—they one and all affirm that it is the Holy House from Nazareth.

In fact S. Catharine with the wheel, the emblem of her martyrdom, was placed over the door, to denote that the Knights of S. Catharine protected the pilgrims to Nazareth in the time of the Saracens.

The fresco representing S. Louis is not less significant. He is arrayed in royal robes, red and white, and in a purple mantle ; in his left hand he holds a sceptre, and hanging from his right hand are chains to indicate the captivity in which he had groaned at Mansourah before his pilgrimage to the House at Nazareth.

* "Dall'armadiolo, colle opportune superiori facoltà, ho estratto una bricciola di cemento delle commissure, che ho sottoposto all'analisi chimico, ed eccone il risultato, che me ne dava il lodato Professor Ratti in un suo foglio con data del 10 del caduto Gennaio :

"'La sostanza trovata da V. S. Illma e Rma aderente a pezzo di pietra calcarea, tolta da antico monumento, e consegnatami perchè ne fosse determinata la natura, è soltanto di calce, ossia gesso, come dicesi comunemente, impastato con piccoli pezzi di carbone vegetale. Non dee recar maraviglia l'averla trovata aderente ad un pezzo di pietra calcarea, inquantochè appartenendo il gesso in qualche modo (come dice Bendaret nel suo tratto di Mineralogia) a tutte le specie di depositi, che si trovano sulla superficie terrestre, e trovandosi per ciò sovente anche nei paesi, dove esiste la pietra calcarea, può benissimo essere stata adoperata in un monumento insieme a questa pietra come cemento, o come materia di decorazione.

"Mi creda qual mi pregio di essere con tutta la stima e rispetto,

Di V. S. Illma et Rma
Umo e Dmo Servitore
FRANCESCO DR. RATTI."

See *Sopra la Santa Casa di Loreto*, di Mgr. Dom. Bartolini. Roma : De Propaganda Fide, 1861.

† "Ma dimando a chiunque abbia un fil di senno, dove mai si è praticato in Italia nelle costruzioni un cemento composto di gesso, cenere o carbone, quando il suolo abonda cotanto di sostanze vulcaniche da poter formare la miglior calce del mondo ? "

These paintings were in the Holy House when it came from Palestine, and stood out clearly on the walls in 1637, when Silvius Serragli of Pietra Santa put engravings of them in his work entitled *The Holy House Embellished;* and later on, in 1791, when Vincent Murri wrote his history dedicated to Anthony Clement, King of Saxony. Time has almost effaced them, and much of the plaster has pealed off, but their work is done and their mission is fulfilled; for many ages they have borne their testimony, and scarcely can men need their witness longer. (The reader will find engravings of them in Part VII. Chapter I.)

Nazareth is situated among the southern ridges of Lebanon, before they sink into the fertile plain of Esdraelon; and every thing that is of cedar in the Holy House, whether it be the lintel of the hallowed doorway, through which God Incarnate passed for nearly thirty years, or whether it be the shelf of the sacred cupboard hollowed out in the north wall, or the remains (still visible in the walls) of an ancient partition, or the pieces of the original woodwork placed beneath the altar by the orders of Clement VII.—all these sacred objects in cedar bear the same testimony as the other materials. *The stones cry out of the walls:* "We have sheltered Jesus of Nazareth." *And the timber between the joints of the building gives answer:* * In Lebanon's vast forests we reared our lofty heads, as lords among all trees; yet kindly was the axe that made our future so much greater than our past, exalting us to form a portion of the habitation of the King of kings and of the Queen Immaculate."

* Habacuc ii. 11.

CHAPTER IV

Visit to Nazareth *—Foundations of the Holy House—The sacred Dwelling as it was when inhabited by the Holy Family—Description of the House given by a Pilgrim of the Twelfth Century.

NAZARETH is built on the side of a hill honeycombed by ancient caves, which form the back rooms of many of the dwellings. The House of the Holy Family opened thus into a cave; and a chapel, called the *Chapel of the Angel*, has been built on the spot where it stood. This chapel occupies only a portion of the site; and the sacred foundations are all round outside it. It would not have been well, for many reasons, to have erected this structure actually on the ancient and hallowed foundations which the Holy House left at its departure. So we find it shorter and narrower, and resting on foundations of its own, enclosed within the holy ground, which the ancient foundations have always clearly marked out. The north side of this chapel abuts against the rock, and has an opening into the Cave.

Possession of the holy Caves at Nazareth was given in 1620 by the Prince of Sidon, the Emir Fakhr ed-Dine, to Thomas of Novara. This Guardian of the Holy Places, finding that the Chapel of the Angel, which had been erected in 1300,† was falling into ruins, determined to have it rebuilt, and he writes as follows about the foundations of the Holy House : " Brother James ‡ .... pulled down the old walls to their foundations ; and then, having diligently and attentively examined them, he found the foundations of the Holy House of Loreto two palms in thickness, and separate from the other foundations. . . . Leaving the former, and beginning at the ancient and the true foundations, on drawing the measuring line from it, the place at Nazareth was found, to the great joy of all, in all things equal to the place of the Holy House at Loreto. And we found that the foundations entirely agreed and were commensurate with the walls, and the house with the

---

* The author has visited the former site of the Holy House at Nazareth.

† Sanutus Torsellus describes this chapel in 1306.

‡ This Jacques de Vendôme had been newly appointed Guardian of the monastery, to which the Franciscans had been permitted to return after an interval of seventy-eight years.

No. VII. A section of the Church of the Annunciation, shewing the Chapel of the Angel, built on the former site of the Holy House in front of the Sacred Cave.

No. VIII.—Interior of the Holy House of Nazareth when inhabited by the Holy Family.

No. IX.—Exterior of the Holy House in the time of the Holy Family. View shewing the Entrance by the West Door through the Lower Cave.

foundations, the place with the place, the site with the site, and the space with the space at Nazareth and at Loreto." *

We have then only to represent the Holy House of Loreto standing in front of the sacred Cave at Nazareth, and the picture will enable us to realise its identity and to form a clear idea of the habitation of the Holy Family.

The doorway that opened into the Cave is the one that we see walled up at Loreto.† The Dwelling had also two doors leading from the Cave into roads or gardens on both sides of the House. The place occupied by the west door is situated in the south-west corner of the large Cave, between the foundations of the Holy House and the lower part of the rock. ‡

The second door, opening out upon the slope of the hill, was at the top of the staircase tunnelled in the rock, and was situated either on the east side of the little Cave, in which we find a walled-up doorway, or else close to it, at the east end of the rock-cut passage alongside of it, where the eastern entrance is at present.§

The Cave was so closely united to the Building that both together they formed the abode of the Holy Family. The Holy House of Loreto is not then the whole of the sacred House of Nazareth; and, as the Cave and the Building were integral parts of the hallowed Dwelling in which the Archangel Gabriel saluted the Immaculate Virgin, we may say of each of these holy places: HERE THE WORD WAS MADE FLESH, and it is most fitting that the same mystery should be commemorated in both Sanctuaries.

To induce the faithful to make the pilgrimage of the Holy House then at Nazareth, John Phocas, a Greek monk, wrote some very interesting details about the sacred Dwelling, which he had himself visited.

Let us accompany him in spirit and admire with him the magnificent Basilica of the Annunciation, such as it was about a hundred years before the translation of the Holy House. (See Plate X. and also Plate XIII.)

Advancing towards the High Altar, you find on your left a doorway decorated with a bas-relief in white marble representing the Annunciation. This is a way into the sacred Cave and, through the Cave, into

---

* Quaresimus, *Terræ Sanctæ Elucidatio*, t. ii. lib. 7, cap. 4, p. 837.

† The other doors in the *Santa Casa* were opened in the pontificate of Clement VII. to give freer passage to the innumerable pilgrims.

‡ The exterior of this door, such as it was in the time of the Holy Family, is represented in Plate IX.

§ In going out by this passage, the traveller leaves the little Cave on his left hand and reaches the choir of the church by passing through the sacristy. A pilgrim of the twelfth century entered the Cave and the Holy House by the *east* door, and another pilgrim of the same century tells us that there was also a *west* door into the Cave and thence into the Blessed Virgin's Chamber. (See Part V. Chapter I.)

the Holy House. "Having entered the Cave through this mouth, you descend a few steps, and then your eyes look upon the ancient Dwelling of Joseph, in which the Archangel announced the good tidings to the Virgin, who had returned from the well. There is moreover in the place of the Annunciation a cross in black stone let into white marble, and over it an altar, and on the right of the altar is the small room which the Ever-Virgin Mother of God used to occupy; on the left of the place of the Annunciation is seen the dark room which our Lord Jesus Christ is said to have inhabited after the return from Egypt until the beheading of S. John Baptist." *

Phocas expresses the admiration of the pilgrim at seeing in a state of perfect preservation the Room which the Ever-Virgin Mother of God was wont to occupy, the very walls which re-echoed the first *Ave*, and the chamber sanctified by the indwelling of the Saviour of the world.

Let us now compare this description given by a pilgrim of the twelfth century with what we find in Nazareth at the present day.

We can still trace out the form of the Church of the Annunciation erected by S. Helena. The cloister and the terrace of the monastery are built on the remains of the ancient walls; in the garden behind the sanctuary there is a piece of wall that is preserved, and probably formed part of the apse of the north transept, and, in the cloister, the bases of two of the columns occupy their original positions.

The present church lies north and south, being built on the transept and a part of the choir of the ancient cathedral, which stood east and west.

The Chapel of the Angel, as we have seen, has been erected on the site of the Holy House, and stands in front of the sacred Caves. On crossing the large Cave, we find the steps that are mentioned by Phocas, and we go up by them into the little Cave. Here we see that the door by which that pilgrim entered from the choir of the ancient Basilica has been blocked up, on account of the rock-cut passage

---

* See the list of engravings accompanied by critical notes. The Latin translation of the text of Phocas is as follows :

"Domus Joseph postmodum in pulcherrimum templum immutata est, in cujus. læva parte prope altare spelunca non in terræ visceribus latens, sed superficie tenus hians, os candido marmore exornatur super pictoris industria : Angelus. . . . Per os in speluncam ingressus paucos admodum gradus descendis ; tum antiquam illam Josephi ædem oculis lustras, in qua regressæ a fonte Virgini Archangelus, ut jam dixi, fausta annuntiavit. Est præterea eo in loco in quo Annuntiatio facta est, ex nigro lapide crux candido marmore incisa, et super eam altare ; et a dextra altaris *pusilla ædicula in qua semper Virgo Deipara se continebat*. In læva parte vero Annuntiationis illa conspicitur ædicula, luminis expers, quam Dominus noster Christus, regressus ex Ægypto usque ad Præcursorem decollatum, incoluisse fertur."—In *Allatii Symmictis*, et *Acta SS. Bolland.* Mai. ii.

No. X.—The Holy House as the Crypt of the Cathedral erected by S. Helena at Nazareth

alongside this upper Cave affording a more convenient way into the choir of the modern church.

Even the Mahometans venerate the portions of the Holy House that are still to be seen at Nazareth, and they believe in the miracles wrought in the sacred Caves through the intercession of the Immaculate Virgin, who, according to their belief, was "never touched by the finger of the devil."

Great as is the sanctity attached to these Caves at Nazareth, the miracle of the Translation is an assurance to us that a still greater sanctity is attached to that portion of the House which God Himself has thus more highly honoured.

CHAPTER V

Testimony of the Sovereign Pontiffs, and their Devotion towards the Holy House.

NO less than forty-seven Popes have rendered honour to the Holy House of Loreto either by their visits, or by their gifts, or by the spiritual favours that they have accorded to pilgrims.

Among the first* of the Sovereign Pontiffs who have conferred privileges on this Sanctuary, we may mention Benedict XII. and Urban VI. A brief written by the former was found in 1525 among the city records by Angelita, chancellor of Recanati and historian of the Holy House.

Many aged and infirm people of that city, being unable to walk five miles to Loreto, Benedict XII., in this brief dated 1351, accorded the same spiritual privileges to those who visited the Church of the Angel in the Piazza at Recanati. This church had been specially erected in commemoration of the Annunciation made by S. Gabriel in the Holy House, and had a painting over the altar representing the Virgin of Loreto. This brief was in letters of gold and was written only forty-six years after the arrival of the Holy House on its present site. †

* The Popes who resided at Avignon from 1303 to 1377 were hindered from visiting Loreto, and the schism from 1378 to 1417 occasioned still further delay in the development of this devotion. The blessed Urban V., the only Pope who returned from Avignon for a time, made preparations for the journey to Loreto, but we have no certain proof that he carried out his intention. However, at Tersatto there is a celebrated Madonna believed to have been sent by this blessed Pontiff in 1367. (See Part IV.)

† This church exists at the present day. Since the seventeenth century it has belonged to the Confraternity of St. Anne, and has, in consequence, taken her name.

Urban VI., in 1389, granted, on the occasion of the miracle of the flames, * a plenary indulgence to pilgrims visiting the Holy House on the festival of the Birth of the Blessed Virgin. This indulgence was extended by Martin V. to the days of the fairs established by him at Recanati "in honour of the Holy Virgin of Loreto."

Nicholas V. paid a personal visit to the Holy House and attached a plenary indulgence to the festival of the Annunciation.†

Pius II. went in 1464 to the *Santa Casa*. Riera and Tursellini relate this visit as follows : Having called on Christian kings and princes to undertake a new crusade against the Turks, Pius II. wished to be present at the assembling of the fleet at Ancona. His state of health rendering this long journey beyond his power, the Pope had recourse to the Virgin of Loreto ; he offered our Lady a golden chalice bearing an inscription recalling the miracles daily wrought in the Holy House, and he besought the gracious Mother of God to heal the fever that consumed him and the cough that exhausted him. The Blessed Virgin accepted the gift. Scarcely had the vow passed from his lips when the cough ceased and the fever abated. He set out upon his journey, and the nearer he approached to Loreto the more his strength returned. On reaching the Holy House, he fulfilled his vow in the presence of a number of Cardinals and Roman barons, as also of generals come from Ancona to meet his Holiness.‡

Cardinal Pietro Barbo, having become seriously affected by the pestilence that raged in that year at Ancona, some fourteen miles from Loreto, had himself conveyed to the Holy House in the hope of obtaining his recovery. He fell into a gentle slumber within its sacred walls, and, in his dream, beheld a vision, and woke up quite restored. The same year, on being elected Sovereign Pontiff, as he had been foretold in the vision, he immediately wrote a Bull about the Holy House, in which he speaks of what he had himself experienced in his miraculous cure. This first Bull of Paul II. bears the date of November 1, 1464, and contains the words: *In which are the House and Image of the Blessed Virgin Mary.* §

In a second Bull, dated February, 1471, Paul II. says: "In the

---

* See Part III. Chapter II.

† This Pope, in a brief addressed to Martin Frangipani, Count of Modrussa, Veglia and Segna, mentions the vow of his ancestor Nicholas Frangipani to build a church at Tersatto, where the Holy House had rested from May 10, 1291, to Dec. 10, 1294. Pope Nicholas V. also forbade the sale of any of the *ex votos* offered at Loreto.

‡ Details of this pilgrimage, which escaped the historians of Pius II., were found by Riera and Tursellini in the archives of the Sanctuary, where there is preserved to this day a brief written by this Pope.

§ *Ubi est Domus et Imago B. Mariæ Virginis.*

Church of the blessed Mary of Loreto, where, according to testimonies most worthy of credit, are preserved the House of the glorious Virgin, and also the Image, borne there in the mercy of God by the hands of angels, one sees, in consequence of the frequent and stupendous miracles that the Most High works there daily, in virtue of the merits and intercession of that glorious Patron in behalf of those who have recourse to her and implore her succour with humility, multitudes of people, delivered by the assistance of this sovereign Protectress, come from the most distant parts of the universe."

Sixtus IV. conferred on the *Santa Casa* the title of *Alma Domus*, signifying that it is worthy of all honour, as being the House where Mary brought up her divine Son. This name distinctly affirms its identity with the Holy House of Nazareth.*

Julius II. visited the Sanctuary, and, by a Bull dated October 31, 1507, augmented its privileges for the following reasons :—" Seeing that not only the Image of the Blessed Virgin Mary is in this church, but also, according to a pious belief conformable to tradition, there is the room in which the Blessed Virgin was conceived and brought up : where, at the Angelic salutation, she conceived the Saviour of the world ; where she nourished † and brought up her Son : where she retired for prayer after the Ascension : considering that this is the first church consecrated to the honour of God and of the Blessed Virgin ; that in it the first Mass was celebrated, and that it was carried by angelic hands from Nazareth," etc.

Other Roman Pontiffs ‡ have spoken of the *Santa Casa* in similar terms. They have assured us that " great, innumerable and continual miracles " were wrought there during their pontificate, and that it had always been held in reverence by all Catholic nations. The successors of St. Peter, animated by the love of Mary, have spared no efforts to increase the splendour of that lowly and yet glorious abode, in which the Queen of Heaven was conceived,§ where she was born ‖ and brought up, ¶ where she was saluted as Mother of God by the Archangel Gabriel ;**

---

* The Bull of Sixtus IV., while confirming the privileges accorded by his predecessors, confirmed at the same time this title, which was already in use. In the Donation of Nicholas delle Aste we find this title of *Alma Domus* recurring several times ; this bishop of the diocese lived during the pontificate of Paul II.

† " Suis castissimis uberibus, lacte de cœlo plenis, lactavit et educavit," etc.

‡ We may mention specially Leo X., Paul III., Pius IV., Sixtus V., Clement VIII., Clement IX., Innocent XII.

§ Julius II., Paul III., Pius IV., Pius IX.

‖ Pius IV., Sixtus V., Clement VIII., Innocent XII., Pius IX.

¶ Paul III., Pius IV., Pius IX.

** Julius II., Paul III., Pius IV., Sixtus V., Clement IX., Clement X., Innocent XII., Benedict XIV., Pius IX., Leo XIII.

they have taken a prominent part in the commencement of the erection of the present Basilica, * in its completion and adornment. † Three Popes ‡ enclosed the Natal House § of the Immaculate Virgin in white marble, and a fourth erected the bronze doors of the cathedral.‖

By the orders of Sixtus V., the façade of the Basilica bears the inscription : *House of the Mother of God, in which the Word was made Flesh.* Gregory XIII. had the relation written by Il Teramano ¶ translated into eight languages. Clement VIII. visited the Sanctuary, and placed outside the east end of the Holy House another account of its miraculous Translations.

The Sovereign Pontiffs exempted the Sanctuary from all other jurisdiction except that of the Apostolic See ; ** they committed it in 1489 to the care of the Carmelites : †† then twelve Canons were appointed ; ‡‡ forty years later the Jesuit Fathers were called to serve the Penitentiary, §§ and the illustrious Society was charged with this care during 215 years. At the end of this period the Penitentiary was confided to the Franciscan Conventuals, ‖‖ who are there to this day. All the powers of Apostolic Penitentiaries have been granted by the Holy See to the confessors attached to the Basilica. ¶¶

The Roman Pontiffs founded the Illyrian Seminary, *** endowed the ancient hospice for poor pilgrims and built a new one ; ††† they erected the Apostolical Palace ; ‡‡‡ they instituted the Order of the Knights of Loreto, §§§ and surrounded the town with ramparts : ‖‖‖ by them also

---

* Paul II. came to the help of the Bishop Nicholas delle Aste, who had undertaken to replace the church built about 1330 by another larger one, or to complete it on the original plan.

† Sixtus IV., Julius II., Leo X., Clement VII., Paul III., Sixtus V., Paul V., etc.

‡ Leo X., Clement VII., Paul III. The second of these Popes visited Loreto in 1533.

§ The Breviary gives it that title.

 Sixtus V.

*' On the subject of the relation by Il Teramano, see Part VI. on the Historians of Loreto.

** Julius II.   †† Innocent VIII.

‡‡ Leo X. It appears that the Chapter of Canons existed in the Pontificate of Julius II., and it has received increased honours from the Popes Leo X., Clement VIII., Benedict XIII., Pius VII., Pius IX., Leo XIII. They wear a violet cassock and a pectoral cross, like prelates. These privileges were conferred by Pius VII.

§§ Julius III.

‖‖ Clement XIV. Later on Gregory XVI. re-established the Fathers of the Society of Jesus in their former college, now secularised.

¶¶ Sixtus IV.   *** Gregory XIII. See Part IV. Chap. I.

††† Eugenius IV., Paul III.   ‡‡‡ From Julius II. to Benedict XIV.

§§§ Sixtus V. This Order no longer exists. It had great privileges and was of use against pirates and brigands.

‖‖‖ Callistus III. and Leo X.

No. XI.—Entrance of the Basilica enclosing the Holy House.
The Illyrian Seminary on the right.

No. XII.—The Apostolical Palace and the Fountain in the
Piazza of the Madonna.

were erected the two fountains, and water was brought from Recanati by a magnificent aqueduct that recalls those of the Roman period.*

Leo XII. declared the town of Loreto to be "worthy of all honour, because in its Temple is preserved the Room in which the Word was made Flesh." Clement VIII. forbade the singing of any other Litanies of the Blessed Virgin except that of Loreto. As S. Jerome called Nazareth "the Flower of Galilee," so S. Pius V. entitled the Holy House of Loreto "truly the House of flowers that was in Nazareth;" † Innocent XII. sang the glories of the *Santa Casa* as "the first Tabernacle of God dwelling in the midst of men." ‡

The Popes have further established the festival of the Translation of the Holy House; they have prescribed solemn Rites for its celebration,§ and placed the anniversary in the Roman Martyrology;‖ they have inserted the history of the Translation into the office in the Roman Breviary and approved a special Mass;¶ they have also authorised the Sclavs, on the eastern side of the Adriatic, to say this Mass and office in memory of the Translation of the Holy House into Illyria on May 10, 1291.**

There exist dissertations of Benedict XIV. on the Holy House of Loreto.†† This most gifted and learned Pope thus expresses his deep conviction : "That the holy Chamber in which the Divine Word took Flesh has been transported by the ministry of angels, all the monuments furnish proof; and constant tradition, the testimony of the Roman Pontiffs, and the miracles that cease not to be worked there, confirm it."

Urban VIII.‡‡ made the pilgrimage in 1625, which was a *Jubilee Year*, and allowed the indulgences of the *Santa Casa* to remain in full force, in spite of the general suspension of indulgences. Pius VI., also, preserved to the Sanctuary its indulgences during the *Holy Year*, and went to

* Paul V.

† *Vere Domus florida quæ fuit in Nazareth*. This inscription was placed by S. Pius V. on *Agnus Dei* which bore the impress of the Holy House. Following this precedent, Innocent XI. had the *Santa Casa* represented on *Agnus Dei* and added the invocation, "Saint Mary of Loreto, pray for us."

‡ See Bull of August 5, 1698, by which Innocent XII. erected the *Congregation of Loreto*.

§ Clement VIII. Urban VIII. extended the privilege to all the March of Ancona.

‖ *Laureti in Piceno, Translatio sacræ Domus Dei Genitricis Mariæ, in qua Verbum Caro factum est.—Martyr. Rom.* Decemb. 10, ex decret. Clement IX. 1669.

¶ Innocent XII. Benedict XIII. conceded its use to several Italian states and to Spain; and Clement XII. to the rest of Christendom.

** Clement XI.

†† See Treatise on the Canonisation of the Saints and on the Festivals of the Blessed Virgin.

‡‡ This same Pontiff established a confraternity *Almæ Domus Lauretanæ* in the city of Rome, April 14, 1633, and Innocent XI. erected the confraternity into an archconfraternity by the Bull *Exponi nobis nuper*, dated July 16, 1677.

the *Santa Casa* to place under the protection of the Virgin of Loreto his journey into Austria.

In this nineteenth century alone, the Virgin of Loreto has received the visits of three Popes; and the present Pontiff, Leo XIII. made the pilgrimage of the Holy House as Cardinal. Every Catholic knows the reason why, as Pope, His Holiness has been hindered from renewing his pilgrimage.

Pius IX., who proclaimed the dogma of the Immaculate Conception, had a great devotion towards that hallowed Dwelling, which three of his predecessors had already honoured as the very place where Mary was conceived. * It was in the *Santa Casa* that he made a vow to take Holy Orders if the attacks to which he was subject should entirely cease through the intercession of our Lady of Loreto. And it was to the Holy House that, on his election to the papal throne, he sent the pectoral cross and ring that he had worn as bishop. From his very childhood he had visited Loreto. "My parents," he said, "were in the habit of going to the *Santa Casa* every year, and they used to take my brothers and myself with them. From the moment I got an inkling of the journey I could not sleep for joy!"

In speaking of a public testimony of his devotion towards the Blessed Virgin, Pius IX. thus celebrates the glories of the Holy House:† "We have placed this testimony in the Sanctuary of Loreto as the most august and the most sacred. Is it not by an unparalleled miracle that this Holy House was brought over land and sea from Galilee into Italy? By a supreme act of benevolence on the part of the God of all mercy, it has been placed in our pontifical domain, where, for so many centuries, it has become the object of the veneration of all the nations of the world, and is resplendent with incessant miracles. With reason then the faithful, who come to visit it in a spirit of true faith, seem not so much to visit the Virgin's House as the Virgin herself. There, in fact, as is proved by innumerable and weighty documents, the Blessed Virgin Mary received the Angelic salutation, and, by the power of the Holy Spirit, became the Mother of God without any detriment to her virginity. There the Word of God—Very God and Son of God, Who was in God from the beginning, by Whom all things were made, and without Whom was not anything created, Jesus Christ our Saviour, the destroyer of sin and of death—came down from heaven upon the earth, drawn by His marvellous love towards man. There, to reconcile man with God, He was willing to clothe Himself with our mortal flesh," etc.

No less than seven times during his pontificate did Pius IX. visit the

* Julius II., Paul III., Pius IV.
† See Apostolical Letter dated August 22, 1846.

H. H. Pius IX., A.D. 1846.

Santa Casa. He conferred also on this Sanctuary the power to affiliate churches and chapels and to make them participate in its own privileges. In a Bull to this effect, dated August 26, 1852, His Holiness thus celebrates the glories of Loreto :—" Among all the churches dedicated to the Mother of God, the Immaculate Virgin Mary, there is one which holds the first place and shines with an incomparable lustre. Consecrated by the mysteries of God, renowned for innumerable miracles, honoured by the vast concourse of people who flock there, the most august House of Loreto fills the Catholic universe with the glory of its name, and is, with good reason and by right, an object of the devotion of every race and every nation.

" It is in truth the House of Nazareth that is venerated at Loreto, that House dear to God by so many claims, built originally in Galilee, separated from its foundations, and carried by divine power across the seas into Dalmatia first, and thence into Italy ; the blessed House where the most holy Virgin, predestined from all eternity and perfectly exempt from original sin, was conceived, was born, was brought up : where Heaven's messenger saluted her as full of grace and blessed among women : where filled with God and under the fruitful operation of the Holy Ghost, without any loss of her inviolable virginity, she became the Mother of the only Son of God, the splendour of the Father's glory and the figure of His Substance, Who did not disdain to be born of this most pure Virgin and to redeem the human race, which by the fall of our first parents had been precipitated into the slavery of the devil.

" One cannot be astonished if, from the earliest days of the Christian religion, this blessed House, adorned and changed into a chapel, has been an object of respect, devotion and veneration on the part of all the faithful ; if every subsequent age, animated with feelings of the deepest reverence, has not ceased to give it glory ; if princes have come from the most distant lands to pay it their homage and lavish upon it their most precious offerings ; if the Sovereign Pontiffs, our predecessors, especially since the time of Boniface VIII. of happy memory, have felt it an honour to enclose the august cradle of the Virgin in a rich and magnificent church, bearing the title of *Basilica,* and possessed of all the privileges attached to that distinction. We, then, with the intent of making the holiness of the spotless Virgin and *devotion towards Our Lady of Loreto flourish from one end of the world to the other,* approve and confirm all the indulgences, and we accord to the Prefect of the Congregation of Loreto the power to affiliate churches," etc.

Among the most splendid documents by which the successors of St. Peter have rendered homage to the *Santa Casa,* we must place the Apostolic Letter of the venerable Pontiff, Leo XIII., in which His

Holiness proclaims a Jubilee in honour of the Holy House of Loreto. In
the words of the Vicar of Christ on the observance of the centenary all
Catholics ought to find a pledge of the approbation of Jesus of Nazareth
of the preparations made to celebrate this most auspicious event, and a
guarantee of many graces to everyone who, following the exhortations of
Pope Leo XIII., shall concur with His Holiness in honouring "*that
most blessed place where the beginnings of man's salvation were wrought.*"

CHAPTER VI

Testimony of the Saints.

THE *Blessed Baptist of Mantua*, superior of the Carmelites, who had
charge of the Holy House at the end of the fifteenth century,
compares the august Dwelling to the earthly Paradise, where Eve was
taken out of the side of Adam; to Sinai, where the Mosaic Law was
given; to the Temple of Solomon, filled with the visible presence of
God; to the Cave at Bethlehem, where the Lord was born; to Mount
Tabor, where He shewed forth His glory; to the Mount of Olives, from
whence He ascended into Heaven; and lastly, to the Holy Sepulchre;
nor does he hesitate to place the Holy House above all these other
Holy Places, because chosen by God in the Flesh for laying there the
foundations of the salvation of the world.

S. Alphonsus Liguori, during the three days that he passed at Loreto, was
heard frequently repeating to himself in the Holy House: "Here the
eternal Word was made Man! Here His most holy Mother held Him in
her arms!"

S. Francis Curacciolo passed two nights in this Sanctuary and received
a divine revelation concerning the glorification of his companion and his
own approaching death.

S. Aloysius Gonzaga was pledged through his mother's vow, even before
his birth, to visit Loreto; and in fulfilling the vow he remained on his
knees all day within the Holy House, and received such unspeakable
comfort from the Lord and from our beloved Lady, that he always
burst into tears at the bare remembrance of it.

S. ALPHONSUS MARIA DE LIGUORI.

S. FRANCIS DE SALES.

S. Peter of Alcantara could not speak of the *Santa Casa* without transports of ineffable sweetness.

S. Francis Xavier received at the feet of the Virgin of Loreto the inspiration to carry the Gospel to the East Indies and Japan; and he healed every kind of disease by applying to the sick the Litany of Loreto, written out for that purpose by his own hand.

S. Joseph Calasanctius after his visit to the Holy House never ceased to daily recite the Litany of Loreto, and used his influence that others should do so.

S. Francis Borgia was healed of a fever in this Sanctuary. And when *S. James of the March of Ancona* came to celebrate Holy Mass in the *Santa Casa*, seeking to obtain health for the ministry of the Word, the Blessed Virgin appeared to him and assured him that his prayers were heard.

S. Camillus of Lellis and *B. Alexander Sauli*, Bishop of Aleria in Corsica, bear witness of the gifts and graces which they derived from this divine spring.

The House of the Holy Family was so dear to *S. Joseph Benedict Labre* that he went there eleven times, journeying on foot across the snowy Apennines, poorly clothed and badly shod. At his last visit, the Lord made known to him his approaching death.

The Blessed Anthony Grassi also made this pilgrimage many years in succession, and when, in the year before his death, the time for leaving the Holy House arrived, he exclaimed: "Let me remain another moment here, it is the last time that I shall visit this Sanctuary!" And when obliged to take his leave of the Blessed Virgin, he said, "O Mary, I commend to thee the end of my life!"

Nor less tender are the expressions of farewell on the part of the *Venerable Peter Traversino*, Vicar-General of the Carmelites: "Without the House of Life, what life remains to me? I am deprived, alas! of the Virgin's Chamber, and soon I shall cease to live!"

The following fervid aspirations terminate the account of the Translation of the Holy House attributed to the *Blessed Peter Compagnoni*, Bishop of Macerata: "O blessed chapel, small, it is true, and poor to the eyes of the flesh, but to the eyes of the spirit richer and more precious than the palaces of kings or even the Temple of Solomon! O venerable Chamber, in which was placed the greatest Treasure which has ever been, or ever will be in this world! O holy Walls, against which often leant the august forms of the Son and of the Mother! O happy Hearth, enough to inflame the hearts of men who reflect how oft the virginal hands of Mary kindled there the fire that warmed the tender limbs of the Child Jesus! O Stones, more precious than orient gems, how often did the words that the Son addressed to His Mother strike upon you, and the gracious answers that the Mother made to her Son! O divine Sanctuary, whence so many prayers of the Son of God were sent up to His heavenly Father, where so many tears of compassion flowed from the eyes of the Son and of the Mother for the salvation of sinners!"

The Mother of fair love has perfumed her dwelling with the purest balm;* and as vases retain the aroma of the perfume they have held, so is this House, which has contained the source of all that is sweet in Heaven and earth, impregnated with the odour of celestial perfume. The presence of Jesus, Mary and Joseph, makes itself felt in their beloved Habitation : it seems, as the *Blessed Grignon de Montfort* expresses it, that we can see them and hear them speaking together ; the " Light of the world " appears always to illumine the interior, and the smile of Mary to rejoice it still. We feel constrained to exclaim : *Show me thy face, and let thy voice sound in my ears : for thy voice is sweet, and thy face comely.* †

The Blessed Juvenal Ancina, disciple of S. Philip Neri, and Bishop of Saluzzo, experienced so great a devotion towards Mary in her Holy House that he said to her : "My heart has only the feeling of life when I am in thy presence! If I cannot be always near thee, I should wish at least here to breathe my last, beneath thy eyes!"‡

S. Francis of Sales, when he came as a pilgrim to this blessed abode, said in a rapture of divine love : "O lovely Spouse of the Eternal King, it is then here that are thy beams of cedar and thy planks of cypress! And it is behind these walls that Thou didst stand, O divine Love, looking through the windows, looking through the lattices!§ Here Thou didst feed among the lilies till the day declined and the shadows fell. ‖ In this place, O Lord, Thou didst become my Brother! And who will grant me the favour to see Thee at Thy Mother's breasts, and to be able to bestow upon Thee my devout kisses?" Whilst praying thus, his soul was melted by love, and the Saint seemed rapt in ecstasy.

---

* 1 Eccles. xxiv. 20.   † Canticles ii. 14.

‡ Vergin, ben posso dire
Che d'aver vita il cor soltanto sente,
Quando a voi son presente ;
Ma, se non m'è concesso
L' esservi ognor d'appresso,
Qui almen vorrei finire
Mia vita innanzi a voi,
Perchè sia 'n ciel l'alma beata poi.

                           See *Tempio Armonico.*

§ Canticles ii. 9.   Canticles ii. 16, 17.

The testimony of so many Saints who in every age have visited the Holy House,* cannot fail to have weight with the faithful.

It may not be out of place to add here the special graces with which the servant of God, *J. B. Olier*, was favoured.   " On entering into the church," he writes, " I felt myself so deeply touched, and so softened by the caresses of the Most Holy Virgin, that I was obliged to give myself up to my Saviour.   Bathed in tears, I besought the Most Holy Virgin that she would obtain death for me, if she foresaw that I should fall back into my past sins !   But, thanks be to God, I have never relapsed into them again.   My God, how salutary to sinners are the places dedicated to devotion towards the Blessed Virgin !   This was the most mighty stroke in my conversion. . . . . It is in this place that I was begotten to grace by the prayers of the Most Holy Virgin, and the Mother of Mercy gave me a new birth to God in the same place where she had conceived Jesus Christ." †

More striking still are the prophecies foretelling the Translation of the Holy House. The Seraphic *S. Francis of Assisi*, eighty years before this glorious event, pointed out the spot chosen by Heaven as the site on which this Sanctuary should one day stand.   The scene of this prediction is Sirolo, ‡ ten miles north-east of Loreto, where S. Francis went and founded a monastery in 1215.   The Saint told the Friars that this particular hill in the district of Loreto, which was at that time without a single habitation, was destined to be honoured with the presence of a Sanctuary not less sacred than the Holy Places of Palestine.

S. Nicholas of Tolentino also, only twenty years before the Translation, and while he was finishing his theological studies at Fermo, was favoured with a prophetic vision of the coming of the Holy House. Looking out over the sea in an ecstatic state, he said, amid ardent aspirations, that a *great treasure* was going to be sent across the vasty deep, beating the billows under it and riding on their backs. §

S. Joseph of Cupertino, like his spiritual father, the patriarch of Assisi, fell into ecstasy at the presence of the Holy House. This great servant of Mary, on his first arrival at Osimo, saw angels flying down from

* Suffice it to mention S. Ignatius of Loyola, S. Francis of Paula, S. Andrew Avellino, S. Cajetan, S. John Capistran, S. Bernardine of Siena, S. Catharine of Siena, S. Seraphin of Monte Granaro, S. Fidelis of Sigmaringa , S. Diego of Alcala, S. John Berchmans.

† A model of the Holy House of Loreto has been erected in memory of this conversion, and may be visited, near Paris, in the country house of the Seminary of S. Sulpice, of which M. Olier became the founder.

‡ It is at the foot of Monte Conero, the promontory seen in Plate I. The *Crucifix of Sirolo* is so celebrated that many pilgrims go there.

§ Father Octavius Falconi, of the Oratory, member of a noble family of Fermo, found the account of this vision related in the archives of that town.

Heaven upon the *Santa Casa*, bringing with them heavenly gifts, and
he exclaimed: "O God, what do I behold! But why should the angels
disdain to descend into this Holy House, into which the Lord from
Heaven did not disdain to descend and to become Man?"

This vision, granted to one so eminently favoured, brings clearly to
the Christian's view the *Santa Casa* as nothing less than *the House of
God and the Gate of Heaven!* * A ladder, similar to that which was seen
by the patriarch Jacob, connects this lower world with Heaven. Its foot
rests upon the Dwelling here below, and its summit reaches the Abode on
high. It is a ladder placed for the sons of the true Rebecca; † a
ladder by which to rise from guilt to favour, and to mount from earth to
Paradise. ‡ At the top of this mystic ladder, we behold God saying
to the Mother of our Lord: *In thee and in thy seed shall all the tribes
of the earth be blessed.* ‖

Angelic strains enraptured the soul of S. Joseph of Cupertino while
he looked upon the vision. It was such a song as makes heaven rejoice
and hell tremble—the song of the deliverance of the human race, and
of triumph over Satan; the song of redemption from death and of the gift
of eternal life.

"Sing with me," said the Saint on coming out of the state of ecstasy,
"sing with me, Brother Peter, the Christmas antiphon." He then
went again into raptures, listening to the heavenly music, and watching
the angels in their downward flight, laden with graces; and in their
upward flight, soaring rapidly in quest of more. "Behold and see," he
cries, "how the mercies of the Lord, like a copious shower, come down on
this Sanctuary! Oh the blessed Place! Oh the blessed House!"

* Gen. xxviii, 16, 17. The mysterious Ladder of Jacob is represented in one of the
new windows in the choir of the Basilica of Loreto.

† Mary is typified by Rebecca: she gives her younger sons the garments of her eldest
son, to obtain for them their father's blessing.

‡ S. Jerome calls Mary the Ladder by which we mount to heaven, and the Blessed
Albert the Great declares her to be the Ladder of ascension from sin to grace and from
earth to heaven. The Mother of God in the flesh is the Ladder by which He came
down to earth and took our nature to redeem us.

‖ Gen. xxviii. 14.

CHAPTER VII

Homage rendered by the entire Catholic world—Pilgrimages of the rich and poor, of the learned and the unlearned, of mighty monarchs and lowly faithful.

HOW shall we sketch out and bring together into one picture the pilgrimages of emperors and kings accompanied by the train of their attendants, the cavalcades of princes, dukes and peers? How give an idea of the magnificent gifts, the costly offerings, the profound reverence, the religious fervour of the great of the earth?

And the multitude of humble parentage but precious in the eyes of God, *the poor in this world rich in faith,*[*] who partake of the labours, sorrows and sufferings of Jesus, Mary and Joseph! Aye, this House is theirs; they form a part of the Holy Family; their prayers, their sighs, their tears have a sublime eloquence; they form a plaintive concert that is wafted to the Throne of God, and the whole Heaven is bowed down to listen to a music so divine!

Picture to yourselves forty thousand [†] pilgrims praying round the Holy House upon one single day! The remembrance of all these pilgrims, and of their ardent supplications, stirs the heart deeply on going to Loreto. We feel we are standing on the same ground where more than fifty million have stood before us; where, during the last six hundred years, vast processions of the faithful have passed; where so many saints have trodden with hearts in ecstasies of love at the thought of the Holy Family; where the retinues of Sovereign Pontiffs and crowned heads have come like the Magi to Bethlehem, with offerings rich and rare.

It would require volumes to relate the visits of illustrious pilgrims, who, at various epochs, have brought to the Holy House the tribute of their homage and their love. The list is well-nigh interminable; let us then be content with naming the Emperor Charles IV., accompanied by the Empress and his children, in 1355; John Palæologus, Emperor of

---

* S. James ii. 5.

† Tursellini says that, during his residence at Loreto, from thirty to forty thousand faithful were assembled on Holy Saturday, and that generally Holy Communion was given to 40,000 during Lent. And Gaudenti says that in May, 1780, 50,000 Communions were made, and in September 63,000.

the East, who came from Constantinople; the Emperor Frederic III.; Charlotte, Queen of Cyprus; Catharine Cornaro of Venice, Queen of the same country; Catharine, Queen of Bosnia; Alphonse of Aragon, King of Naples; Alexander and Stephen Batthori, Kings of Poland; the two Janes of Aragon, Queens of Naples; Bona Sforza, Queen of Poland; the Emperor Charles V.; * Mary of Austria, mother of Margaret, Queen of Spain; Jane of Austria, daughter of the Emperor Ferdinand I., and wife of Francis de Medicis; Mary-Ann, sister of Philip IV., King of Spain, and mother of the Emperor Leopold; Christine, Queen of Sweden; the Grand Duchess of Tuscany, Mary Magdalen; Mary Casimir, wife of John III. of Poland; the Archdukes of Austria Leopold, Ferdinand and Maximilian; Charles IV., King of Spain, 1814; Mary Louisa, Queen of Etruria, in 1815; Mary, Princess of Wurtemberg in 1817.

Among the first to shew zeal for the Holy House have been the Princes of Italy, the Dukes of Savoy, of Tuscany, of Parma, of Urbino, of Modena and Mantua. We may mention that the Duke Raniero Farnese went barefooted to the Holy House from his hotel.

We find among the personages of distinction who have made the pilgrimage of Loreto the Duke William, and his son the Elector Maximilian of Bavaria, the Elector of Cologne, and a number of the nobility of England, Germany, Hungary, Flanders, Bohemia, Poland and Transylvania.

From France we may record the visits of the Princes of Condé, the Counts of Soissons, the Dukes of Joyeuse, and many other noble families too numerous to find a place in this abbreviated list.

Spain also has furnished her quota of Knights of the Golden Fleece, of Cardinals and bishops.

In a word, illustrious pilgrims have come from every kingdom and province of Europe; kings who could not come in person have sent their ambassadors to present their vows and offerings; and even Daimiyos of Japan have emulated the devout generosity of the princes of the West.

A number of philosophers, historians, and eminent men of every kind have likewise paid their tribute of respect and homage to the *Santa Casa*.

Christopher Columbus, after his discovery of the New World, sent a faithful friend to fulfil the vow that he had made to Our Lady of Loreto.

The French moralist, Montaigne, shewed a marked confidence in Our Lady of Loreto. In his account of his journey into Italy in 1580, he speaks with admiration of a miracle wrought in behalf of a young Parisian of noble birth, who was cured of a painful disease of the knee, considered incurable by all the doctors. " It would be impossible,"

* See Calcagni, *Memoirs of Recanati.*

says Montaigne, "to form a better or more exact idea of a miracle." He stayed there three days and hung up a silver tablet in the Holy House. Later on, Descartes made a vow to undertake the pilgrimage *on foot* from Venice to Loreto, and he fulfilled his vow in 1624.

Tasso, author of *Jerusalem Delivered*, an epic poem which places him almost on a par with Virgil and with Milton, made a vow when in prison to visit the *Santa Casa*, and, when he reached it, composed some beautiful verses in honour of Our Lady of Loreto.

> Qui gli Angeli innalzaro il santo albergo
> Che già Maria col santo figlio accolse,
> E il portar sovra i nembi e sovra l'acque.
> Miracol grande ! a cui sollevo ed ergo
> La mente ch' altro obbietto a terra volse,
> Mentre da' suoi pensier oppresso giacque.
> Questo è quel monte ch'onorar ti piacque
> Delle tue sante mura,
> Virgine casta e pura.
> Del re dei regi— e tuo l'umil soggiorno
>   .   .
>
>   .   .   .   .   .   .
> E tragge a rimirar la santa imago
> Dall'estremo Occidente a stuolo a stuolo
> Peregrinando con tranquilla oliva
> Quei che dianzi bevean l'Ibero e il Tago,
> E da'segni soggetti al freddo polo
> Di là dall'Istro, e da più algente riva.
> E mille voti alla celeste Diva,
> Che scaccia i nostri mali,
> Solvon gli egri mortali,
> Il cui pregar per grazia al cielo arriva :
> E i magnanimi duci a Dio più cari
> Offrono argento ed auro,
> Sacro tesauro—a'tuoi devoti altari.

The above is but a small portion of the poem, *Ecco fra le Tempeste e i fieri Venti*, and may be rendered thus :—

> And here the Angels placed the Sacred Home,
> Which welcomed Mary and the Holy Child,
> And bore it o'er the clouds and o'er the sea.
> A wondrous miracle ! that raises and uplifts
> The soul, which other objects earthwards turn,
> The while it lies oppressed with its own thoughts.
> This is the mount, O Virgin chaste and pure,
> It pleased thee thus to honour with these walls of thine
> A humble sojourn for the King of kings
> And thee. .   .   .   .   .

It draws in crowds to gaze upon thy holy form,
Those from the distant West in pilgrimage
Who bear the peaceful olive in their hands ;
Those who erst-while drank the Iberian stream or Tagus,
By signs made manifest beneath the freezing Pole,
Beyond the Danube and yet colder shores—
The sick and suffering mortals bring their thousand woes
To her the heavenly Queen,
Who our ills dispels,
Whose prayers for grace so surely reach the Heavens :
And to thy holy altars
The great ones of the earth—those dear to God
Their gold and silver—holy treasures bear.

Riera, in his history of Loreto, * refers to the *Pilgrimage of the White*, in 1390, when a great multitude of men and women, of every rank and age, all clothed in garments of white linen, came down from the Alps to Loreto. Everywhere they passed, their example had a great effect ; multitudes left everything to adopt their dress and follow them. There were to be seen in the long procession princes and merchants, bishops and inferior clergy, rich and poor, great and small, old and young, all walking two and two with the same grand object of paying their homage to the Holy House of the Incarnation, conveyed by angels from the East to the West as a gift of Heaven to the piety of the Catholics of Europe.

The great renown of Our Lady of Loreto dates from the Jubilee of 1300, which had the effect of drawing to Rome and to Loreto representatives from all parts of Europe. They saw the great antiquity of the building that stood without foundations on a high road ; they conversed with the nobility, magistrates and people of the neighbourhood. They knew these men could not have been deceived ; for the House had passed from one place to another twice since its arrival in the district of Recanati. These repeated changes of position, of which the inhabitants were witnesses, were so many repeated proofs of the fact ; and the most incredulous of the pilgrims could not doubt, when they beheld it standing in the middle of a public highway. Men of exalted intelligence among them reflected on the power of the Omnipotent, Whose *fiat* all existing things obey ; they called to mind other wonders God has wrought by the ministry of angels ; they felt that no mere mortal on this earth can compute the strength of even one of those immortals sent from heaven ; they gave proof of true greatness of mind by acknowledging that the reason of the creature must bow before the higher reason of the Creator, and that the more the works of God surpass the ideas of man, so much the more is the glory of the Sovereign Ruler of the

* *Hist. Lauret.* cap. 10.

universe enhanced. They realised, in proportion to their grasp of intellect,
what it is for God to have taken human nature, and to have a human
Mother; they were not surprised at any wonder wrought in honour
of her House, the great monument of the Incarnation, and the very
place in which the Archangel S. Gabriel declared : *No word shall be
impossible with God.* *

CHAPTER VIII.

*The Pilgrimage of Loreto in the present day—Memories of the Holy Family
and of the sublime Mysteries of which the Holy House was the
divinely chosen scene.*

DEVOTION towards the Immaculate Mother of God in her sacred
Dwelling has been kept up continuously to our own times. The
hallowed Walls have never ceased to be surrounded by pious
pilgrims, specially on the festivals of the Birth of the Blessed Virgin,
her Annunciation and the Translation of the Holy House into Italy.
Thousands of pilgrims arrive yearly in Loreto. The twenty-seven thousand
tickets given up annually at the station, † so far from exceeding the
number of pilgrims, falls very far short of it; for the great majority are
Italian peasants, who do not come by railway, but on foot, from Naples
and across the Apennines—a pilgrimage far more attractive and inspiriting.
Listen how the valleys and the forests resound with their thrilling strains !

On approaching the City of Mary on the festival of her Nativity, there
are to be seen outside the gates covered waggons and vehicles of every
kind, drawn up at the side of the road and extending to a considerable
distance.

The Roman Gate *(Porta Romana)* leads into the central street, which
is the direct road to the Sanctuary. No one could fail to be struck with
the spectacle that here meets his eyes. Crowds of pilgrims throng the
way. Processions advance towards the Basilica. The singing is most
stirring. The whole town rings with the refrain: *Evviva Maria e Chi la
creò !* ‡ Radiant with joy is every face, while pressing on towards the
Shrine. One thought alone fills every breast—*The Holy House !*
Making their way through the bronze doors of the Basilica, they catch

* Luke i. 37.   † In the years 1887-1892, the average passenger traffic was 27,000.
‡ Live Mary, and He Who created her.

the first glimpse of the object of their pilgrimage, and the sight of the Holy House moves many to tears.

Sublime indeed are the moments spent in this blessed Dwelling. Scenes divinely ineffable pass before the eyes of the mind. The birth of Mary, her early years and the coming of S. Gabriel; the childhood and hidden life of Jesus ; the incomparable spectacle of the humility of the Son of God, veiling the splendour of His Majesty beneath the outward appearance of the son of a carpenter, and working under his orders.

At the end of a long day of toil at the workshop, we see the Lord taking a little rest at the family hearth, and sitting at the table to eat what His Mother's loving hands have prepared for Him. Like the three angels in Abraham's tent, the Holy Family partake together of the evening meal. We seem to stand beside this table in the Holy House, even as our father Abraham stood beside that table in the vale of Mambre, and as Sara listened from behind the door. We seem to hear their blessed converse, to behold the divine smile of Jesus and to listen to the gracious words that proceed from His lips. With what sympathy He enters into all their feelings ! As a devoted son He shews, by His every look and gesture, His deep and filial love, and as the Christ He opens out to them the treasures of His Sacred Heart.

Happy the Christians who, visiting this cottage-home, are able to summon back within its walls the memories of Nazareth. It is to make those scenes live in our mind and nourish our soul, that this hallowed Dwelling has been given to us. All the actions of the Holy Family are a light to illumine our hearts. None others were so much like Jesus as Mary and Joseph, and it is a very great grace to be privileged to enter their Home and picture them fulfilling their duties with a perfection so much in accordance with their heavenly model.

To honour the domestic work of Mary, princesses have often asked permission to sweep the floor of the Holy House upon their knees. And who can stand unmoved within those Walls, where the Queen of Heaven performed such menial tasks ? True, in the service of God no task is menial ; and Mary's faith in the God she served ennobled her most commonplace actions. While in this humble cottage the most blessed among women was engaged in her household duties, all that she did was permeated with divine love.

If on entering the Holy House we cannot with these eyes see the Blessed Virgin occupied in spinning, nor even, like S. Antoninus the Martyr, bend our looks upon her spindle, her basket and her seat, we may realise that, while her hands were turning that spindle, her mind was turning over the words of Jesus, and her heart meditating on the utterances of the Eternal Wisdom Incarnate.

Mary, so simple in the ordinary duties of daily life, was capable of rising to the most sublime contemplation of the Deity. Her acts of adoration surpassed those of the Seraphim, and her heart was the *Censer of the Holy Spirit.*

Let us make a mental picture of the Virgin of Nazareth in prayer in the Holy House. The little lamp sheds a glimmering ray upon a form whose grace and beauty are the image of her soul. A loveliness that seems not of this earth, belongs to her whose nature is Immaculate. In her presence we breathe the atmosphere of Paradise.

It is the hour of prayer. Her long veil falls down to her knees. She is turned towards the Holy City. Her hands and eyes are raised towards Jerusalem above. The heavenly light that pervades her soul illumines her whole countenance. Upon the wings of love her spirit soars to those realms that await her as their Queen. No cloud hides out the vision of her God. Her eyes behold unveiled the marvels of the Deity. She is lost in wonder and adoring contemplation of the beauty and the glory of her Maker.

Mary in prayer in the Holy House! Picture her as you will, it is a scene that must thrill the pilgrim, as he kneels where the Holy Mother of God has prayed. What a help to devotion to unite our supplications and our thanksgivings to those offered by our Immaculate Mother during her almost life-long residence in this sacred Dwelling!

Let us represent her again as lifting up her heart to God at Holy Mass. After the Ascension of the Lord a portion of the Holy House became a chapel. An altar marked the spot hallowed by the Incarnation. The Lamb of God was immolated on that altar there where He took Human Nature. Calvary was brought to Nazareth. At that self-same spot where Mary said, *Be it done to me according to thy word,* she stood by the mystic Sacrifice. By her side, as at the foot of the Cross, were to be seen the Magdalen, Salome, and Mary of Cleophas, who had been associated with her in her dolours—at the altar S. John, the beloved disciple of her crucified Son.

Were Masses ever so devoutly offered as where Mary herself was present? Was there ever such a reception given to Jesus descending on an altar as where His own Mother was there to receive Him? And in what place would her maternal heart receive her Son with so much rapture as in that Room, where first she had received the Lord from Heaven at the message of the great Archangel?

In remembrance of those fervent Masses offered in the Holy House, where Mary both conceived and cherished her Divine Son, let us assist with heart and soul at the Masses offered at Loreto. Mary will come with us to the foot of the altar, and will present to Jesus our adoration and our vows.

II

" I will glorify the place of my feet."—ISAIAS LX. 13.

PART II.

Honour rendered to the Holy House when it was at Nazareth—Detailed account of its Translations.

CHAPTER I

*Honour rendered to it by the Son of God, by the holy Apostles, by S. Helena, S. Francis of Assisi, S. Louis King of France, and other Saints; * by the Crusaders and Pilgrims of all nations. †*

THE Holy House belonged to the Virgin of Nazareth by succession from her father, S. Joachim, and became the heritage of Jesus. The Divine Heir held it in great esteem, as coming to Him from his dearly beloved Mother, and for her sake resolved to preserve it from age to age through all the vicissitudes of time.

It was befitting that this heritage of the Son of God should be neither destroyed nor defiled, and his watchful care over it is strikingly manifest from the first years of His return to Heaven. For while the Fathers of the Church had to denounce the sacrilegious pollution of the Holy Sepulchre and the cave of the Nativity by a temple erected to Venus and a grove planted to Adonis, the Holy House of Nazareth, far from being desecrated or dishonoured, was "the first church consecrated by the holy Apostles in honour of God and of the Blessed Virgin," ‡ and always retained the altar that S. Peter had set up.

As God preserved the house of Rahab in the destruction of Jericho, so was the Holy House preserved at the time when Vespasian sacked Nazareth.

When Constantine the Great proclaimed Christianity the religion

* Suffice it to mention S. Nicholas of Myra, S. Firmilian, S. Jerome, S. Paula, S. Cyriac, S. Petronius, S. Antoninus the Martyr, S. Willibald, S. John of Damascus, S. Macarius, B. Simeon Salus, S. Anastasius of Persia, S. Theophanus, S. Bonfiglio of Osimo.

† Among the more celebrated pilgrims we may name Alexander, Bishop of Cappadocia, Theodorus, Archimandrite of the same territory, Rusticiana, a lady of Constantinople, the two brothers Candidus and Gabrius, fifty Normans, William Duke of Aquitania Vandulph of Brabant, Cardinal de Vitri, Rodrigo, an English hermit, Sigefroy, Bishop of Mayence. Pilgrimages of Britons to the Holy Land are spoken of by S. Jerome and S. Chrysostom in the fourth century, and by Palladius and Theodoret in the fifth. It is not commonly known how much the apostasy of the Emperor Julian increased the number of pilgrims, on account of the series of miracles that hindered his rebuilding the Temple of Jerusalem.

‡ Julius II., Bull, dated Oct. 31, 1507.

of the empire, his holy mother, Helena Augusta, came to Nazareth, and
"found the House of the Angelic Salutation."* The sacred Dwelling had
been still preserved from profanation, and the saintly empress had merely
to restore the ancient altar on which Apostles had celebrated the holy
Mysteries. Deeply was S. Helena moved at the contemplation of so
poor a habitation in which the Sovereign Lord of all had deigned,
for love of us to dwell; and, being mistress of the treasures of the
empire, she resolved to make them serve to the glory of the Lord
so lowly, to Whom she had given her heart. The Sanctuary she
erected was one of the most beautiful in the East,† and became, eventually,
the metropolitan cathedral of the whole of Galilee. The empress
dedicated it to the Mother of the King of kings; and over its portal
she placed the inscription, "This is the altar on which were first laid the
foundations of human salvation." ‡

The memorable zeal of the Empress Helena greatly increased the number
of pilgrimages to the Holy House. Christians flocked from every part
of the world to that chosen dwelling where S. Gabriel announced
salvation—that hallowed Chamber where the great Virgin gave to her
God her substance and her virginal milk. Borne upon the wings of love,
these ardent pilgrims traversed land and sea, that they might enter the
House which God selected out of all others on the surface of the globe, as
the one in which to take our human nature and in which to live. Men
of every clime and nation, fired with a sacred flame of divine fervour,
journeyed with eager expectation to its hallowed precincts. They felt it
was *no other but the House of God and the Gate of Heaven.* They longed
to pray beneath the shadow of those Walls rendered so holy by the long
residence of the Son of God made Man; those Walls wherein Mary
was born and lived, where she gave that consent which is the joy of
heaven and earth, and the reparation of the fatal conversation between the
first Eve and the prince of fallen angels.

No serious perils were incurred in these pilgrimages so long as Palestine

---

* Niceph. Callist. *Hist.* lib. viii. cap. 30.

† The remains of this Basilica so closely resemble the Basilica at Bethlehem that they
attest the fact of their erection at the same epoch. Cardinal Bartolini, when reading
his discourse on this subject before the Archæological Academy at Rome, says; "We still
see fragments of the cornice and the frieze. The style of these ornaments is very superior
to that of Constantinian basilicas in Rome. This is a proof that the decadence of art was less
rapid in the East than in the West." Up to the time of the conversion of Constantine, the
Hebrews in Nazareth had hindered the Christians from building a church. See S. Epiphanius.
S. Paulinus, A.D. 431, says of S. Helena, "Ædificatis basilicis, contexit omnes et excoluit
locos, in quibus salutaria nobis mysteria pietatis suæ *Incarnationis*," etc. S. Antoninus
about 570, saw this "*admirandam basilicam magnam*" at Nazareth.

‡ "Hæc est ara, in quâ primo jactatum est humanæ salutis fundamentum."—Niceph.
Callist. *Hist.* lib. viii. cap. 30.

was under the Christian emperors. But when the banner of Islam was unfurled, and the Holy Land came under the power of Arabian Caliphs, Saracens and Fatamites, it became necessary to institute the Order of the Knights of S. Catharine to protect the pilgrims on their journey to Nazareth.

At a subsequent period, nomad tribes of Seljukian Turks were a great cause of suffering to the pilgrims and native Christians in Palestine.

The danger to pilgrims, however, only rendered many the more eager to visit the Holy Places ; and some, like S. Francis of Assisi at a later date, went hoping to shed their blood. The spirit and devotion of the pilgrims excite our highest admiration. Impelled by holy zeal, constrained by heartfelt gratitude, no difficulties or dangers hindered them from kneeling within those sacred Walls where Redemption had its beginning ; men ready to pour out their life-blood, to return to Jesus blood for blood and life for life, forced their way to Nazareth, where He took Flesh that He might die !

Those who escaped the scimitar of the Mahomedans gave so heart-rending an account of the persecutions endured by the Christians in the East, that a great cry of grief and indignation arose throughout Europe.

From this cry of pain the crusades took their birth. S. Urban II. and Peter the Hermit had only to speak, and all Europe rose up as one man, ready to take the cross and rush to the succour of their brethren in distress. A great number of those who started died on the way, and those who reached there failed, in spite of their heroic efforts, to permanently improve the position of the native Christians, or to open up lastingly a safe way for the pilgrims. The kingdom of Jerusalem was founded, it is true, with Godfrey de Bouillon as its first king, and Galilee was placed under Tancred as governor ; but, eighty-eight years after, the crusaders were vanquished at Tiberias, and the Holy Places fell again into the hands of the Mahomedans.

The chief protectors of the pilgrims to the Holy House during the crusades were the Knights of the military Order of the Templars. And when the son of Saladin attacked Nazareth, a small band of one hundred and thirty Knights of the Temple, accompanied by some four hundred men, defended the Sanctuary foot to foot against seven thousand Arabian horsemen. After feats of heroism that deserve to be immortally recorded, the Master of the Temple, Jacquelin de Maillé, thought by the enemy to be S. George, fought almost alone on his white charger, till it fell exhausted beneath him ; then, continuing the unequal combat on foot, this brave defender of the Holy House went to the Lord of the House to receive his crown.*

* Michaud, Croisades.

All seemed lost; but the Virgin of the Holy House herself watched over her Dwelling. On the night of July 8, 1192, a supernatural light appeared at a post of the crusaders outside the walls of S. Jean d'Acre, and in the midst of the light the Christian warriors beheld the great Virgin of Nazareth. She had come to this city that was nearest to the Holy House to make this promise: "In four days you shall be masters of this city." For more than three whole years in vain had the crusaders besieged Ptolemais, but on the fourth day it fell.

This fortress, the key of the whole North, being in the hands of Richard Cœur de Lion, Philip Augustus, and Guy de Lusignan, the route to Nazareth was re-opened; and among the pilgrims was the Greek priest John Phocas, already mentioned, who tells that he had the joy of visiting the *little Room of the ever-Virgin Mother of God*, which formed part of the *ancient House where the Archangel announced the good news*.

Fifty-five years later, Louis IX. of France received the crusaders' cross at Notre Dame, Paris, and left the capital on June 12, 1248, at the head of a powerful army. Pestilence and famine, however, decimated his brave followers, and, in spite of prodigies of valour, this heroic and saintly king was taken in chains to Mansourah. When S. Louis had gained his liberty, A.D. 1252, he went as a pilgrim to the Holy House at Nazareth. His reverence for it was so deep, that he prepared himself by fasting and by putting on a hair-shirt. As soon as this pious king came in sight of the sacred precincts, he descended from his horse, and on bended knees bowed low. Then he walked slowly and prayerfully into the town, and entered the cathedral. He had come for the festival of the Annunciation, that he might receive the Body of the Lord on the same day and in the very Place where *the Word was made Flesh*.

The Holy House formed, as we have seen, * the crypt of the Basilica, and the king had to descend the steps in the tunnelled rock, which exist to this day.

The royal counsellor and historian, Peter Matthew, tells us that S. Louis, with eyes bathed in tears, his heart overflowing with heavenly consolation, "*received the Holy Eucharist in the very same Room where the Virgin Mary, Our Lady, was saluted by the Angel.*"

The king's confessor, Geoffrey de Beaulieu, who had accompanied him to Nazareth, also describes S. Louis's touching devotion, and says that, after Mass and Holy Communion at the *Altar of the Incarnation*, the king caused the Office of the day to be celebrated with great solemnity, and that Odo Tusculanus, legate of the Holy See, preached an

* Part I. chap. IV. Plate X.

No. XIII—Visit of St. Louis to the Holy House.   Interior of the Basilica erected by St. Helena.

11

impressive discourse, and sang Pontifical Mass at the High Altar of the Basilica.

Ten years after S. Louis's return to France his deep devotion towards the Holy House was manifested anew in a telling manner never to be forgotten. Hearing from Pope Urban IV. that the Mameluke Sultan of Egypt, Bibars-Ben-Dokdar, had made sad havoc of the Church of the Annunciation, which contained the Holy House, the king entered the Council Chamber of the Louvre wearing a *crown of thorns*, and called upon his nobles to join him in a new crusade. An army was hastily equipped and a fleet fitted out, and this pre-eminent votary of the Holy House set sail for S. Jean d'Acre, the port of Galilee and Nazareth.

The Holy House did not need any human protector; but the ardent vow of S. Louis obtained for him to enter without further delay into the heavenly Dwelling, of which the House of the Holy Family below is so beautiful a figure. So felt the saintly king when expiring at Tunis upon his way to Nazareth; for raising himself upon his death-bed strewn with ashes, and heaving a deep sigh, he exclaimed: *" O Lord, I will come into Thy House, and will worship Thee in Thy holy Temple."** And saying this he fell back dead.

What death hindered this sainted monarch from achieving, Edward of England,† supported by the Knights of S. John and of the Temple, was enabled in a measure to effect. He advanced to Nazareth with 7,000 men, and won it at the point of the sword. The victory was complete, but its results were transient. Edward returned home without restoring the Basilica or providing for the safety of the Christians.

Some seventeen years later, the Christian cause in Palestine was permitted, by an inscrutable Providence, to fall into a hopeless condition. Tripoli and Acre held out for a time, but when Tripoli was taken in 1289, and Acre in May, 1291, the last remnant of Christian power in the Holy Land was gone. The Mahomedans slaughtered thousands of Christians, and the monks on Mount Carmel were massacred while singing the *Salve Regina*.

At the sight of these woes the Knights of the Temple, who had fought so bravely to defend the Holy House of Nazareth, shed tears of rage and grief; and one asked with bitterness if God intended to allow the Moslems to turn the Sanctuary of Nazareth into a mosque. No, the Lord will not suffer this. If needs be, the Holy House will be found no longer there. God will know how to withdraw it from profanation or destruction. No blows of destructive axes shall ever lay it low, nor shall sacrilegious rites ever desecrate it. Tripoli may fall; Acre, the last stronghold, may fall too; the Christian power in Palestine may be

* Psalm v. 8.   † Son of Henry III.

entirely overthrown ; not a single soldier of the Cross may remain to
defend the sacred Walls wherein God became Man ; the fanaticism of the
followers of the false prophet may profane all other Christian churches ;
but the Omnipotent can place limits to the blind fury of unbelievers ;
and when there are no human hands and hearts to protect the hallowed
Chamber of the Incarnation, God *will give His angels charge over* it ; if
necessary, *in their hands they shall bear* it up ; they shall snatch it
away from profanation, and it shall be found in a Christian land,
where it shall be venerated. Yes, the Creator of the Universe, Who
could remove this whole planet to another orbit more easily than we
can pick up a particle of sand and put it elsewhere, will by His
Almighty power remove the immortal Shrine of the Incarnation and put
it in a place of safety and of honour.

No. XIV.—MOUNT CARMEL AND ST. JEAN D'ACRE.

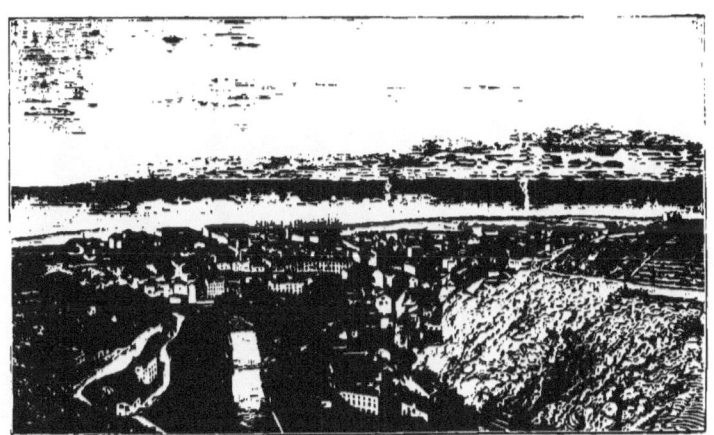

XV.—FIUME AS SEEN FROM THE HILL OF TERSATTO.

CHAPTER II

The Translation of the Holy House into Illyria.

AT the break of dawn on the eastern shores of the Adriatic, May 10, 1291, some woodmen went to fell trees on the hill of Tersatto, that rises up behind the city of Fiume, at the head of the beautiful Gulf of Quarnero. On reaching an open space in the woods, they were astonished to find there a small stone building. They could scarcely believe their eyes; for all the cottages in the neighbourhood were built of wood, and on this particular spot they had never seen a building of any kind. They had even passed on the previous day, and there was nothing.

All nature was smiling, and the birds singing their most joyful notes; but these awe-struck men stood dumb with amazement. Signing themselves devoutly with the holy sign of the Cross, they ventured to approach it and look in. Directly opposite the door there was an altar. The Holy Mother of God was represented by a statue, holding in her arms the Infant Saviour, and a large wooden cross, attached to the wall, bore the figure of Our Lord painted on it.

The surprise of the woodcutters was increased on observing in this Chapel eating vessels in a cupboard, and what seemed to be a fire-place blackened by smoke, as if it had been the habitation of some family.

The walls were covered with plaster, on which were painted the Immaculate Virgin and some of the Saints honoured in the East. Among the different frescoes, there was also a representation of a king holding chains in his right hand, as if to denote that he had visited this shrine when liberated from captivity. The woodmen knew nothing of S. Louis, or this picture might have aided them to solve the mystery; but their fear gave place to holy joy, when they found their hearts filled with a heavenly sweetness; and, after praying devoutly, they hastened to call others to behold the mysterious Sanctuary.

The inhabitants of Fiume and Tersatto were as much astonished as the woodmen. The antiquity of the building; its construction and materials, so different from their own buildings; above all, its position on the grass, without any foundations to rest on—all this filled them with wonder and awe. Whence could it be? No human power could have made this shrine suddenly appear. Meanwhile, a father who had a sick child found it healed, and others brought their sick and they were cured; the

sorrowful found their hearts filled with an unwonted joy ; many could not
tear themselves away from the spot, and remained all night in fervent
aspirations.

In the meantime, the parish priest of St. George's Church, named
Alexander de Giorgio, while lying on a bed of suffering, heard descriptions
of the Sanctuary that had miraculously arrived, and it grieved him much
that he had no hope of ever being able to go and visit it. Whilst he was
thus full of desire to behold what God had wrought, there appeared to
him the Blessed Virgin, and with the sweetest voice she said : " My son,
thou hast called me ; behold, I am here to give thee effectual help, and
to reveal to thee the secret that thou wishest to discover. Know, then, that
the sacred dwelling, recently brought to this territory, is the same House in
which I was born, and where I was chiefly brought up. It is in it that,
at the message of the Archangel Gabriel, I conceived, by the operation
of the Holy Ghost, the Divine Child. It is in it that the *Word was made
Flesh*. Wherefore, after my leaving this world, the Apostles consecrated
this Dwelling, rendered great by such ineffable Mysteries, and here they
devoutly celebrated the august Sacrifice. The altar conveyed with it
to this country is the same that the Apostle Peter consecrated. The
crucifix in it was formerly placed there by the Apostles. The statue in
cedar is an Image of myself, carved by the hand of Luke the Evangelist,
who, by reason of the intimate acquaintance that he had with us, has, as far
as was possible to a mortal, represented my form and coloured it. This
House, so loved by Heaven, and for so many years treated with the
greatest honour in Galilee, has now, at length, owing to a decline in devotion
towards it, due to the decay of faith, departed from the town of Nazareth
and come to your shores. Nor let faith doubt. The Author of this work
is God, *with Whom no word is impossible*. * And that thou thyself mayest be
witness and herald of these things, receive thy restoration to health. Thy
so sudden recovery from so long an illness will produce faith in the miracle."

The vision disappeared, leaving the room redolent with a heavenly
odour, and the sick priest felt that he was indeed healed. Overflowing
with gratitude, he hastened to the Holy House to thank his Benefactress.

A suppressed cry of surprise burst from all at the sudden appearance in
their midst of their parish priest, whom they thought to be beyond recovery.
They saw no remains of disease upon him ; and he related to them, amid
tears of joy, that the Blessed Virgin had revealed to him that it was her
House from Nazareth, and that she had healed him that he might bear
testimony to this truth. †

* Luke i. 37.
† Farlatus, in his *Illyrici Sacri*, gives the title of *Antistes* to Alexander de Giorgio.
We find him sometimes called bishop, and sometimes parish priest, owing to writers

The Holy House had been placed near the little valley of Dolaz, at Raunizza, where there was land belonging to a widow named Agatha, and the Archangel Gabriel appeared to her, to announce that the Sanctuary had come from Nazareth.

At the distance of a bow-shot stood the castle of Count Nicholas Frangipani.* The Count was absent from Tersatto at the actual moment of the arrival of the Holy House; but he soon returned.†

Once upon the spot, he lost no time in sending four delegates to Nazareth. ‡ They took with them the dimensions of the sacred Building, and every particular about its materials, structure, and contents.

Before the return of these delegates, some Christian captives, who had escaped from the hands of the Turks in Galilee, arriving at the port of Fiume, related what astonishment there had been at Nazareth on finding that the Holy House had disappeared; and when they were taken up the hill

differing as to the meaning of *Antistes*. It appears to have here its classical signification of one who presides over sacred rites (hence a priest), and not its ecclesiastical signification, of one who presides over a diocese. Hence, Tursellini is careful to say *sacrorum antistes*, as if to correct Riera, who put *episcopus*. Glavanich and Pasconius, writing at the Monastery at Tersatto, and Marotti, Bishop of Pisino, in Istria, only mention his cure of souls in the Church of S. George, Tersatto. The parish existed in 1280 (see *Schematismus Cleri Diœcesium Segniensis et Modrusiensis*, British Museum Library, under *Fiume*, pp. 2441, zt.), and even a hundred years before, for we have the name of the parish priest in 1180, John Vazmina. S. George is still the patron of the parish, and his banner is placed in a position of honour, near the entrance of the church.

Chiolich's list of bishops of this diocese is so imperfect that no names whatever are given between Saraceno, 1236, and Vitus, 1435: but Farlatus shews that a bishop named Peter succeeded to the see about 1300. If Saraceno were still bishop at the time of the arrival of the Holy House, he had held the see for 55 years; so that he may have needed an auxiliary bishop to assist him, and may have placed him at Tersatto. Why Tersatto should have been chosen for his residence might be explained by there having been bishops of *Tersactum* as late as the time of S. Charlemagne. (See list of bishops during the reign of this emperor, kept in the Archives of Udine. It is known that Charlemagne destroyed a town where Fiume now stands, and that its name was Tersatica.)

* This castle remained a stronghold of the Counts of Frangipani up to 1671. It was purchased a few years ago by an English General, whose mausoleum is in its donjon. A picture of it is given in Part IV.

† He may have been only at his other castle at Modrussa; but a more probable cause of his absence was the war of succession to the throne of Hungary. Ladislas IV. having been assassinated in his tent in 1290, the Emperor Rodolph of Hapsburg thought he could dispose of the crown in favour of his son Albert; but Andrew, called *the Venetian*, seized the crown and sought the help of the Doge of Venice. The Frangipanis had always combated the pretensions of the Doges (on the subject of the Frangipanis of Illyria, see the book of Baron Trasmundo dei Frangipani), and, in 1291, Count Nicholas Frangipani would certainly take the side of his relative, Rodolph, against Andrew, *the Venetian*. If the Emperor Rodolph had lived, he would perhaps have succeeded in putting his son Albert on the throne of Hungary; but death put a stop to his projects, and Andrew kept the crown.

‡ Suffice it to name Sigismond Orsich, John Gregoruzchi, and Alexander de Giorgio.

I

to Tersatto, they recognised immediately the Holy House and the sacred objects in it.

An aged pilgrim, who had been to Nazareth thirty years before, and upon whom the Holy House had made a profound impression, ardently desired to see it once more before his death. What he most loved on earth was his only son, and, to draw down the blessings of Heaven upon him, he determined to take him with him on this pilgrimage. The port of Fiume lay upon his way; and, on reaching it, he learnt with grief the fall of Acre, and the complete overthrow of Christian power in Palestine. Behind the harbour there rose up before his eyes the hill of Tersatto, with the little Church of S. George, shaded by rich foliage, and the strong castle of Count Frangipani overhanging a deep ravine. He is told that a mysterious Chapel has arrived miraculously there, and he sees the people pouring in from the surrounding country and climbing eagerly the steep ascent. He joins the crowd, and takes his turn to enter. No sooner do his eyes behold the interior and the image of the Blessed Virgin, than, filled with transports of joy, and trembling with emotion at the sublimity of the miracle that has brought it there, he falls with his face upon the earth and adores the great Omnipotent. At length, arising from his knees, he declares to those assembled that he himself had prayed within this very portion of the Holy House when he was at Nazareth.

Meanwhile, the delegates sent by Count Frangipani arrived in the Holy Land, and by the payment of blackmail obtained a safe-conduct and a mounted escort to accompany them to Nazareth. Here they saw at a glance the exact state of the Church of the Annunciation, and the position that the Holy House had occupied in front of the sacred Caves. Some of the stonework and roof of the Basilica, together with a column or two,* may have fallen down into the space where it had stood; but, evidently, the foundations were readily discovered after the removal of a little débris. They then took the dimensions, and found that they agreed perfectly with the measurements that they had brought. They examined the nature of the stones in the foundations, and saw that they were exactly similar to those forming the walls of the Holy House of Tersatto. They compared the date of its disappearance from Nazareth with that of the arrival in their country, and they exactly corresponded.

Thoroughly convinced by all that they had seen and heard at Nazareth, the delegates returned to Tersatto; and Count Frangipani, in his public capacity, had a formal document drawn up to serve as a testimony to posterity.

---

* Two columns, that remain on the site of the Holy House up to the present day, seem to have belonged to the nave of the original Basilica.

The result of the deputation to Nazareth becoming known, the people of the provinces of Croatia, Dalmatia, Istria, Bosnia, and Servia, eagerly hastened to visit the sacred Walls where the Immaculate Virgin first drew breath, where she received the angelic Annunciation, and where the eternal Word took Flesh and lived until the time of His public ministry.

Count Frangipani had a strong wooden building erected over the sacred Edifice to protect it from the weather, and determined to raise in its honour a church more worthy of so precious a treasure. But Jesus of Nazareth and His most holy Mother had other purposes respecting the glory of their sacred Dwelling.

CHAPTER III

Translation of the Holy House into Italy, December 10, 1294.

AMID the darkness of a stormy winter night upon the coast of the province of Ancona, there suddenly appears far out at sea a brilliant light that approaches nearer every instant. Like the pillar of fire that led Israel across the Red Sea, it is passing over the Sea of Adria. Like the fiery chariot of the Prophet S. Elias borne upon a whirlwind, it is seen to be advancing rapidly through the air. Resembling a halo of glory, it surrounds some object that is as yet wrapt in mystery. Is it a bright band of angels bearing in their hands some servant of God, as erst they carried the Prophet Habacuc from Jerusalem to Babylon, and the body of S. Catharine from Alexandria to the desert of Mount Sinai? Is it a choir of cherubim escorting the Ark of the Covenant, and have they received the commission to place in the centre of the Church that holy Ark which held the Manna that came down from Heaven? Nay. Note well the direction of their flight. This heavenly convoy is coming in a straight course from Tersatto's hill! All this flood of light upon the sea encompasses, and this celestial train escorts, the true Ark in which *the Living Bread* from heaven dwelt. These flaming spirits have received this high behest of the Eternal; and this approaching wonder given to Italy, amid the songs of angels and the brightness of God, is none other than the earthly Home of Him Who deigns to be the

Bread of our immortal souls. Behold! The advancing light is passing over the billows from the Port of Fiume. Like a vessel, with bright angels as the navigators, comes that ship in which the Lord from heaven embarked when He came from the celestial shores. It has the cross for its mast, the mantle of Mary for its sail, and the breath of God, like a favouring breeze, to make it glide swiftly over the waters. At the helm stands the Queen of Angels, at her side the Archangel St. Gabriel. See! it has already reached the shore! Now it has traversed half-a-league on land! It descends into the wood of the Lady Lauretta! The trees are become like the bush on fire that Moses saw! And, as in Joseph's dream, his brother's sheaves bowed down before his sheaf, so the trees bear silent testimony to the greatness of that which has arrived among them. With heads bent low they bow in homage; and so will they remain, in attitude of reverence, for nigh 300 years, that untold thousands may behold and learn the honour due to the sacred Walls that held Incarnate God.

The shepherds of the district, keeping the night-watches over their flock, view with awe this heavenly refulgence, and strain their eyes to discover what it is. Feeling sure that it is not a mere vision, but a reality, they determine, at approaching dawn, to go down into the wood and see this thing that the Lord has shown to them.

Their surprise is as great as that of the woodmen of Tersatto, and, as in their case, fear gives place to joy: they pray with an unwonted fervour, and then hasten to the nearest town to recount all that they have witnessed.

At first only a few of the inhabitants of Recanati heeded the message of the shepherds; but when they returned and told their fellow-citizens the wonders of the chapel that rested on the earth without foundations, many were constrained to go and see it for themselves. At length the people flocked in crowds to the wood on the estate of the noble Lady Lauretta, and there became a general feeling in all the surrounding country that it must be the work of God. The inhabitants spoke of nothing but of the mysterious Chapel; and the paths in the wood were filled with people of every position in life. Even the aged and infirm made great efforts to get there; and the faith of all was powerfully seconded by miracles of healing. So much fervour took possession of their hearts, that they could not tear themselves away from the place, and preferred kneeling on the cold hard earth in those nights of December to reposing quietly in their beds.

It soon became necessary to erect huts around the Sanctuary, to dig a well, and provide other accommodation for the pilgrims.

It was a time of civil war,* and banditti, taking advantage of the

* All Italy was torn by the factions of the Guelphs and Ghibellines.

No. XVI.—Translation of the Holy House into Italy.

unsettled state of the country, waylaid pilgrims benighted in the dark and tortuous paths of the wood. But God turned the malice of the devil to His glory ; to it we owe a greater certitude of the miracle of the Translations of the Holy House. For pilgrims, being afraid to enter the wood through fear of the robbers, and the Holy House becoming thus neglected, it abandoned the wood exactly as it had left Nazareth, where the pilgrims were massacred and it was deserted.

This second miracle in the vicinity of Recanati confirmed the first. And when, on a morning in August, 1295, the people of the neighbourhood found that it had left the wood, and, borne through the air, had descended on the hill, this fresh Translation produced an immense effect upon them.

Its new site was about a mile further inland, and, being near the road from Recanati to Porto Recanati, could be visited without the same amount of peril. It was a cultivated hill, and the joint property of two brothers, the Counts Stephen and Simon Rinaldi de Antici.

The honour and joy of having this mysterious Sanctuary in their field made them ignore at first any difficulty as to their respective rights of property in the piece of land on which it stood ; but the rich offerings of the pilgrims soon aroused their love of gain, and stirred up the question of ownership of the plot on which it had been placed. The dispute between the brothers became, at length, so violent that the land, sanctified by the presence of this most sacred Building was in danger of being defiled by fratricidal bloodshed.

The Holy House was then suddenly withdrawn from the hill of discord. The two covetous brothers rose one morning in December * to discover that their attachment to the goods of earth had deprived them of the heaven-sent gift; that their hearts, full of rancour and *greedy of filthy lucre*, † had displeased the Holy Family, and that the object of their dispute had quitted their polluted field.

This last removal of the Holy House was, in one respect, more striking than the previous ones ; for it was put down " in the middle of the road of the Commune of Recanati ;"‡ and the authorities were obliged to divert the course of the road so as not to disturb it.

The people of Recanati and the neighbouring towns were also stunned with amazement at the miracles wrought there ; for " with great signs and innumerable graces and miracles was the august Chapel placed on that road."§

The place where the Immaculate Virgin chose to fix her permanent dwelling is on the same ridge of hills as the hill of the two

---

* A.D. 1295.　† 1 Tim. iii. 8.　‡ Jerome Angelita, Chancellor of Recanati.　§ Il Teramano.

brothers, and at little more than a hundred yards from it. No private individual could now any longer claim possession of it, or be tempted to make it a source of personal gain. The magistrates of Recanati had already done what they could to avoid these evils; for, when it stood in the field of the brothers, they had sent a delegate with a letter to the capital to ask that the piece of land should be made over to the city, as the Sanctuary ought not to be the property of one family. Before, however, a reply could come from Rome, a higher Power had transferred it to its present position, which, being a public road, was the property of the city of Recanati.

This third miracle, in the same locality and in the space of one year, rendered more manifest the reality of divine interposition. God foreknew all the difficulties that would arise at each spot; but He saw fit to give us these additional proofs of His love for the Sanctuary of the Incarnation, that we may learn the more to honour it.

CHAPTER IV

Delegates are sent to Nazareth and Tersatto.

"PEOPLE began to say it was from Schiavonia; and the inhabitants gave credence, because it stood without foundations." So relates the chancellor of Recanati, Angelita.

Ancona lying almost opposite the Port of Fiume, its inhabitants became aware of the disappearance of the Holy House from Tersatto by conversations with merchants and sailors; and these men, who had seen it at Tersatto, had their curiosity aroused by what was being said in Ancona about a miraculous chapel recently arrived, and on going to see it, recognised it immediately—the same building, the same image, the same cupboard, the same frescoes, the same altar, and the same crucifix.

It pleased the Mother of God to appear in a vision to a holy man * who prayed much in her sacred Dwelling. Full of kindness, she told him that it was indeed her Holy House from Nazareth, the place of her conception, as well as of her birth and the Annunciation: the humble Sanctuary where the only-begotten Son of God became Man for our

---

* He is called the *Hermit of Mount Orso* from the name of the hill on which his cell was situated.

salvation ; where she suckled Him until the flight into Egypt,* where she ministered to Him up to the age of thirty, and where she often received Him during His ministry. She said also that, God having enriched her there with many spiritual gifts and made her mediatrix, He had determined to receive in the Holy House the prayers of the faithful, and display the treasures of His grace. In conclusion, she told the hermit to make known far and wide the dignity of the Holy House and the greatness of the gift conferred upon the West, in order that this Sanctuary, chosen of God, might be adorned with fresh honours.

The Immaculate Virgin disappeared, and her faithful servant, in spite of being mocked as a visionary, persevered in proclaiming her message, until at length a general assembly of the leading men of the March of Ancona was convened at Recanati.

This assembly determined, in accordance with the wish of Boniface VIII., to send delegates to Palestine ; and sixteen men of eminent virtue were chosen to examine into the truth of so great a marvel.

The delegates were first sent across to the harbour of Fiume. There the inhabitants expressed universal regret at the great loss they had sustained by the departure of the Holy House. They led the delegates to the spot that it had quitted, and shewed them the Chapel erected in commemoration of its stay among them. When they heard that the delegates were on their way to Nazareth, they shewed them, in the archives of Tersatto, the account signed by the four chosen men sent to Palestine by Count Frangipani—an account which affirmed the identity of the Holy House as the result of most careful investigations.

Setting sail from Fiume, the delegates went on to Palestine. The Mahometans were sole masters of the Holy Land, but by the payment of a heavy blackmail, they were allowed to go to Nazareth, under the protection of an escort. Some five years having elapsed since the last Christian warriors had left Galilee, warlike feeling had quieted down ; and there were inhabitants who could point out to them the spot the hallowed Chamber had occupied, when it stood in front of the mouth of

---

* Luke ii. 39 :—*After they had performed all things according to the Law of the Lord, they returned into Galilee, to their own city Nazareth.* St. John Chrysostom thinks that they were in the Holy House at Nazareth when they received the order to fly into Egypt. The Holy House would, in this case, be associated with the *Dolour of the Flight*, and there is an *Altar of the Flight* in the Cave of Nazareth. According to a tradition at Nazareth, related by Daniel, a Russian abbot, who visited the Holy House in 1114, Mary suckled Jesus in the room he saw. They shewed him also the little bed of the Holy Child on the floor of Mary's private chamber. Some commentators think that Mary and Joseph went back to Nazareth for only a short time, intending to bring up Jesus in the city of David. According to this theory the Divine Infant would have been nursed in the Holy House of Nazareth until the return to Bethlehem, which ended in the flight into Egypt, after the visit of the Wise Men.

K

the sacred Cave and formed part of the crypt of the cathedral. They found that the measurements coincided exactly with those they had brought; and they could see that the stones in the foundations were of the same kind as those in the Chapel that had arrived in their country. An inscription also relating the date of the departure of the Holy House was shewn to them, attached to a wall.

We may imagine the joy that fills their hearts in having these proofs before their eyes. When they reach their native shores they will be able to assure their compatriots that they have among them, not merely a miraculous sanctuary, in which the Lord Jesus is pleased to pour out His gifts, in answer to the intercession of the Mother He so loves, but the very Chamber in which the Incarnation was wrought; the very Nursery of the Infant God ; the very Habitation in which God the Son dwelt among men for the long space of nearly thirty years !

So eager are the delegates to tell the news in Recanati, that the days of the voyage seem like months. At length they come in sight of the Mount of Ancona; the Holy House is visible upon its hill, and they salute it with enthusiasm. On landing, they go forthwith to pay the homage of their love and gratitude to the Immaculate Virgin. Then they make their entry into Recanati, where their return is already known ; they are surrounded and asked a thousand questions, but the expression of their countenances sets at rest all doubt. The municipal authorities receive them at the Town Hall, where they listen to an exact description of all they saw, and, after having taken minutes of their testimony, resolve to transmit it to posterity by means of a document bearing the signature of the sixteen delegates.

This document was placed in the archives of Recanati, and copies of it sent to be kept in neighbouring towns and in several private families. Tablets were also put up in the sacred precincts of the Holy House relating what the delegates had found.*

The report of the return of the delegates spread rapidly, and the inhabitants of all the surrounding places poured out of the towns and villages. Many were the processions with sacred banners and with bands of music that advanced with holy joy to salute that sacred Dwelling, whose presence made their province a second Galilee with a new Nazareth in their very midst. Well might these privileged people rejoice, for were they not become the most favoured of all the children of Mary, who had brought her beloved House among them, that she might dwell amidst them as in her earthly Home ?

The inhabitants of Tersatto, and the other Slavs that peopled the neighbouring provinces, inconsolable at the loss they had incurred,

* Riccardi, *Santuarii piu celebri di Maria SS.*

came in their turn to pour out their grief at the feet of their kind Mother and implore her to give back to them her precious Dwelling. When the ships that brought them over were about to return, numbers of them could not make up their minds to leave the Holy House; they felt that their true country and their home was that place in which their Mother, Mary, had chosen to fix her abode.

Many families of Slavs permanently established themselves in the locality, under the shadow of these sacred Walls, and aided thus in founding the town of Loreto,* which was beginning to spring up, to supply accommodation for the vast concourse of pilgrims, flocking from the whole of Christendom, to visit the earthly abode of the Incarnate Word and His Ever-virgin Immaculate Mother.

On the feast of the Annunciation the devotion of the inhabitants of Recanati was so great that the town was left almost empty, everyone thronging to the *Santa Casa.*

And as each anniversary of the Translation came round, all the city kept it as a festival; and in the evening there were illuminations and festive fires lighted, and other rejoicings. The devotion towards the Virgin of Loreto became so popular that in the open space before the town hall of Recanati the Litany of Loreto was publicly sung every Saturday evening. Later on, in the centre of their city, a grand monument in bronze, girt round with marble, was erected to celebrate the coming of the Holy House to their shores.

---

* The *district* of Loreto existed in pagan times, and took its name from a laurel grove containing a heathen temple, but the *town* was not built till after the arrival of the Holy House. By a coincidence, the lady who owned the wood where the Holy House remained for eight months, was named Lauretta, and her memory has become immortal by being associated with this great sanctuary.

" No word shall be impossible with God."—S. Gabriel.
" Quis ut Deus"?—S. Michael.

PART III.

Sanctity of the Holy House of Loreto shewn by the Testimony of God.

CHAPTER I

*Miraculous Separation of the Walls built up to support the Holy House—
Forced Restitution of Stones taken out of the sacred Walls—
Chastisement inflicted on a rash Architect.*

SOON after the arrival of the Holy House upon its present site, the
civil authorities of Recanati hastened to surround it with a wall,
with porticoes to shelter the pilgrims and a house for the clergy.

This first enclosure of the Sanctuary was built of brick, and adorned
with pictures of its miraculous Translations and of the principal mysteries
of our holy Faith which were wrought in the blessed House of Mary. An
altar was also erected outside, that all the pilgrims might see the priest
while he was saying holy Mass.

One of the objects of the external walls was to support the Holy House,
on account of its having no foundations; but the sacred Walls would
never adhere to the new walls. Riera relates what took place as follows:
"As soon as the work was finished, the new walls were found to be
so separated from the old that a little child could pass easily between,
with a light in his hand, to show the people, when it was necessary, the
truth of this separation. This phenomenon struck the minds of the
people very forcibly, and the more so because they knew with certainty
that the two walls were so closely united before, that there was not
between them the thickness of a hair. . . . . . Whatever was the
cause of it, the truth of the fact is above all controversy; for many
witnesses still live who have seen this wonderful sight with their own
eyes. Also when, in the time of Clement VII., Rainero Nerucci, architect
of the holy Chapel, who, since his work, has lived with me on terms of
sweet intimacy, wished, by order of the Pontiff, to pull down the brick
wall, which time had already almost destroyed, and to erect in its place
the magnificent marble casing that we see there now, he remarked, not
without great astonishment, that, contrary to the rules of architecture
and the plans of human art, all the material foreign to the Holy
House was separated from it, as if to render it a just homage."

Riera adds that there were long and wide fissures in these external
walls, through which the ancient building could be seen. This was not

the effect of a mere settlement of the brickwork, but the separation was on all sides at once, and left considerable intervals.

Jerome Angelita, who was personally present in 1531, says the same thing on this subject in his history, dedicated to Clement VII.

The present space of about $4\frac{1}{2}$ inches between the sacred Walls and those faced with marble is a standing monument of the fact of the receding of the former walls.* No one will imagine that without reason the present casing of the Holy House was so constructed as not to support the ancient fabric. The walls may be seen to be out of the perpendicular. It would have appeared the height of folly not to let them rest against the new walls, and their mode of construction is only to be explained by the belief of those who directed the work that the former separation of the walls was wrought by divine power, and "that absolutely nothing can remain attached to the walls of the august House of Loreto, the Blessed Virgin wishing it thus, to hinder anyone from thinking that she has need of the help of men to support her venerable Dwelling."†

The state of preservation of the sacred fabric, which has neither external walls to support it nor foundations to rest upon, is an evident confirmation of its true origin and of a divine protection over it.

Another sign that God watches over the *Santa Casa* is the divine care taken of its stones. The Holy House has shown itself inviolable by allowing no one with impunity to take away a single one of its stones or a fragment of its cement.

John Suarez, Bishop of Coimbra, in 1562, wished to take a stone of the *Santa Casa* to Portugal, and place it in a chapel in his diocese, built in imitation of the Sanctuary at Loreto. His private chaplain, Francis Stella, who took the stone to him at Trent, where the Council was then sitting, seemed to be pursued on his journey by an avenging power, and told the Portuguese bishop what it had cost him to bring it there. But the lesson was unheeded; and the bishop was smitten with a malady that the physicians could not understand or relieve. Prayers were offered for his recovery, and the following message came from two convents : " If the bishop wishes to recover, let him restore to the Virgin of Loreto what he has taken away." Bishop Suarez lost no time in sending Stella back to Loreto with the stone ; and his recovery was so rapid that, by the time the stone was replaced, his health was perfectly restored. The bishop wrote a long account, which exists now in the Vatican archives,

---

* Tursellini also, who wrote fifteen years after Riera, says : " Ut satis appareret, Dei parentem ad sustentandam suam domum excludere hominum industriam voluisse, quo divina vis insignior foret, si tectum longe antiquissimum sine fundamentis, ullove humano auxilio, per tot sæcula staret." (*Lauret. Hist.* i. 16.)

† Riera.

and a copy of which is to be seen at Loreto. Riera, the historian, heard the whole account from the lips of Stella. Tursellini also, fifteen years later, published a copy that he made of the Bishop's letter in the castle of San Angelo, Rome.[*]

There are many other examples of the same kind with reference to the mortar of the Holy House. An inhabitant of Palermo suffered for twenty years; an avenging storm followed a ship of Sclavonia; a lady of the March of Ancona brought fever into her family; Helena Aloysi had to redeem her life by restoring some of the cement; and a lady of Alessandria and two priests of Plaisance only recovered their health by a prompt reparation for their indiscreet abstraction of some mortar from the walls of the Holy House. Unless punishments of this kind had been divinely inflicted on those who removed portions of the Holy House, there would not probably be any of it remaining.

Such chastisements did not occur when stones and cement were taken to be analysed, because the investigations tended to the honour of the Holy House, and were, in a sense, necessary to help the weak faith of many.

The sanctity of the Holy House was further shown when the architect Nerucci approached his work in a wrong spirit. This architect it was who erected the marble building that encloses the Holy House, and at that time Clement VII. ordered him to make three new doorways in the walls of the Sanctuary, and close up with some of the sacred stones the ancient entrance, because one entrance was not enough, and it was unseemly that the pilgrims should crowd through the very doorway God Incarnate and His Immaculate Mother used to pass.

What occurred at the making of these new doorways is related by Riera, who knew the architect Nerucci, and also by Tursellini.

They relate that the workmen, out of reverence for the Holy House, were afraid to strike its sacred Walls; and so the architect himself, filled with greater confidence in his art than reverence for the place, came forward and struck impatiently the first blow. His right hand withered instantly, and he remained unconscious for eight hours. His wife, being called, came and threw herself down at Mary's feet in the Holy House, and with many tears besought the forgiveness and recovery of her husband. The *Virgin most merciful*, touched with compassion, obtained from her divine Son the healing of this man, who immediately recovered his senses and the use of his hand.

They hastened to inform Clement VII. of what had taken place, and to ask his decision as to what was to be done. His Holiness replied that it was lack of reverence that had caused this chastisement, and that they should proceed with the work in hand. After this verdict, a

* Tursell. *Lauret. Hist.* iv. 4.

L.

cleric belonging to the choir, named Ventura Perini, prepared himself by prayer and fasting for three days, and then, reverently approaching the Holy House, fell upon his knees and said: "O sacred House of the Virgin, pardon my innocence. It is not I who pierce thy walls with this hammer, but Clement, God's Vicar, in his ardour for thy adornment; he desires thee embellished, he wishes thee accessible. May that be pleasing to the Mother of God which is pleasing to His Vicar." He then struck the wall in the appointed place, and no chastisement followed. The workmen took courage and put their hand to the undertaking. They also were fasting; and the new doorways were soon cut through the walls.

This memorable event in the history of the Holy House is analogous to the chastisement inflicted on an Israelite who ventured to touch the Ark of the Covenant,* and it shews how jealous God is for the honour of the *Santa Casa.*

CHAPTER II

Descent of Fire, the emblem of the Holy Ghost—Marauders turned into donors—Pirates and Mahometans repulsed—Demons forced to quit the Holy House, after having publicly acknowledged its identity.

AS on the Tabernacle in the wilderness of Sinai and the Temple of Solomon, which successively contained the Ark, a column of fire repeatedly came to rest, so a flame from heaven has often been seen to descend upon the Holy House.

A hermit called Paul della Selva had taken up his solitary abode in a neighbouring wood, and he was the first to observe this light, apparently twelve feet long and six feet wide. As the star stood over the House † at Bethlehem, so this miraculous light came and stood over the House that used to be in Nazareth. The hermit saw this phenomenon about three in the morning on the feast of the Nativity of Mary. He determined to wait another year to see if it recurred on the same day, and, in the midst of the darkness, he beheld again a brilliant column of fire come down and remain upon the Sanctuary. The next year a vast concourse assembled and witnessed this marvellous spectacle. This miracle, frequently repeated, was regarded as a divine indication that the

* 2 Kings vi. 6.

† The Holy Family were no longer in the cave, for the Magi *entered into the house.* (*Matt.* ii. 11.)

Nativity of Mary took place in the Holy House of Loreto, and ought to be observed there in a special manner.

Riera was himself present, in 1555, when flames were seen to descend and rest on the Holy House, and then surround the congregation that were assembled during a sermon. As an eye-witness, he bears this testimony in his *History of the August House of Loreto*. He prostrated himself on the floor of the church, and was filled with a heavenly joy. He saw also in the countenances of those near him, in their expressions and in their attitude of adoring wonder, that they felt the same as he did.

Two years after this a heavenly light again encircled the assembled listeners. It was as a second Pentecost—the hallowed chamber from Nazareth became like the "upper room" at Jerusalem. Visible was that emblem of the invisible gifts which the blessed Spirit ever pours into the hearts of those who seek Him in that sacred place, where He descended from on high and overshadowed Mary. These flames were as the seal of heaven put upon the Holy House.

A band of marauders, when devastating the March of Ancona, came to pillage the treasury of the Holy House. Their chief, the Duke of Urbino, tried to keep them back from such a sacrilege; but they would endure no restraint, and set forward to besiege Loreto. No sooner did they approach the town than suddenly a mysterious cloud enveloped the Basilica. Seized with terror, the depredators fell upon their knees and besought the Blessed Virgin to forgive them. From plunderers they were turned into liberal donors. The soldiers gave to the Sanctuary the most precious things they had upon them, and the Duke hung up his sword before the altar, vowing to leave the whole territory in peace.

On another occasion a robber, who had managed to conceal himself in the Basilica, put together a great many jewels during the night, but on going out of the church it seemed to him as if the whole piazza in front of the cathedral was full of soldiers. He dared not leave the church, and, when the guardians came in the morning, he was arrested and condemned.

A similar fate attended two others, who had managed to put out to sea with their sacrilegious plunder, but were driven back to the shore by a sudden and violent tempest.

When we consider the immense accumulation of wealth from the offerings of emperors, princes, and nobles, and all the great in Christendom, it is no slight mark of divine protection that pirates, tempted by a booty so unrivalled, never attacked the little town to enrich themselves with the plunder. Supernatural must have been that religious awe that held them back, and divine must have been that invisible rampart that surrounded the ancient dwelling of God in the flesh.

Of this we may give two or three instances. Mahomet II., who had taken Constantinople from the Christians, made an irruption into Italy about 1470 : and, after ravaging the south, one of his generals landed at Porto Recanati, thinking to seize the treasure at Loreto. So far from succeeding, he found the Holy House to be an impregnable fortress against the followers of the false prophet ; for as soon as they began to march against it, such terror was struck into their hearts by an invisible power that they dared not approach it. *More terrible than an army with banners*, the great Virgin hurled back the Mahometan forces to their ships.

Another incursion was made by Selim I., son of Bajazet II. and grandson of Mahomet II. In this case, as in the preceding, the very sight of the Sanctuary deprived the soldiers of all strength, and they had to re-embark without attacking Loreto.

Christian slaves have often borne witness that no efforts of the pirates could bring their galleys to shore, when they wanted to plunder the Holy House. And when, in the pontificate of Paul III., the famous corsair Barbarossa thought to pillage the Sanctuary, all his galleys were dashed to pieces on the promontory of Monte Conero, and their débris washed up upon the beach in front of the sacred Shrine which they had dared to approach with sacrilegious armaments.

Every Catholic is supposed to know that the title *Help of Christians* was added to the Litany of Loreto after the great victory obtained over the Turks at Lepanto. Many writers attribute this crushing defeat of the enemies of Jesus of Nazareth to the prayers said in His hallowed Dwelling by the orders of S. Pius V. After the victory, Don Juan of Austria came with his principal warriors to Loreto, to offer the banners and the scimitars taken from the Mahometans, and the chains of the liberated Christian captives. Ever since this triumph of the Christian arms, the Virgin of Loreto has been invoked as *Auxilium Christianorum*.

Let us pass on now to another order of miracle. A citizen of Grenoble, illustrious by birth and fortune, had the deep sorrow of finding his wife possessed with seven devils. Peter Orgentorix, under this painful affliction, determined to take his beloved Antonia to the chief shrines in Italy. He had her solemnly exorcised at the church of St. Julius at Novara, then before the altar of St. Geminian at Modena, then at Rome in presence of the Sacred Column. But all was of no avail, and he finally went to Loreto in 1489.

There his wife offered such great resistance that it required ten men to drag her into the Holy House. The custodian of the *Santa Casa*, Canon Stephen Francigena, set himself to exorcise the demons according to the prescribed rites of the Church. They readily gave their names, but

No. XVII. The Annunciation in the Holy House.

refused to come out of their victim. The priest, however, by the power
of the names of Jesus and of Mary, prevailed over four out of the
seven ; and they came forth, filling the Sanctuary with their clamour.
Canon Stephen then attacked the remaining three with greater vigour,
invoking the Blessed Virgin Mary with a loud voice. At this command
the fifth had no power to resist, and cried out on coming forth : " It is
not you who drive me out, it is *Mary* who expels me !" The sixth also
followed, uttering the bitter plaint : " Thou art too cruel towards us, Mary !"

There now remained but one, and he poured forth his wail of woe,
feeling that he had no more strength to stay : " Thou art too powerful,
Mary, in this place, where thou forcest us to quit against our will the
habitation we have chosen."

The respectful manner in which this demon spoke of the place in
which they were, led Stephen to adjure him, in the name of God and
of the Virgin, to speak the truth and declare in all sincerity what
this place was. Nor was the priest disappointed in his hope ; for at
length the demon, brought under control by the exorcisms, affirmed that,
overcome by the power of God, he was obliged at that moment to
speak the truth, and that in very deed this was the room in which, at the
message of the Angel, the Mother of God conceived her divine Son.

Stephen then became very desirous to know where the Angel stood
when he saluted our blessed Lady, and where the Virgin was at the
moment of the Salutation. Yielding anew to the power of God, the
demon pointed, by the hand of the lady whom he possessed, to the
left side of the altar (the Gospel side) as the spot where Mary
was, and to a point near the corner on the right hand side
of the altar in a transverse direction, towards the wooden cross
at the foot of the *Santa Casa*, as the place from whence S. Gabriel gave
the heavenly message. *

The vanquished demon now relinquished his hold of the lady, showing
how completely he was under the power of God, Who compelled him to
make this revelation.

After the forcible expulsion of the demon, the lady lay unconscious,
stretched out upon the pavement of the Holy House ; but she was soon
able to join her grateful husband in his heartfelt thanksgivings.

There were present at this miracle the Chancellor of Recanati, John

* The altar at that time stood in its original position about the middle of the south wall,
and it faced the only door then existing. Angelita sent this account to Clement VII. ten
years before the altar was moved into its present eastward position. We now add this
historian's own words : " Ostendebat in cubiculo locum in quo stabat Maria, cum salu-
taretur ab Angelo, a sinistris aræ cubiculi, in quo Angelus a dextris, prope angulum in pede
cubiculi, versus crucem ligneam a traverso." *(Historia Lauretana Hieronymi Angelitæ.)*

Francis Angelita; Anthony Bonfini of Ascoli, historian of the kingdom of Hungary; and also the greater part of the nobility and leading men of the neighbourhood. The account was sent to Clement VII. during the lifetime of most of the eye-witnesses, some of whom were personally known to the Pontiff. The historian Jerome Angelita received the account of it from the lips of his own father, and published it only thirty-six years after the event.

The Holy House is that *closed garden* into which the serpent could not penetrate to infect with his poison the Conception of the Immaculate Virgin; and neither he nor any of his evil spirits are able to remain in that sacred chamber, in which the mystery of the Immaculate Conception was wrought.

CHAPTER III

Further Examples of the Testimony of God.

THE Sovereign Pontiffs are unanimous in declaring in their Bulls and Briefs that the *Santa Casa* has been, during their Pontificate, the scene of great, innumerable, and continual miracles; and Benedict XIV. states that these miracles "prove that this place is the same as that in which was accomplished the ineffable mystery of the Incarnation of the Word." * When, then, Heaven has wrought such countless signs and wonders to render manifest the identity of the House, the Virgin of Loreto has no need of letters of commendation written by the hand of any mortal. Might she not say with St. Paul : *Do we begin again to commend ourselves? Or do we need (as some do) epistles of commendation?* Nay, might she not exclaim with that great Apostle of her Son : *Ye are our epistle, known and read by all men?* Ye prodigals, brought back to your Father's home; ye Jews, Mahometans, and heretics converted; ye sick cured; ye innocent liberated; ye wounded healed; ye are our *letters of commendation known by all men.* Ye, Thomas of Parma, Romano of Faenza, and Bernardin of Sardinia, who recovered your sight; thou, John Ubaldi, of Padua, to whom was restored thy lost power of speech; thou, Erasmus of Cracow, cured of total deafness, while offering the Sacrifice within the Shrine; thou Turkish Pasha, Corcuto, whose painful abscess thy slave's

* See *Treatise on the Feasts of the B. Virgin Mary.*

invocation healed; * thou, Lucius Venanzio, delivered from the ulcer in thy cheek; thou, Signora Longa, whose paralysis in all thy members disappeared, while the celebrant was singing in the Holy House the gospel, *He saith to the sick of the palsy, I say to thee, arise;* thou, Julian Cesarini, Roman baron, who, by invoking the Virgin of Loreto, when at the door of death from dysentery, didst recover instantly; thou, Creusa, wife of Sebastian Jerome, who, at thy last gasp, wast suddenly recalled to life; ye, Raffredi of Bergamo, and Delphini of Mantua, to whom an apparition of the Virgin of Loreto gave back the life well-nigh extinct; thou, fair Sicilian, a second Magdalen, who, in the forest of Ravenna, robbed of all thy ill-gotten gains and bathed in blood, receivedst life and grace from Mary of Loreto, who appeared to thee; † thou, John Philip Ambrose, called by the people a *second Lazarus,* thy mortal wounds, inflicted by assassins' hands, being healed on thy address to the Virgin of Loreto; thou, Migliorini, illustrious youth of Genoa, whose parents wept for thee as dead, while the broken dagger was in thy wound; ‡ thou, Augustus of Rocca Valdonia, whose chains fell off thy feet and whose prison doors flew open; thou, Francis of Ferrara, who, when hung unjustly as a spy, wast twice delivered by the snapping of the cord by the Protectress of the Innocent; thou, lady of Sclavonia, Paula, who only foundest deliverance from demons when beside the Virgin of Loreto, and stayedst there to the end of thy days; thou, scoffing Franciscan brother, who didst faint away, and when thou camest to thyself, didst exclaim: " It is the birth-place of the Blessed Virgin! it is the Sanctuary in which the Word was conceived! I have beheld the Mother of God with the Infant Jesus frowning on me!" thou, Hungarian knight, who, with thy horse, wast miraculously carried across the Adriatic; § thou, James II., Marquis of

* This Pasha himself relates his own recovery in a letter sent to Loreto by the hand of his former slave. "One of my slaves," he writes, "comes to me and says: *If you promise me my liberty, I will invoke the Mother of my God, and she will restore your health.* I call a notary and promise to set him free, provided he obtains for me the healing of an enormous abscess which had formed in my breast. Immediately the slave throws himself upon his knees, makes certain signs with his right hand, and asks me to repeat after him the following words: *I implore the succour of the Blessed Mary of Loreto.* Three days after I was healed of my abscess. I then emancipated this slave, and I have given him this testimony written by my hand." (Tursel. *Hist. Lauret.* iii. 18.)

† This Sicilian woman went to Loreto and passed the rest of her life there. Riera, eyewitness of the cicatrice in her neck, attests this fact in his *History of the August House of Loreto.*

‡ "He came to Loreto," says Tursellini, "while I was writing this history, and he left the point of the dagger that had pierced him." That dagger is mightier than any pen to tell the healing power of the Virgin of Loreto.

§ Jerome of Radiolo, in his History of the Holy House, dedicated to Lawrence of Medici, about 1473, thus relates this miracle: "Some years previous to the fall of Constantinople, an Hungarian chief, John, surnamed the White, defended a fortified place on the sea-coast,

Baden, who, when on the point of dying from a gunshot wound, wast
immediately healed on making a vow to go on a pilgrimage to Loreto;
thou, Christine, wife of Francis I., Duke of Lorraine, paralysed and
enfeebled by age, who didst walk without help all round the *Santa Casa*,
to the great astonishment and joy of thy suite; thou, Anne of Austria,
who didst offer the weight of thy infant in gold in acknowledgment of
the marvel of his birth after twenty-three years of sterility;* thou, John
Copra and countless others, saved from shipwreck; thou, Castellino Pinelli,
delivered from a devouring fever; thou, Marquis of Bergan, son of the
Archduke Ferdinand of Austria, whose knee-cap, fractured in several
places, was miraculously cured; thou, Jewish captive amid the Turks,
who, on invoking Mary, wast conducted by her to Loreto and there
baptised; thou, George Ivanovic, Dalmatian priest, who, after cruel eviscera-
tion by the Turks, wast kept alive by a marvel of divine power and able
to reach the Holy House before thy death;† ye inhabitants of Venice,
Udine, Palermo, Poggio, Recanati, and Lyons, delivered from a pestilence;
in short, all ye countless cities and peoples favoured with the protection of the great Virgin of Loreto, are so many vouchers guaranteeing
the truth of the history; ye are living documents, signed by the hand of
the Holy Mother of God, and bearing her seal. Nay, shall we not say:
Ye are the epistle of Christ, written, not with ink, but with the Spirit of

which was being attacked by the Turks. Betrayed by a Greek, he throws himself upon the
enemy with a mere handful of men, and for the moment arrests their advance by prodigies
of valour. But the strife is altogether unequal; he is driven back to the water's edge, and
captivity or death awaits him. In his extremity he calls to mind Our Lady of Loreto, and
makes a vow to go and thank her in the Holy House, if she will save him; then, urging
on his charger, he dashes into the sea. A short time after his horse stops upon an unknown
shore. The inhabitants tell him that he is in the neighbourhood of the sacred Dwelling
of the Holy Virgin, whose hand has snatched him from inevitable death and transported
him to the opposite shore of the Adriatic. He goes on immediately to Loreto, followed by
an ever-increasing crowd, and he leaves to the Treasury of the *Santa Casa*, in testimony of
his gratitude, his armour, his horse, and his portrait."

* This infant became Louis XIV., King of France.

† The details of this miracle, as related in an inscription to be seen at Loreto, are
word for word as follows: "In the year of Our Lord 1513, when part of Dalmatia
was under the dominion of Selim I., a certain George Ivanovic, Dalmatian priest, prepared himself for making the devout pilgrimage to Loreto. Seized by the Turks, those
fierce enemies of the Christian name used every art to induce him by soft words to
embrace the Koran and to give up his holy pilgrimage. But this unvanquished athlete
of Christ, taking for his shield the sweet Names of Jesus and Mary, stands against his
persecutors firm as an immovable rock. They threaten to disembowel him if he does not
curse these Names,—but in vain. Then, as furious wild beasts, they rush upon him;
and he, in the midst of his martyrdom, changes into a vow his pious purpose of making
the pilgrimage of the Holy House. His murderers cut open his breast, and, drawing
out his intestines, put them in his hand, saying in mockery: *Go and carry them to
Mary!* The great Mother of Mercy turned on him a pitying eye; and, with his

CHAP. III]   TESTIMONY OF GOD   99

the living God, * and sealed with the signet of the **King** of kings?

Who could count up all the myriads that will be eternally grateful to Our Lady of the Holy House? How many with infirmities of soul, that seemed incurable elsewhere, have there discovered the sovereign remedy! How many, once covered with the leprosy of sin, have obtained their cleansing there! How innumerable the multitudes that in the courts of heaven will bless for ever the Virgin of Loreto for favours she procured for them, for imminent perils escaped, for overwhelming grief alleviated, for arduous undertakings happily accomplished, for long-sought vocation found; for painful sickness cured, for moral infirmities that she has deigned to calm or banish for ever!

The Blessed Canisius exclaims: "O blind and ungrateful men, who perceive not the sublimity of such marvellous operations of the Spirit, and who have no hearts to celebrate the countless gifts that are wrought in this place at the invocation of Mary! The miracles worked in this Sanctuary are so numerous that they cannot be counted, so manifest that they cannot be denied, so stupendous in their greatness that the most eloquent cannot worthily extol them: they are marvels that can only be compared with those wrought at the tombs of the early martyrs. "When I came," says the Blessed Baptista of Mantua, "to the sacred Dwelling of the most Holy Virgin Mary, and beheld miracles of such a kind and of such number, most manifest signs of the power and mercy of God, a sudden dread came over me, and I seemed to hear the voice of God speaking to Moses: *Come not nigh hither, put off the shoes from thy feet: for the place whereon thou standest is holy ground.* †

entrails in his hand, he set forth upon his way, pursuing his journey amid the enthusiasm of the peoples he passed through, and reached Loreto, where the citizens welcomed him with holy joy. Then, fortified by the Blessed Sacrament, at the feet of Mary he breathed forth his blessed soul. His bowels, after being long exposed to public view, were buried near his body in the Chapel of S. Anne, at the spot where a heart in red marble is let into the pavement, on the left side of the transept of the Basilica. To perpetuate the memory of so great a prodigy, an oil painting was substituted for the buried viscera during the Pontificate of Paul III. This painting is still to be seen on one of the four grand pilasters which support the dome of the Basilica, where an inscription records the circumstances of the miracle. In 1877, on the occasion of the episcopal Jubilee of Pius IX., when Dalmatian pilgrims, led by Monsignor Doino Maupas, Archbishop of Zara, went to Rome, they visited, with feelings of fervent piety, the Holy House of Loreto; and, seeing that the above picture had somewhat suffered from the injuries of time, they had it restored at their expense."

* *2 Cor.* iii. 1, 2.   † *Exodus* iii. 4, 5.

" We have found it in the fields of the wood."—Ps. cxxxi. 6.

PART IV

Monuments of the various Translations of the Holy House.

CHAPTER I

Monuments connected with the stay of the Holy House at Tersatto*—Pilgrimages of Slavs to Loreto—Coronation of the Virgin of Tersatto by a Decree of the Chapter of the Vatican—Celebration of the Sixth Centenary.

INTIMATELY linked with the fact of the Translation of the Holy House are the monuments that we find of it at Tersatto, where it first stayed. We see on this commanding eminence, that rises up behind the Port of Fiume, a celebrated sanctuary whose existence commemorates the fact we are relating. Count Nicholas Frangipani, who held the most influential position in this place at the time of the arrival of the Holy House, made a vow to erect a church upon the spot, but only lived long enough to build a chapel on the site that it had quitted. Martin Frangipani, however, fulfilled the vow of Nicholas by constructing a church in 1453; † and at his death he was buried in the very earth on which the Holy House had stood. To him is also due the

---

* The author has made the pilgrimage of Tersatto and stayed there for six weeks.

† His ancestors had been hindered from building it by wars. In a Bull addressed to this Count of Modrussa, Veglia and Segna, Pope Nicholas V. speaks of the vow of *Nicholas*. This document bears the date of July 5, 1453. It would have been clearer if it had specified *which* Nicholas Frangipani had made the vow referred to in it, as Martin's own father was a Nicholas.

The Frangipanis are of the family of the Anicii, as also were S. Cecilia, S. George, S. Ambrose, S. Gregory the Great, S. Thomas Aquinas. Flavius Anicius was the first who received the name of *Frangipani*, from having distributed *bread* to the poor in Rome during a famine.

A Nicholas Frangipani of Rome and two of his brothers founded branches of the family in Illyria A.D. 833; and the kings of Hungary made their descendants Counts of Veglia, Vinodel, Modrussa, and Segna, for assistance given in wars. Tersatto, together with seven other fortified places in Vinodel, were received by Wido Frangipani from Andrew II., King of Hungary, A.D. 1223; and the Frangipanis remained lords of Tersatto till 1671. Baron Trasmondo dei Frangipani, in his *Genealogy of the Frangipanis of Illyria*, says that the Frangipani family ruled at Tersatto in the years 1291-1294, and built a church in honour of the Holy House of Nazareth. The Baron adds that he can affirm for certain their having jurisdiction and their helping to build the Sanctuary. The monastery had to be rebuilt after a fire in 1629, at which time there perished in the flames the valuable documents signed by the delegates who had been sent to Nazareth by Count Frangipani in 1291.

erection of the Franciscan Monastery, which joins the church. The original chapel stood as chancel of this church till 1614, when it had to be rebuilt by the Guardian of the monastery, Francis Glavanich.

Another monument of the stay of the Holy House at Tersatto is an ancient inscription placed in a chapel on the steps leading up from Fiume to the sanctuary and village. After mounting about 200 steps and passing several wayside chapels, we arrive at this special one, which has always stood at the middle of the ascent. In it we read : *Venne la Casa della Beata Vergine Maria da Nazaret a Tersatto l'anno* 1291 *alli* 10 *di Maggio e si partì alli* 10 *di Dicembre,* 1294. ("The House of the Blessed Virgin Mary came from Nazareth to Tersatto on May 10, 1291, and left on December 10, 1294.") Glavanich assures us that this stone tablet was ancient in his time, and adds : "We hold by tradition that this chapel on the steps was erected at the time of the Translation into Italy ; it has been restored several times since." This steep ascent to Tersatto and the castle always existed, but most of the steps were not cut in the rock till the time of Peter Krusich, 1531. The incription is in Italian, as Fiume was founded by Italians.*

The 10th of May being the anniversary of the coming of the Holy House to Tersatto from Nazareth, the miracle of its arrival is celebrated by a special office. At this festival the church does not suffice to contain the multitudes,† and the ways leading to the holy mount are thronged.

The clergy and people still sing the ancient hymn : "O Mary, here didst thou come with thy House, to dispense grace as the loving Mother of Christ. Nazareth was thy cradle, but when thou didst seek a new country, Tersatto was thy first harbour. Thou hast borne away thy holy Dwelling elsewhere ; but, Queen of Mercy, thou hast none the less remained with us. We congratulate ourselves that we are accounted worthy to keep thy maternal presence."‡

* Italian is still exclusively employed in the notices put up in the public garden. It is also used in the law courts, in preaching, and in newspapers. Anyone who stumbles over the above inscription being in Italian has certainly never visited *la gentile città di Fiume, di costumi italiani. (La Varietà.)*

† Endeavours are being made by the Guardian of the monastery to add a south aisle, corresponding to the north aisle added by Count Nicholas Frangipani in 1644, and lengthened in 1824.

‡ O Maria,

Huc cum domo advenisti,	Ædem quidem hinc tulisti,
Ut qua pia Mater Christi	Attamen hic permansisti,
Dispensares gratiam.	Regina clementiæ.
Nazarethum tibi ortus,	Nobis inde gratulamur
Sed Tersactum primum portus	Digni quod hic habeamur
Petenti hanc patriam.	Maternæ præsentiæ.

The metre of this hymn favours its antiquity. It is inscribed on the north wall of the chapel which stands in the place of the Holy House.

Formerly, according to Father Bart Kassich, a Dalmatian, and the *Fasti* of Fiume, a stone

No. XVIII.—Chapel commemorative of the stay of
the Holy House in Tersatto.

No. XIX.—Sanctuary of Tersatto, Parish Church of St. George, and
Ruins of the Castle of the Frangipani.

Desirous of having clergy educated under the shadow of the Holy House, these people sent, for three centuries, to the Illyrian College at Loreto, young men of their race to be prepared for the priesthood.* A confraternity of Slavs was also established at Loreto in the fifteenth century, and two hospices were founded there for pilgrims from Illyria. The Slavs have further a chapel of their own in the Basilica; and their pilgrimages to the *Santa Casa* have manifested age after age their deep-rooted belief in the identity of the Holy House.

The loss of the sacred Dwelling produced so deep a wound in the heart of these people that even centuries failed to heal it. Two hundred and fifty years after its removal into Italy, we still find them praying amidst tears that the Holy House might be restored to them. Riera thus describes a pilgrimage in 1559: "Three hundred, or perhaps even five hundred of these pilgrims came to Loreto with their wives and children. Holding in their hands lighted candles, they knelt before the doors of the church and implored the divine mercy, invoking the Blessed Virgin Mary. They then entered into the Basilica, in two lines, upon their knees, and weeping, they cried out, as they advanced towards the Holy House, 'Return, return, to us, Mary! Why dost thou abandon us? Return to us with thy House, O Mary, Mary!' When they entered the Holy House, their cries and sobs redoubled, and were enough to melt the hardest rock." Riera tried to stop them; "for I feared," he says, "lest the merciful Lord, Who does the will of those who fear Him, and grants their petitions, should see fit to deprive us at that moment of so great a good."

Tursellini says that in his time they continued to come with the same cry of "Return;" Renzolio, one hundred years later, bears the same testimony; and Gaudenti later still speaks of their bitter wailing, and adds that pity for them when, worn out with weeping, they had sunk down to sleep where pilgrims of no other nation would be allowed to remain, caused the rules to be laid aside in their favour, so that no one should disturb them; "for we possess that Holy House whose loss they so deplore."

When, according to the Annals of Tersatto,† the blessed Urban V. visited

also bore the following inscription : *This is the place where once stood the Holy House of the Blessed Virgin Mary of Loreto, which is now honoured in the territory of Recanati.* Kassich composed his history in 1617, and Tursellini, who wrote in 1597, also refers to this inscription in the words : " Quin etiam marmorea inibi tabula exstat perantiqua tanti miraculi ad posteros testis. In quâ incisum : *Hic est locus in quo olim fuit sanctissima Domus B. Virginis de Laureto, quæ nunc in Recineti partibus colitur.* Harum ego rerum auctores habeo haud dubiæ fidei viros complures, qui mihi se vidisse narrarunt." (*Lauret. Hist.* i. 9.)   * The invasion of 1860 caused the suppression of this seminary.

† See Pasconius, *Triumph of the Crowned Queen of Tersatto*, 1731. We have no confirmation of this pilgrimage to adduce, and the blessed Urban sent the sacred picture from Rome.

the Holy House at Loreto in 1367, His Holiness witnessed the grief of the Slav pilgrims; and he was so deeply moved at the sight that, by way of consolation, he sent to Tersatto, by the hand of Father Boniface of Naples, an ancient picture of the Blessed Virgin, attributed by tradition to S. Luke the Evangelist, and painted on cedar. The people received it from the Pope with great gratitude and veneration. The fervour of their vows soon obtained for them so many miraculous graces that the Virgin of Tersatto became fitly called *Our Lady of Grace.*

No. XX.—OUR LADY OF GRACE, SENT TO
TERSATTO BY THE BLESSED URBAN V.

The blessed Gregory Barbadico, Cardinal Bishop of Verona, on his visit to this sanctuary in March 1709, conceived the idea of obtaining the coronation of the miraculous icon, and determined to plead the cause himself at Rome. This devout client of Our Lady of Tersatto procured for her an honour that had never yet been granted to any Madonna out of Italy—that of being crowned by a decree of the Vatican.*

* This distinction has since been conferred on several Madonnas in other parts of Europe. The nearest to England used to be *Notre-Dame de Boulogne*, but now Great Britain has her own crowned *Queen of Consolation* at West Grinstead.

About sixty thousand Catholics came to this solemnity. At Tersatto alone Communion was given to thirty-six thousand, and many thousands communicated in the churches of Fiume. In this pilgrimage there were some noble ladies of the Carniola who had come on foot for three days, and who ascended the sacred hill barefoot.

A triumphal arch had been erected in front of the church, and the miraculous icon of the Madonna of Grace was placed on a throne beneath it, that all the pilgrims might see the coronation. The bishop, who acted as Papal delegate, sang the hymn *Veni Creator Spiritus*, and set the crowns upon the heads of the Mother and Child.

The sight of the coronation moved the assembly to tears, and they burst forth into cries of joy, when the bishop blessed them with the crowned Virgin.

The fêtes, which lasted three days, were chiefly celebrated in Fiume on the second day. The nobility, magistrates and citizens awaited on the confines of the city the procession that descended from Tersatto; and, at its arrival, all without distinction fell upon their knees; the bells of all the churches pealed forth a joyous welcome to their Queen, and all the cannons on the ships and in the fortress boomed forth their glad salute. And never was salute so merited as by her who is the *Cause of our joy* and the *Mother of Divine Grace*.

Twenty young men, clothed in white, strewed flowers before the Immaculate Virgin ; four-and-twenty councillors surrounded her canopy, behind which came the nobles, followed by the people. Conspicuous among the banners were those of the crowned Queen of Tersatto, S. Michael, S. George, S. Roch, S. Sebastian, and S. Vitus, patron of Fiume.*

This imposing procession, bearing lighted candles, passed beneath triumphal arches, and through streets richly decorated and hung with affectionate expressions of welcome.†

Thus did the inhabitants of Fiume shew their gratitude for the treasury of grace opened to them by the sojourn of the Holy House upon the hill that towers above their city.

A like enthusiasm was again manifested on May 10, 1891, which was the sixth centenary of the arrival of the Holy House from Nazareth.‡

The *Voce del Popolo*, a newspaper of Fiume, spoke of it in the following terms :§ " From noon, on the eve of the fête, Tersatto was the scene of such animation as we have never before witnessed. And at the decline

---

* The city used to be called *Vitopolis*, after its patron saint. Fiume simply means a river *(flumen)*.
† See Pietro Francetich, Venice, 1718.
‡ It remained at Tersatto from May 10, 1291, till Dec. 10, 1294.
§ The author made this extract during his stay at Tersatto.

of day, when the special trains began to arrive, the pilgrims were too numerous to be counted even approximately. On the flight of four hundred steps leading to the sanctuary it was a true rising tide of human beings, a ceaseless flow! In the open space before the church, the concourse was such that the hail, so frequent at this season, could not have fallen on the ground. The stream continued to flow, the tide to rise and rise.

"The pilgrims arrived from the neighbouring places in Croatia, from Trieste, from Istria, from Carniola, from Styria, from Dalmatia, from Italy, and even some from France. The trains were crowded to excess with old and young men, women and children, some under the escort of the Nestor of the village, some led by their parish priests.

"After a little rest at the fountains of Sasso Bianco and of Muster-chione, they went in procession along the Corso, the Deak and the Fiumara (on the north bank of the river), singing hymns and advancing towards Tersatto, which shone forth on the heights like a beaconlight.

"The illumination was splendid, there was not a house, nor even a cottage, which did not shed forth beams of light. The castle of the Frangipanis, with its embattled towers, produced, amid the darkness of the night, a magic effect. The Church of the Blessed Virgin was resplendently bright, and hung with garlands surrounding a transparency of the Translation. The whole flight of steps from Fiume was illuminated, and the arch at the entry of it was more brilliant still. It was quite a fairy scene when beheld from the city below.

"The arrival of the pilgrims continued until midnight. The threatening state of the weather had no effect upon them. The prospect of passing the night in a hovel imperfectly roofed, or in a cloister, or even under the open sky, did not disquiet them. The faith with which they were animated was too strong to allow them to falter before the little miseries of life. Tersatto is there with its sanctuary of the Virgin of Grace! Forward towards the beaconlight of consolation! Soon we shall be in the harbour!

"Blessed are those for whom, on the path of life strewn with so many thorns, there spring up roses called into being by the vivifying power of Faith!"

The greater part of the pilgrims were Croatians and Sclavonians; and during the three days of the centenary festival not less than thirty thousand came. Fervent discourses were delivered in their languages, as well as in Italian, and Pontifical Mass was sung in Slavo-Glagolite, the ancient liturgical language, in which the Holy Mass was celebrated in that country at the time of the Translations of the Holy House.

In imitation of the *Santo Camino* of the Holy House of Loreto, there is a fire-place behind the altar, which is surmounted by the miraculous

icon of Our Lady of Grace, sent from Rome to console the inhabitants
for the loss of the *Santa Casa.*   After Mass or Benediction the faithful
are accustomed to go round the altar kissing the walls and the fire-
place.   It is usual to make the circuit many times in succession ;
some continue to go round and round for an hour, walking slowly and
praying all the time.   Many pilgrims describe this circle on their
knees.   The most devout traverse the entire length of the church
upon their knees ; and pilgrims are to be seen ascending on their
knees the four hundred and eleven steps leading to the sanctuary from
Fiume.

It would be impossible to make a stay at Tersatto at any time of
the year, and not to come to the conclusion that the inhabitants and
the pilgrims from surrounding countries are most profoundly convinced
of the sanctity of this spot—a sanctity that depends entirely upon
the truth of the Translation of the Holy House from Nazareth to this
place.

Numerous and rich offerings made by emperors, princes, and nobles
shew also the confidence of the great of the earth in the miracle of
the Translation to Tersatto.   Among these gifts we may mention a
golden eagle sparkling with diamonds, presented in 1536 by the
Emperor Charles V., and a chasuble, the gift of Maria Theresa.

CHAPTER II

Monuments at Loreto recording the Arrival of the Holy House and its Changes of Site.

THE present memorial of the alighting of the Holy House in the wood of the Lady Lauretta is about to be replaced by a beautiful chapel erected by the Italians as a *Voto Nazionale* in honour of the sixth centenary.

Pius IX. had given orders to build a chapel here; but scarcely had the foundations been laid, when the Revolution interrupted the progress of the work.

The inhabitants of the neighbourhood have always been in the habit of visiting this spot on certain festivals; and Riera built a wall on the depression left in the earth by the weight of the Holy House. The east end of this wall is still standing, and contains a bas-relief of the Translation, which is adorned on fête-days with flowers, branches of trees, and hanging lamps.

Angelita says: "This spot on which the House of Our Lady stood has not been encroached on by the thistles and briars, which grow on all sides round; but, on the contrary, it is filled with sweet-smelling herbs, beautiful grass, and a variety of flowers according to the season."

For nearly three centuries there existed another of nature's memorials of the coming of the Holy House to this particular spot in the centre of a wood. The inanimate trees, as silent witnesses, bore their constant testimony as long as they stood. For, in spite of the force of the wind from off the sea, they remained bowed down towards the coasts of Illyria, in the very same attitude of reverence that they had assumed at the moment of the passage of the Adriatic by the angelic convoy. Tursellini says: "They were shown to pilgrims as evidence of the wondrous event. The memory of it is still recent. A person of unquestionable veracity told me that he himself had often seen many of these trees not more than twenty years ago." "There is certainly clear evidence," says Serragli, "that on the arrival of the Holy

House the trees of the wood bent down, and thus remained inclined even to our days." By 1575 several of these trees had died ; and some peasants, finding the remaining ones in their way in tilling the ground, inconsiderately cut them down.

When the Holy House rested in this wood, a flag was hoisted by sailors on a tree close by it, in order that ships might salute it as they passed, and that pilgrims might find it more readily. The name of the spot is Banderola,* meaning a banner ; so that the very name of the place serves as an additional evidence to the fact of its having stayed there.

The second site occupied by the Holy House in the district of Loreto is still pointed out on the west side of the *Piazza di Maria*, in front of the Basilica. Placed in a side wall of the Apostolical Palace, and near the south-west corner of the Piazza, there is a bas-relief in terra cotta representing the Translation of the Holy House. Formerly according to Vincent Murri, there was a stone, on which could be distinguished the words, *Visitatio custodivit.*†

Riera grieved that no oratory had been erected there. ‡ Old men led him to the spot where, in their youth, they had seen numbers of pilgrims on their knees, mingling tears with their prayers.

An English traveller in Italy, in 1802,§ actually suggests that the *Santa Casa* might be a cottage long buried in the pathless forest, and that the Lady Lauretta declared it to be the Holy House. But it did not stay in the wood ! How did it get up to the top of the hill ? It is strange how prejudice blinds. Even if it had stayed down below in the wood of Lauretta, its stones, mortar and timber, and its standing without foundations, would have shown it was no Italian cottage.

To get over the difficulty of the absence of foundations, some have had recourse to the hypothesis that it might be a cottage separated from its foundations by an inundation, or washed away by torrents of melted snow. Such objections are absolutely worthless ; for there are no snowy mountains nearer than the Apennines, and the Sanctuary is situated on the summit of a hill, where inundations could not take place, and where it could never be carried by any torrent.‖

* "Certe parvum vexillum Itali Banderolam appellant."—Tursell. *Lauret. Hist.* i. 9.

† A canon, named Agostini, made this spot his oratory towards the middle of this century, and, at his death, one of his friends took away this stone into the former kingdom of Naples. It is much to be desired that it should be restored to its place.

‡ There is a movement towards building a chapel of S. Joseph on this site, and the faithful are invited to co-operate in its erection.

§ *A Classical Tour through Italy*, by J. C. Eustace.

‖ None who have visited Loreto would attach any weight to the hypothesis. Monreale is very little higher than Loreto, and was separated from it by a valley till the seventeenth century, when it was filled up to render the road more level.   o

Others have spoken of landslips, and brought forward examples of houses being carried away together with the ground they stood upon. But phenomena of this kind have clearly no power to change brick dwellings into stone ones and to transform a Loreto cottage into a Nazareth house.

Others, again, wishing to get over the successive changes of site at Loreto, have thought that a mistake might have arisen through several chapels having been built in imitation of the Holy House. Imagine three representations of the same thing erected close to one another: one a mile off, and the other two only at the distance of a stone's throw! Who could think that probable?

The theory of its being merely a commemorative chapel has no basis to stand on. No example anywhere exists of such a mistake as taking a model of any of the Holy Places for the original. The model at Tersatto never claimed to be anything but an imitation, and no copies anywhere, either of the Holy House or of the Holy Sepulchre, have ever been imagined to be the Holy Place itself.

It being impossible to deny that the stones are the same as those at Nazareth, the conjecture has been raised that a band of crusaders might have brought them. But had they done so, there would have been evidence of it; whereas there is no trace whatever of such a thing, and the annals of the neighbourhood furnish a diametrically opposite account. Who again could reasonably imagine that crusaders could land all these stones, convey them two miles from the shore, and build them up on the summit of a most commanding eminence without being seen? Further, why should they choose this spot if they did not live near? And if they were crusaders from the locality returned home, all the inhabitants of the ten ancient towns round about would know it. The event of constructing such a chapel would have excited public attention; it would have been erected in a town, and not in the country; some tradition would have existed with regard to its origin, so that the inhabitants of the March of Ancona could not have suddenly begun to regard it as a building that had recently appeared among them.

The sacred building also itself bears decisive testimony that it was not built where it stands: its entire lack of foundations shows that they were left elsewhere; its standing in the middle of a former roadway proves that no one erected it there; its mortar, being quite different from that of Italy, and exactly the same as that of the Holy Land, tells us that its stones were cemented together in Palestine; and, lastly, the monuments of its stay in the wood and on the hill of the Antici show that it was no mere commemorative chapel, for that would have been stationary.

All around Loreto there are ancient towns, whose inhabitants are mostly descended from those who lived there in the thirteenth century, and there are the castles of many noble families whose ancestors were contemporary with the Translation of the Holy House. "We have heard it related," they say, "by our fathers; and it has been handed down in our family from father to son, ever since the event occurred. Going back thus from age to age, till the arrival of the sacred Dwelling, we find that the account of the miracle has been always received in every generation as an acknowledged fact. It was not wrought in distant lands and among a barbarous people; but in this country, which was then the most civilised in Europe, and in the very presence of our ancestors. An event so portentous could not have happened without their verifying it, neither could it have been fabricated without their rising up to deny it."

Cardinal Bartolini appeals to the tradition of Nazareth: "The inhabitants of Nazareth have always held, and still hold, as true, the miraculous Translation of the hallowed Chamber, and still point out the site it occupied."

We may recall also the testimony of the Croatians, Dalmatians and Sclavonians. The Holy House, situated on a hill, was exposed to the view and veneration of the city of Fiume, and the inhabitants of all the surrounding places; and then, after three years and a half, it is found to have suddenly disappeared, and is discovered on the opposite shore of the Adriatic. The Slavs of Illyria attest its departure; the people of Italy attest its arrival; and monuments of the event exist in both countries.

The removal of the Holy House from Tersatto has greatly increased the proofs of its removal from Nazareth. The inhabitants own that they have only an imitation at Tersatto; they say that the genuine House abandoned them. The Translation into Italy must then be a real event, for they acknowledge a great humiliation, such as no impostor could foist into the traditions of any people.

" The Angel Gabriel was sent from God into a city of Galilee, called Nazareth."—S. LUKE I. 26.

PART V.

Testimony of Pilgrims before and after the Translation, attesting its preservation at Nazareth and its miraculous removal.

CHAPTER I

Preservation of the Holy House in Nazareth until the thirteenth century, the
epoch of its Translation into Europe.

IN the beginning of the twelfth century (A.D. 1114), a Russian
abbot named Daniel* visited the Church of the Annunciation, and
saw there the Blessed Virgin's room. "A large and beautiful church,"
he writes, "stands in the middle of the town, and has three altars. On
entering it one perceives on the left side a cavern which has two entrances.
One descends into it by steps. Then one sees on the right the cell of the
Blessed Virgin, in which she dwelt with the Child Jesus, our God, and
where she suckled Him. On going into the cavern by the west door, one
sees on the left the tomb of S. Joseph, where his body was laid by the
sacred hands of Jesus Christ Himself. They shew also in this
underground place, near the door, the spot where the most Holy
Virgin was occupied in weaving a purple texture, at the moment when
the Archangel Gabriel, sent by God, presented himself before her. The
spot is three sagenes † from where the Archangel was when he pronounced
the words, *Rejoice thou that art full of grace*, and foretold to her the Birth
of Christ. An altar is erected on this spot for the celebration of Holy Mass.
The place, which is now underground, was the house of Joseph, and it is
there that this event occurred. It is over this subterranean place that the
Church of the Annunciation has been erected."

A French bishop, Arculphus, visited Nazareth in the seventh century ;
and his *Memoirs* were written by Adamnan, abbot of the monastery
founded by S. Colomba on the island of Iona, where he is said to have
stayed after being shipwrecked. In these *Memoirs*, allusion is made to
the Church of the Annunciation as standing in the very "place where the
House had been constructed in which Gabriel the Archangel spoke to
Blessed Mary."‡

* A complete list of all the manuscripts and editions of this Hegumen's travels in the
Holy Land is given in *Bibliotheca Geographica Palestinæ*, Reinhold Röhricht, Berlin, 1890.

† That is, six metres forty-two centimetres, or about seven yards.

‡ *Altera vero ecclesia habetur in loco ubi illa Domus fuerat constructa, in qua Gabriel
Archangelus ad Beatam Mariam eadem hora solam inventam est locutus.* In a book on

It is thus that John Phocas speaks first of the Holy House as having been "changed into a beautiful temple,"* and then goes on to describe, as an eye-witness, what he saw in the crypt; how he had the privilege of entering "the ancient House of Joseph, in which the Archangel announced the good news to the Virgin," and how he was led into "the small chamber of the Ever-Virgin Mother of God," and "the dark room inhabited by Our Lord Christ after the return from Egypt." In the same way Daniel tells us of the grandeur of the Church of the Annunciation at Nazareth, and how he visited in the crypt "the room of the Holy Virgin, where she dwelt with the Child Jesus, our God, and suckled Him."†

The silence here as to the existence of the workshop of S. Joseph is explained by the workshop having been separate from the House. At Nazareth the shops are not part of the dwellings, but are situated in the Street of Bazaars. After S. Joseph's marriage, the paternal home‡ of his Immaculate Spouse became his, and so is styled by Phocas and

---

the Holy Places attributed to the Venerable Bede, we find this passage reproduced : *Altera vero est ecclesia, ubi Domus erat, in qua Angelus ad Beatam Mariam venit.* Pope Benedict XIV. says that we may readily concede that the church had been built where the House had stood, and yet at the same time hold as certain that one room of the House had been preserved—namely, that in which the Divine Word clothed Himself with our flesh,—and that it is this part of the House which has been translated by the ministry of angels.

Anthony Riccardi, in his *Storia dei Santuari più celebri di Maria Santissima*, says that there are a great many similar cases, and cites the following example : "When we state simply, without entering into details, that a church has been built where there was the oratory of S. Eusebius on Mount Oropa, should we be right in concluding that the oratory has been destroyed ? Certainly not ; and if anyone should understand it in that sense, it would be contrary to fact."

Divine Providence often gives more than is absolutely necessary. It might have seemed enough if only the hallowed room in which the altar of the Incarnation stood had been preserved. But Phocas, a pilgrim to Nazareth in the twelfth century, assures us that there existed also the private room of the Blessed Virgin on the right of the altar, and the dark room of our Blessed Lord on the left of the Holy Place of the Incarnation. (See, in the List of Illustrations, the explanation of Plate XVIII., accompanied by plans).

* This expression means the same as that of S. Antoninus the Martyr, who visited Nazareth about 570, and says, "The Holy House is a Basilica." Similarly we say, "The house of S. Cecilia is a Basilica," meaning that a Basilica has been built over the portion of her palace that remains, specially the scene of her martyrdom.

† Phocas and Daniel, in thus explaining their own meaning, have interpreted Adamnan and the Ven. Bede, who, not having visited Nazareth, are less graphic. It appears clear that the church had not taken the place of the House, but that the House had become the most sacred part of the church.

‡ The Blessed Canisius points out that, on the testimony of Eusebius of Emisa, Mary, having no brother or sister, inherited the whole of her parents' property ; and he quotes Nicephorus Callixtus, who states that there were other possessions besides the House.

No. XXI.—The "Fountain of Mary" at Nazareth.
(From a photograph by Bonfils.)

No. XXII.—Church of the Archangel Gabriel at the spring which supplies the Fountain.

Daniel *the House of Joseph;* but he did not cease to frequent his workshop. Here, when the Lord was a child, S. Joseph earned the bread which built up the Body of Him Whose *Flesh* is *the Life of the world.* (John vi.) Here was labour truly ennobled and sanctified by the toil of the Divine Carpenter and of His Foster-father, the descendant of fourteen kings.

The remains of the workshop are in the *centre of the town;* [*] so that it is probably the second house mentioned by the Venerable Bede, following Adamnan. Jerome, also,—an ancient writer whom we must not mistake for the great saint of that name,[†]—speaks of a second church erected at the place where our Lord was brought up. As the Divine Son of Mary passed so much of His Childhood in the workshop, He may, in a certain sense, be said to have been brought up there; but the private House was the scene of His domestic life, and was His Home. Tradition assigns these two Houses to the Holy Family at Nazareth, and no others.[‡]

When referring to the most sacred scenes in Palestine, it is usual to speak of them as *the Holy Places.* Accordingly we find the confessor of St. Louis, Geoffrey de Beaulieu, describing thus that sainted monarch's visit to the Holy House: "The king entered into the Holy Place of the Incarnation." [§] This is equivalent to what is said by the historian of the

[*] It lies to the north-east of the site of the Holy House, and at a distance of 140 paces. There is not only a chapel at the workshop, but also the foundations of an ancient church, measuring 120 feet by 50. Only a portion of an *inner* wall of the workshop remains: it is of the soft stone *Nahari,* like the cupboards of the *Santa Casa.*

[†] "Sancti Hieronymi non esse ex eo colligitur quod ipsum citat Hieronymium." See *De Actis Apostolorum,* Marian. Victor. ad opp. S. Hieron. tom. i. p. 1440. Paris, 1609.

[‡] It was at the House of the Annunciation that they lived after the return from Egypt, and in that House S. Joseph died (see Phocas and Daniel). There is no reason for thinking that they had a house at the public well; for the church at the "Fountain of Mary" commemorates something quite different. It is dedicated to S. Gabriel, in accordance with an oriental tradition to the effect that the voice of the Archangel was first heard at the well. This may be read in the apocryphal Gospel of S. James, which says that Mary looked about her to see whence the voice proceeded—like the men with Saul of Tarsus, who *stood amazed, hearing a voice, but seeing no man.* Being a Greek, Phocas accepted this tradition; but he states distinctly that the real Annunciation was after Mary's return from the Well to her House at the Cave. The second House, "*in the centre of the town*" (mentioned by the Ven. Bede), could not have been at the Well, which was situated "*just inside the city gate.*" (See Phocas).

[§] The Holy House of Nazareth, venerated at Loreto, may be called a "Holy Place;" as well as "the Holy House," and over one of the doors there is the inscription : *No place is more holy than this place.* The Blessed Baptist of Mantua calls it "the most celebrated place in all the world." Thus the word "place" is used to indicate the House; and so it was at Nazareth. The contemporary author of the Life of S. Willibald, Bishop of Eichstadt, A.D. 775, relates that several Christians of Damascus "went on foot through Galilee, praying as they went towards that place where Gabriel first came to Holy Mary. There is a church there now." The same Jerome referred to above also says: "There is a church at the place where the Archangel entered to announce the good tidings to Mary."

kings of France, Peter Matthew, who calls the Holy Place entered by S. Louis, " The very chamber in which the Virgin Mary, our Lady, was saluted by the Angel." In both of these accounts it is pointed out that the royal pilgrim received the Body of the Lord at the same spot where the Eternal Word took Human Nature. Now the fresco of S. Louis, painted, not in the Cave, but inside the Holy House that was transferred afterwards to Loreto, shews that the sainted king went rather to visit the portion of the Dwelling built up in front of the Cave than the Cave itself. This fresco placed by the piety of S. Louis, and the altar in Galilean stone, form, in the opinion of Cardinal Bartolini, an irrefragable proof that it was at this altar in the *Santa Casa* that S. Louis received Holy Communion when he visited Nazareth.

Some pilgrims and writers on Palestine, as if they had foreseen that future ages would look to them for greater precision of language than they could find in other annalists and travellers, have given so clear a testimony as to the existence of the Holy House, or the most sacred portion of it, that they have left no handle by which to overturn this monument of deathless fame. It is with no faltering hand that they write the word *House*. Thomas Celano, contemporary of S. Francis of Assisi, says that that great saint went to *venerate that House*.* It was a *House* that S. Helena found, and over which she erected the magnificent Church of the Annunciation. The ancient documents relating to the visit of the sainted empress to Palestine were kept by the Church of Constantinople, and the librarian Nicephorus relates in his Ecclesiastical History that the mother of Constantine " found the House of the angelic salutation, and erected there a very beautiful temple." † We have seen also, already,

We may illustrate the passage in the *Itinerary* of S. Willibald by the "hired lodging " of S. Paul in Rome, or by his prison, and the house of S. Cecilia mentioned above. We may say : " They went to the places in Rome where Epaphroditus ministered to the wants of S. Paul in his captivity, and where S. Luke visited SS. Peter and Paul in chains, and where the heathen persecutors tried to suffocate S. Cecilia." And of each of these places we may add ; " *There is a church there now*." The existence of churches on those sites does not exclude the existence of S. Paul's hired house, or the Mamertine Prison, or the bath-room of S. Cecilia's house, which many of us have seen in the Corso, near the Forum, and in Trastevere. We might also say : "They went through Rome to the *Via in Piscinula*, to visit the place where S. Benedict, Patriarch of the Monks in the West, lived as a youth (about A.D. 510), and to pray before the same picture of the Blessed Virgin before which he prayed. *There is a church there now*." The existence of the church does not exclude that of the room he occupied.

If any wish further illustration from Loreto, we may quote Riera's *History of the Holy House* : "Qui sanctum hunc *locum* invisebant . . . . qui scipsos et ejusdem *loci* parietes prolucbant." (Riera, *Hist. Almæ Domus*, c. 21.)

* "Tandem Nazarethum pervenit adoraturus *Domum illam*."

† "Pervenit Nazareth, et salutationis angelicæ Domo reperta, peramœnum inibi condidit templum." (Lib. viii. cap. 30.) His Ecclesiastical History extending only up to A.D. 911, the Translation of the Holy House has, of course, no place in it.

that the words "House" and "Chamber" are equally employed by the
Russian Daniel, the Greek Phocas, and the French Peter Matthew;
so that the Holy House and its sacred Chamber of the Incarnation can
be traced by direct testimony as existing at Nazareth till towards the
middle of the thirteenth century, which is the century of its Translation

CHAPTER II

*The Preservation of the Holy House of Nazareth during the War analogous
to that of many other ancient Sanctuaries—Letter of Pope Urban IV.
to S. Louis of France—Testimony borne to the truth of the Translation.*

THE author of the life of St. Willibald tells us that the Christians of
Palestine were often obliged to pay large sums of money to save
the Church of the Annunciation from destruction ; so that the cupidity
of the Mussulmans has acted as a safeguard to the Sanctuary of Nazareth
in the same way as it has to the other holy places.

The Church of the Holy Sepulchre at Jerusalem has been frequently
laid in ruins, but the tomb of the Lord has always remained uninjured,
although it stands exposed in the middle of the nave, and it would
have been extremely easy to cut away the rock and level it to the
pavement.

The Holy House of Nazareth, far from being exposed like the Holy
Sepulchre, was singularly sheltered from any participation in the devasta-
tion of the church. It formed the crypt of the basilica, in much the same
way as the Oratory of S. Clement of Rome,* which is mentioned by S.

---

* Those who know Rome will also call to mind other rooms sanctified by the presence of
saints, and preserved in that city of martyrs ; for example the room beneath the Church
of S. Agnes, on the Piazza Navona, the scene of her cruel persecution and invincible
chastity. This and the Mamertine prison, as also the hired house of S. Paul already
mentioned, are crypts of churches, and less hidden away than the Holy House was at
Nazareth ; yet no destruction of the churches over these sacred buildings would affect
them.

From the time of S. Helena, the Holy House stood at Nazareth like the Grotto of the
Druids beneath the cathedral of Chartres. In the one the chosen Virgin conceived
her God, and in the other, a hundred years before her birth, the Druids placed a statue
with the prophetic inscription *Virgini parituræ* (" To the Virgin about to give birth.")

Jerome ; and, although the Basilica of S. Clement was destroyed in the invasion of 1084, these chambers of the imperial age exist to our day.

Daniel relates, in A.D. 1114, that the Church of the Annunciation at Nazareth had been devastated before his visit, and that the Franks had restored it with the greatest care.* The Holy House had suffered no damage, for not only did this Russian abbot see "the Room of the Most Holy Virgin," but after him S. Francis of Assisi † "venerated the House," as did Phocas and S. Louis. Again, in A.D. 1263, the south side of the cathedral was much damaged by the Mameluke Sultan of Egypt, Bibars-Ben-Dokdar ; but the whole of the crypt was preserved as well as the north side of the basilica.‡

Pope Urban IV. wrote to S. Louis, as we have already mentioned, to persuade him to undertake a fresh crusade. In that letter the Pontiff speaks to the king of the destruction of this "venerable church of Nazareth, within whose precincts the Virgin of virgins was saluted by the Angel and conceived by the power of the Holy Ghost." It is not of the humble cot of Mary that Urban speaks, but of the "*noble structure*" erected in its honour. What was grand and met the eye above ground, suffered wreck ; but what was lowly and out of sight escaped. That magnificent cathedral might even have been levelled to the pavement without the crypt being in the least affected. §

The site of the House of Nazareth, however, being situated in a valley and at the foot of one of the lower ridges of Lebanon, more nearly resembled that of the primitive chapel of Our Lady of Laghetto in the Maritime Alps near Monaco. That ancient oratory forms the crypt of a miraculous sanctuary of Our Lady of Mount Carmel, somewhat as the holy place of the Incarnation formed the crypt of the Church of the Annunciation at Nazareth. And, if Nazareth is the source of the waters of life, Laghetto is a lake of Grace, *(a)* in which is reflected "that Sun that never was obscured by the blemish of sin." (S. Thomas Aquinas.)

(a) Laghetto is the diminutive of *Lago*, a lake.

* It was under Tancred, as governor of Galilee, that it was restored. The pillage had taken place at the epoch of the siege of Jerusalem by the first crusaders.

† The mention of S. Francis reminds us that the chapels of the *Portiuncula* and of the death of the saint remained uninjured when the church built over them was destroyed by earthquake in 1832.

‡ Quaresmius.

§ See Plate X. in Part I. Chapter IV. The text of Urban's letter is as follows : "Sic venerand am ecclesiam Nazarenam, infra cujus ambitum Virgo virginum salutata per Angelum de Spiritu Sancto concepit, et ipsius partus angelico extitit prœnuntiatus afflatu, manus non solum occupatrices, sed etiam destructrices injecerit, quod ipsum per sacrilegos et nefandos iniquitatis suœ ministros desreviens redegit ad solum, ejusdem structura nobili omnino destructa."

Raynaldo says on this passage : "Urban speaks of the sumptuous and elegant temple (and not of the House of Mary) that enclosed in its compass the sacred Chamber, in which was wrought the great mystery of the Incarnate Word, which, *preserved by kind Providence*, was translated," etc.

Although, as in former sacrilegious attacks upon the Sanctuary, the Holy House remained intact, yet the violence of the Sultan had so dishonoured the Holy Place of the Incarnation that the Pope had just cause for indignation and lamentation; and it may have had much to do with the Translation of the sacred Dwelling into a Christian land. " My house remained at Nazareth," said the Mother of God to the hermit of Mont Orso, " to the great consolation of Christians, my children, who venerated it until their expulsion by the infidels, when, as it ceased to be honoured and was exposed to profanation and destruction by the unbelievers in contempt of the name of Christian, it pleased my beloved Son to have it translated by the hands of angels from Nazareth into Illyria, and thence into your country."

No. XXIII.—THE CHAPEL OF THE ANGEL, NAZARETH.
(The Front view of the Crypt is seen in No. VII.)

In the summer of the year of the Translation to Tersatto, the four delegates of Count Frangipani went to Nazareth, and in 1296 the sixteen Italian delegates made the same journey. They saw on one of the walls of the formerly beautiful basilica an inscription relating the departure of the Holy House.*

Four years later, A.D. 1300, Franciscan Fathers took up their abode at Nazareth and built a chapel on the site of the Holy House. They

* "In uno pariete ibi prope est scriptum et sculptum in muro, quomodo ista ecclesia fuit ibi, et postea recessit." See Teramanus, *Translatio miræ Ecclesiæ B. Mariæ Virginis de Loreto.*

also erected *three altars* for the celebration of the Holy Mass.* The basilica a little after that time is described as "almost destroyed," and Mahomedan soldiers kept guard over the Holy Place.† An alms-box was placed near a column of the church to receive the offerings of pilgrims.‡ The Franciscans remained there unmolested till A.D. 1365, when Mahomedan intolerance drove them out for a period of one hundred and three years, during which the Sanctuary remained "desolate,"§ and the *Chapel of the Angel* fell into ruins.‖

About 1473, Jerome of Radiolo relates, in his account of the Holy House of Nazareth (dedicated to Lawrence of Medicis, styled the Magnificent, or the Father of Literature):—"All those who have visited the Holy Land from pious motives declare with one mouth that this is the Chamber in which the Archangel S. Gabriel appeared from Heaven to the Virgin Mary, and that it was brought hither to save it from profanation at the hands of the Mahomedans. The Sanctuary of Loreto is the first of all the temples of Mary, Mother of God, and the most adorned with votive offerings."

The Franciscan Fathers, who had been driven out of Nazareth in 1365, were able to return in 1468; and in 1509 Anselm of Poland, Observantine, attests that when at Nazareth he was told that the chapel in which the Archangel Gabriel announced the Incarnation of the Son of God to the Blessed Virgin, had been translated from that place to Loreto by the ministry of angels.¶

Again, in the first half of the same century, the three delegates of Pope Clement VII. declared on oath that they had found the measurements at Nazareth to correspond exactly with those at Loreto. Of great help to them in their researches were the Franciscan Fathers, who had been back in Nazareth since 1468. The Fathers were obliged to leave it again soon after, in 1542; but we possess an account written by Sir John Zuallard,** a Flemish knight, in 1586 :—"One descends twelve steps, and there are the foundations of the House of S. Joseph, in which the Lord was brought up and nourished; the rest of which was miraculously transported by the angels, and is at present in the city of Loreto."

Andricomius, writing on the Holy Land in 1590, says that the House of the Blessed Virgin was carried by angels to Fiume, and thence to Loreto, where its four Walls stand without foundations.

* Sanutus Torsellus, A.D. 1306.
† William Baldensel, 1337.   ‡ Sir John Maundeville, A.D. 1350.
§ Bernard of Brandenberg, A.D. 1427.   ‖ *Topographia Terræ Promissionis*, A.D. 1463.
¶ *Descriptio Terræ Sanctæ.* Cracow, 1514.   ** *Viaggio a Gerusalem.* Rome, 1586.

" You shall say to this mountain : ' Remove from hence thither,' and it shall remove."—S. MATT. XVII. 19.

PART VI.

Historians of Loreto—Opinions of Theologians—Narrations, Poems, Discourses, Letters—Miracles similar to the Translation of the Holy House of Nazareth.

Q

CHAPTER I

Historians of the Holy House of Loreto, and Opinions of Theologians.

THERE came to Loreto, in 1430, the Provost of the Church of
S. Sinideo, at Teramo, in Abruzzo. Being a native of Teramo,
he is commonly called *Il Teramano,* but his name was Peter George
Tolomei. After twenty years' service in the Sanctuary, he was appointed
rector, and he is spoken of very highly by the celebrated Bishop
Nicholas delle Aste in a document still extant. *

About thirty-five years after his coming, † he wrote a work on the
Sanctuary of Loreto, in which, among other important information, he
gave us the results of a personal examination of two witnesses, whose
evidence he had taken down.

The first witness, Paul Rinalducci, being interrogated on oath, answered
with the greatest precision that he had often heard his grandfather relate
what *his* grandfather used to recount in his presence, namely, that with
his own eyes he had seen the Holy House cross the sea, gliding over the
waves like a ship, and that he had beheld it come to land and descend
into the wood.

The second witness, Francis Prior, native of Recanati, put upon his
oath, deposed that he had heard his grandfather, who lived to the age
of one hundred and twenty, ‡ say that he had often prayed in the Holy
House when it stood in the wood; that, in his time, it had ascended
to the hill of the Two Brothers; and that his grandfather had a cottage
near it while it was in the wood.

Il Teramano erected a tablet in the Sanctuary, containing the evidence
of both these witnesses, together with his own history of the Holy
House. Copies of the original document are preserved in the Vatican

---

* See *The Donation of Nicholas delle Aste,* Turselllini, lib. i. cap. 28.

† Vögel puts the date forty-two years after his arrival, and only one year before his
death at Loreto.

‡ In the relation given in the text we have followed Baptist of Mantua and Angelita,
who agree in saying that it was Francis' grandfather, and not Francis himself, who
was 120.

Library, the Library of S. Augustin, Rome, and the National Library at Paris. Translations also of this tablet are to be read in eight languages on the walls of the Basilica at Loreto.

Sixteen years after the death of Il Teramano (1473), there came to Loreto an illustrious man of great learning—an orator, poet, philosopher, and theologian. He had left the world and become a Carmelite; and when that Order, which had had charge of the Holy House for a thousand years in Nazareth,* was appointed by Innocent VIII. to take charge of it once more at Loreto, he came there as superior. His proper appellation is the Blessed Baptist de Spagnuoli, but he is commonly called *Il Mantovano*, as he came from Mantua.

The Blessed Baptist tells us that he saw a tablet on the wall of the Sanctuary "almost consumed with decay,"† and that he studied it carefully before writing his History of the *Santa Casa*.

Riccardi, in his *History of the Celebrated Sanctuaries of the Blessed Virgin*, thinks that the description given of this tablet shews that it could not have been the one put up by Il Teramano, but must date "from the origin of the pilgrimage, or near the time of the coming of the Holy House." And, indeed, in the short space of time that elapsed between the erection of the tablet written by the former rector, Il Teramano, and the publication of the history penned by the superior, Il Mantovano, it does not seem probable that the tablet could have arrived at such a state of decay. Riccardi adds that it is customary to place such tablets in miraculous sanctuaries, that pilgrims and travellers may see before their eyes the origin of the shrine; and according to his opinion this tablet was erected in the Sanctuary of Loreto at the time of the building of the first church over the Holy House under the pontificate of Benedict XII. It may have been put up earlier still— for example, on the return of the sixteen delegates, who were sent to Nazareth; or again, by the bishop of the diocese, the Blessed Peter Compagnoni, to whom, as we shall see, a relation of the translations is attributed. However this may be, the tablet had existed in the Sanctuary until decay had almost destroyed it, and the Blessed John Baptist of Mantua regarded it as worthy of credit and a source of valuable information.‡

In conjunction with his history of the Holy House, he also depicted in a poem the marvel of its Translation.

After Il Mantovano, we have Jerome Angelita, perpetual Chancellor

---

* See Papebrock.   † "Ecce sese mihi offert tabella situ et vetustate corrosa. . . . Volui de tabella illa carie et pulvere jam pene consumpta, rei gestæ seriem colligere."   ‡ His History of the Church of Loreto is to be seen in the Vatican Library. The Latin text will also be given at the end of this work.

of the city of Recanati. This illustrious man, in whose family the
position of chancellor of the city was almost hereditary, his father and his
grandfather having been chancellors before him, had great knowledge of the
history of the locality. And although, in 1322, the city had been taken,
burnt, and destroyed, this learned chancellor was enabled to bring to
light ancient annals of the city by diligent investigation. As chancellor,
he had access to everything that remained, and to the archives of
neighbouring cities, and to documents relating to the Holy House that
were kept in private families of note. He received also, from Fiume
and Tersatto, manuscripts that were sent to the magistrates of the
city of Recanati; and thus he was enabled to compose a complete account, with the exact days of the arrival of the Holy House at Tersatto,
and afterwards at Loreto. His researches are very valuable; the information is drawn, he assures us, "from the ancient annals of that city,
which he had attentively examined;" and, as he wrote under the eyes
of the magistrates of Recanati, all that he states in his circumstantial
history of the *Santa Casa* has the ratification of the civil authorities.

The *History of the August House of Loreto*, A.D. 1560, by Raphael Riera,
who was Penitentiary there, is also very valuable. He wrote before the
archives of the monastery of Tersatto perished in a fire; and from those
archives he received an authentic copy of the report of Don Alexander
and his three fellow-delegates, who went to Nazareth. This author
supplies us also with information respecting the delegations from Recanati and Rome. He says that a copy of the official report, drawn up
on the return of the sixteen delegates, was preserved till 1565, adding:
"Many persons have given me a plain assurance of this fact; among
others, the very excellent Dr. Bernardin Leopold, who has declared to
me that several times he had seen and read this narration that his
father and grandfather had received from the chancellor of Recanati."

With regard again to the third deputation, which went from Rome to
Nazareth under the pontificate of Clement VII., Riera had the advantage of personal conversation with one of the delegates, about twenty
years after his return. He was thus enabled to ask many questions,
and was perfectly convinced of the satisfactory result of the mission.

The last of the historians of the Holy House who may be called the
Fathers of the History of Loreto, is Horace Tursellini. Like Raphael
Riera, who was sent to Loreto by S. Ignatius of Loyola, he was of the
illustrious Society of Jesus, to which the Penitentiary of the *Santa
Casa* was entrusted for more than two hundred years. Clement VIII.
shewed the high estimation in which he held his history by writing a
diploma, in which are praised the great care and research manifested
in its composition. It was published fifteen years after the death of

Riera, whose manuscript was in the author's hands, together with all the documents he could find in Loreto, Recanati, and Rome.

Coming now to the writers who have only treated of the Translation to Tersatto, Glavanich assures us that he had himself made notes from the original document signed by the four delegates sent to Nazareth by Count Frangipani in 1291. The truth, also, of the account given by Pasconius is certified by the magistrates of the city of Fiume, who signed an official document, to which is appended the name of Joseph Cavaliere, public notary and doctor in civil and canonical law. The enquiry was invested with all legal guarantees, and the history written by Pasconius is declared to be in exact accord on every point with the ancient manuscripts and the archives of the monastery of Tersatto.*

We see that the original documents were preserved at Tersatto till 1629, and that authentic copies of them existed in 1735. The early historians, including Tursellini, wrote while the originals were still in the archives of Tersatto. In the time of Angelita, a parchment brought over to the magistrates of Recanati came under the notice of this chancellor, and it was considered so important that the magistrate sent it on to Leo X. Riera also received, in 1560, an authentic copy of the archives sent him by the Vicar General, as well as a public declaration proceeding from the citizens of Fiume.

Benedict XIV. observes on this point : "The annals of Fiume in which this history is written, and which had been seen and read by Angelita, are sufficient to hinder our being reproached with the lack of contemporary documents. And the loss of these annals matters little, as we see in the appendix to George Marotti's dissertation ; for we ought to have confidence in distinguished historians such as Angelita and Tursellini, who had them in their hands when they wrote their narration, and drew their accounts from them, after the manner of Dionysius of Halicarnassus, who composed his work on Roman antiquities after having prepared it for twenty-four years, partly by conversation with learned men, and partly by consulting the memoirs of distinguished persons of preceding ages. And is not Dionysius a great authority, although the documents which he consulted have disappeared ? "

Unless a person is determined to refuse to listen to any human testimony, says Tursellini, he cannot doubt an event supported by such a weight of evidence. And the jurist Lambertini said in 1584: "*It is certain it took place : I have read the legal process.*"†

---

* The document bears the date of Feb. 19, 1735, and is given in full by Martorelli in his *Teatro istorico della Santa Casa.*

† " Ut certum est fuisse factum de S. Æde S. Mariæ de Laureto, quæ fuit vera Domus Virginis gloriosissimæ .   . . et fateor me vidisse et legisse processum hujus rei,

One hundred and twenty writers have treated this subject, and many of the greatest ecclesiastical authors of Europe have been fitly described as *holding torches to light up the road to Loreto.* Suffice it to mention such names as Baronius, * Raynaldus, † the Blessed Canisius, ‡ Leander Alberti, § Vasques, ‖ Gretser, Suarez, ¶ Theophilus Reynaud, ** Natalis Alexander, †† Papebroch, ‡‡ Henschenius, §§ Stiltingus, ‖‖ Laurentius Masellus, ¶¶ Graveson, ** Guido Grandi, ††† Honoratus a S. Maria. ‡‡‡

These learned men have regarded the proofs that existed in their days as incontestible; and, though the translation of the Holy House is one of the most extraordinary miracles in the annals of Christianity, yet these great minds have found it to be one of the best attested.

With Catholics the constitutions of the Sovereign Pontiffs should have great weight. Many of them, even in the order of nature, have justly acquired a high reputation for wisdom and prudence.

The earlier of the Popes gave decisions while the original documents were in existence, and it should suffice for us that they have taken all necessary means to be assured that the Holy House at Loreto is really the sacred Dwelling which the august Virgin inhabited in the town of Nazareth.

in loco fuisse, et plura miracula fieri oculis propriis vidisse."—*De Jur. Patron.* lib. I. p. i. quaest. 2, art. 9, n. 8.

* *Ann. Eccl.* ad an. Dom. 9.   † *Ann. Eccl.* t. iv. an. 1291, 1294.

‡ *De S. Maria Deipara,* lib. v. c. 25 ; *De M.V.L.* 5, 25.   § In descriptione Piceni. Disp. 126, in III. Part. cap. 3, n. 24.   ‖ Tom. III. in part. iii. D. Thom. disp. 9, sect. 5.

** *Opera,* tom. viii. p. 144, *Antemurali adversus fortia.*

†† *Histor. Eccles.* saec. XIII. pag. 37.   Paris, 1689.

‡‡ *Respon. ad P. Sebastian,* ad Art. 25.   §§ *Acta Sanctorum* (25 Mart.)

‖‖ Ad diem 25 Augusti in annotatis ad. n. 38, litt. g, page 551.

¶¶ *Vita della B.V. Madre di Dio,* lib. x. c. 12.

*** *De Vita et Mys. Christi,* tom. I. dissert. 2.

††† *Dissert. Camald.* 3, cap. 8, n. 12.   ‡‡‡ *De Hist. Fam. Sacr., de Christo,* c. i.

CHAPTER II

Quotations from " Italy Illustrated" and from " The Topography of the Saints"—Poem by Luigi Lazzarelli—Discourse of Anthony Bonfini, Rector of the College at Recanati.

IN an Italian work called *Italy Illustrated*, whose author, Flavius Blondus, was born within a century after the Translations of the Holy House, Loreto is spoken of as " *the most celebrated Sanctuary of the Blessed Virgin in the whole of Italy.*"

It may astonish some that all the far-famed shrines of the great Virgin in Rome and every part of Italy should be eclipsed by that which stood upon the country hill of Loreto ; but to us, who believe it to be the Holy House from Nazareth, its great fame is but what we should expect. Those who doubt it to be the Holy House can scarcely find a reasonable explanation for the pinnacle of glory on which it is placed by such an early writer : not only must they see that it existed there, but that it had acquired for itself, in a brief space of time, an unrivalled lustre. " There," says this writer, " the prayers of the suppliants never fail to be heard, witness the offerings in gold and silver which hang before the altar ; the entire church is filled with them."[*]

Luigi Lazzarelli, a poet crowned by Frederick III. (who was elected in 1440, and died in 1493), in his *Poems on the Christian Festivals*, thus sings the history of the different Translations : " I have not allowed the House in which I received the Angel's Salutation to remain amongst my enemies ; I transferred it and placed it on the Illyrian shore. Yet that shore did not keep it long. Indignant at the cruel crimes of a barbarian race, I passed thence across the Adriatic Sea, and, shifting my House, I arrived at Picenum, and stationed my temple on the hill of the three brothers. The brothers began to quarrel on account of the great gifts made to my House. Hence I occupy the grove of Lauretum. A robber put the pilgrims to flight, and the base hand of brigands was stained with righteous blood. Therefore I placed my temple to be frequented in

---

[*] Flavius Blondus of Forli was secretary to Pope Eugenius IV., who transferred to the Holy House the possessions of the neighbouring Abbey of St. Mary of Mount Orso.

the middle of the road which leads from the shore to the walls of Recanati. Behold the foundations of the House appearing above ground ; they were not built in that place. Religion increased the small temple, and, with large buildings, broad walls surrounded the little House. The temple of Lauretta still retains its old name. Thousands of votive offerings you behold in the temple, gifts you see everywhere, proofs of my favour, for I often relieve those who call upon me. What wonder if I now build new towns there, towns made by crowds hastening to my temple? Would Delphos now gain credence to the fiction of Phœbus and a continuous multitude throng its deceitful temple?" *

John, Bishop of Châlons, speaks in the following manner of the *Santa Casa* in his *Topography of the Saints:* † "There (at Recanati) is the Room of S. Mary of Loreto, which at Nazareth was the Room in which the Blessed Virgin received the salutation of the Archangel."

In 1478, Anthony Bonfini, who was rector of the college of Recanati for eight years and afterwards historian of Hungary, made a speech before the Senate, which is preserved in the archives of that city: "We may

* *Maria loquitur:*]

Ipsa Domum angelica qua copi voce salutem,
Non sum passa hostes inter adesse meos.
Traduxi, Illyrici posuique in littoris ora :
Non tamen illa diu præbuit ora locum.
Barbariæ indignans immitia crimina gentis,
Adriacum super devehor inde fretum :
Traduceusque domum Picenis applicor oris,
Deposui fratrum templaque colle trium.
Cœperunt fratres alterna lite furorem
Miscere, ob nostræ munera magna Domus.
Hinc Lauretanum nemus occupo : prædo fugavit,
Latronumque pio sanguine fœda manus.
Ergo Recineti quæ ad mœnia littore ducit,
In media posui templa colenda via.
Fundamenta Domus super apparentia terram
Respice : non illo structa fuere loco.
Auxit relligio breve templum ; et ædibus amplis
Circumdant parvam mœnia lata Domum.
Nomen adhuc retinent Lauretæ templa vetustum.
Votiva in templis millia dona vides—
Dona vides passim, nostri argumenta favoris,
Dum mea clamantes nomina sæpe levo.
Si nova quid mirum est nunc illic oppida condo,
Quæ facit accelerans ad mea templa cohors?
Jam potuit Phœbi figmentum condere Delphos,
Subdola dum celebrat templa caterva frequens.

In 1817 Vögel found the original manuscript in the possession of Peter Pintucci, mansionary of the cathedral of Recanati.

† That is, description of the places where the saints have lived. See the Martyrology of Francis Maurolico.

R

say of this favoured town what is said of the Holy City by S. John in the Apocalypse: *Behold the Tabernacle of God with men, and He will dwell with them. And they shall be His people ; and God Himself with them shall be their God. And God shall wipe away all tears from their eyes : and death shall be no more, nor mourning, nor crying, nor sorrow shall be any more.* For the Blessed Virgin has established her seat in this most holy territory, in order to dwell among a holy people and give a token of affection to the friends whom she had chosen in preference to others. This is the *Promised Land*, flowing with milk and honey. This is the true *Tabernacle of God* upon the earth. This is the *House of God and the Gate of Heaven*, where the angels descend by mystic ladders, and where they tarry. This is most holy ground, by which it is not lawful to swear in vain, and which it is not permitted to pollute by any iniquity." *

---

* Bonfini refers also to the stay of the Holy House in Illyria (as may be seen in the Latin), and in his *Historia Pannonica* he speaks of the power of the Frangipani family in Croatia and Dalmatia. The following is the text of the speech : "Proinde vere de hac fausta urbe exclamare licet, quod de Sancta Civitate per Apocalypsim Joannes exclamat: *Ecce Tabernaculum Dei cum hominibus, et habitabit cum eis: et ipsi populus ejus erunt, et ipse Deus cum eis erit ipsorum Deus: et absterget Deus omnem lacrymam ab oculis eorum: et mors ultra non erit, neque luctus, neque clamor, neque dolor erit ultra.* Beata enim Virgo unica salutis nostrae propugnatrix, profana Dalmatorum scelera abominata, ex Illyrico sinu fugiens, in hoc sanctissimo vestro agro consedit, ut inter sanctos sancta versaretur, ac suis quos elegerat amicis prae ceteris benignum numen offerret. . . . Haec est igitur Vinea electa, ut Hieronymus cecinit, quam plantavit Dominus, in qua omne verum semen seminavit. Haec est Terra Promissionis, ubi lac et mel affluit. Haec in terris est verum Dei Tabernaculum. Haec est Domus Dei et Porta Coeli, ubi per stantes scalas angeli descendunt et remanent. Haec est sanctissima tellus, per quam pejerare non licet, nec aliquo scelere funestari." (Ex Archivio Recanati).

CHAPTER   III

Accounts of the Translations attributed to the Blessed Peter Compagnoni, to the Magistrates of Recanati, and to Paul della Selva.

THIRTEEN miles south-west of Loreto there stands on an eminence the walled city of Macerata, with a cathedral and university. The district of Loreto was, at the time of the Translations, in the diocese of Macerata, and the Blessed Peter Compagnoni, the bishop, is said to have written an account of the origin and sanctity of the Holy House of Loreto.

Its publication is placed in the year 1334, which was shortly after his death.

This venerable bishop speaks of the truth of the translations being " confirmed by many and stupendous miracles." He gives the year in which the Holy House was conveyed to Tersatto, and also the year of its arrival in Italy ; and relates its stay in the wood and on the Hill of the Brothers, and how, finally, it alighted on a " public road."

Riera says that his account was taught in the schools, and that old copies of it were to be found at Recanati in his day. Tursellini affirms that Il Teramano did little more than reproduce it. Bernardin Cyril put it into his treatise on the Holy House, written about 1550, * and printed at Macerata in 1576. Calcagni speaks of it also in his Memoirs of Recanati.

We have seen that, while the Holy House stood upon the hills of the Counts Stephen and Simon Rinaldi de Antici, a quarrel arose between these two brothers. The magistrates, thinking that the best way to put an end to this unseemly dispute would be that the land should be made over to their city, sent a man of mark, Alexander de Servandis, as a delegate to Rome. He went in the name of the magistrates and citizens of Recanati, bearing the following letter of instructions :

" In the name of God, Amen. The Elders of the Community of Recanati, Salutation to thee, illustrious Alexander Q. Anthony de Servandis, our beloved delegate and honoured fellow-citizen. When thou hast arrived at Rome, thou shalt consult with our illustrious and honoured agent, and together with him, as soon as possible, shalt go, in the name of this city, into the presence of His Holiness, presenting our testimonial letters ; and after thou hast rendered due homage by humbly kissing his feet, thou shalt inform him how, in these days just passed, the Holy House has been translated from the site of the miraculous wood to the hill of the illustrious Simon and Stephen Rinaldi de Antici, our honoured citizens. Then thou shalt ask him the favour that the said hill and site may be made over to our city, that we may be able to build for the accommodation of the devout people who daily come to visit it, and that the offerings made may be expended for the benefit of the fabric ; so much the more, because concord does not exist between the said brothers, according to the voucher given thee. Thou shalt further set forth what has been told thee by word of mouth, that thou mayest obtain this favour. Thou shalt do everything, however, in concert with our kind Cardinal D., in virtue of the credentials given thee, and thou shalt negotiate the matter in such a way that the

* It is not known whether Cyril found it in the form in which he gives it. He may have changed some words and phrases of the fourteenth century into those of the sixteenth century, or he may have translated it from Latin into the Italian of his own day.

aforesaid brothers may not be informed of this proceeding. May God conduct thee and bring thee back safe.

" FRANCIS PANTA, Chancellor.

" Recanati, September 9, 1295."

Before any answer could come from Benedict VIII., the Holy House had been removed from, the land of the de Antici; but the Holy Father sent as his commissary Monsignor Frederick di Nicolo di Giovanni, a native of Recanati, to watch over the Sanctuary and erect hospices for priests and pilgrims.

Cinelli, a patrician of Florence, relates that he found the original in the hands of the Marquises Jerome, Philip, and Thomas Anthony Antici, and that it bore the wax seal of the city of Recanati. These marquises allowed Cinelli to make a copy, which he gives in his manuscript work on Loreto, written about 1705. The chancellor of the city of Recanati, Febo Febi, had also shown him an authentic copy of this commission, which was kept in the archives of that city.*

A letter attributed to Paul della Selva repeats what the reader already knows; so that we need only point out that it is addressed to a king who, according to the writer, had sent to him to enquire particulars respecting the Translations of the Holy House. It is thought by some that the king was Charles II. of Sicily; and, as the missive is signed "Paul," it has been attributed to Paul della Selva, the pious hermit, who called out the inhabitants to witness the miraculous flames that appeared on the feast of the Nativity of the Blessed Virgin.

The letter begins by referring to the king's having asked for a narration of the Translation into Italy; the names of distinguished men in Recanati, who could confirm what the letter states, are given to his Majesty; and documents in the archives are mentioned to which, also, appeal could be made. The writer relates further that a general assembly had been held, and that sixteen chosen men had been sent to Nazareth. Among these delegates from the March of Ancona, the following, he says, were leading men of Recanati: "For the Quarter of S. Mary, Polito, son of Count Marzio dei Politi; for the Quarter of S. Flavian, the young Marquis and Count Matthew, son of Count Simon Rinaldi degli Antici; and for the Quarter of the Angel, the illustrious jurist Cicotto di Monalduccio de Monalducci."

He quotes the 131st Psalm: *We found it in the fields of the wood* (referring to where David said he would not give sleep to his eyes till he

---

* Angelita, Riera, and Tursellini make no mention of this letter, and Trombelli says: " Marchio Thomas Abbas Antici exemplar ipsum litterarum ad Bonifacium VIII. missarum mihi dedit, ut illud expenderem. Sed procul dubio illud ipsum difficultatibus non paucis subest." (*De Ædibus quas incoluit SS. Virgo*, cap. x.)

found out a place for the Ark, which, having contained the manna, was a type of the Holy House that contained the *Living Bread that came down from heaven,* and for which a place had been found in the wood of laurels.) * He adds: "I contemplate with my own eyes the continual graces accorded to those who come there to make their prayers. These heavenly wonders demonstrate that this humble Abode was the dwelling of the Mother of God, the place where the Word was made Flesh." Paul thanks his Majesty for offerings sent, and ends: "In the name of the Father, and of the Son, and of the Holy Ghost."

The attestation of the magistrates is as follows:

"We make known to all, and attest, that the facts above related are true, and in conformity with our annals and our public archives. In testimony and in faith of which, we have ordered that this document should be sealed with our seal, and subscribed by our public notary and master of the acts.

"FRANCIS JACOBI, Master of the Acts.

"June 12, 1297."

This parchment, thus judicially legalised, was preserved in the noble family of the Antici, and was copied on June 26, 1674, by the imperial notary, Dominic Biscia, who signed the copy as authentic, with Anthony Masi and Joseph Percivalle, in the Quarter of S. Flavian, and the street Monte Volpino. This copy was placed for safety in the archives of Recanati, the original remaining in the hands of the Bishop of Amelia, John Baptist Antici. The patrician Cinelli, of whom we spoke above, put a copy of this document into his work entitled *The Beauties of Loreto;* and Martorelli, patrician of Osimo, near Loreto, and Bishop of Monte-Feltro, found Cinelli's MSS. in the library of a canon at Rome, and collated Cinelli's copy with two others in the possession of the families of the Luciani and the Antici, and gave it to the world, together with the proofs of its authenticity, in his great work in folio, *Teatro Istorico della Santa Casa Nazarena.* †

Moroni says that Charles II., King of Sicily, erected a church at Naples in honour of the Virgin of Nazareth, and became a benefactor of S. Mary of Nazareth at Marseilles, which was at that time under his rule. ‡

* The letter describes this wood as being situated "between the Aspido or Musone and the Potenza." A copyist may have added the Aspido to the original text. This torrent, descending into the Musone near its mouth, did not flow into it till the pontificate of Clement VII., when the course of the Musone was changed on account of its proximity to the town of Loreto being unhealthy for the inhabitants. At the same time all the plain was drained and many trees cut down.

† Rome, 1732. 3 vols. folio.

‡ "Vivere desivit anno 1309, sepultus in templo divæ Virginis Nazarethæ a se fundato." See *Summa Aurea de B.M.V.* t. xi. p. 38. Trombelli, in his *De Aedibus quas incoluit SS. Virgo,* says: "De litteris quas ad Carolum Neapolitanorum regem a Paolo eremita

missas aiunt, judicent alii quod iis libet : affine commodum ex eis eruimus : scilicet co
tempore, quo compositae eae litterae sunt (fuere autem jampridem compositae), vul-
gatissimam fuisse Picenos apud de Nazarene aedis translatione famam atque opinionem.
Annon enim, si aliter iis persuasum fuisset, obstitissent narrationi rei tam inauditae ac
mirabilis, justissimasque ac severas de illarum auctore sumpsissent poenas? Idem dic
de monumento, quod apud nobiles *Anticios*, seu, si vis, *antiquos* servari indubitatum est :
neque enim, etiamsi vis subsequenti aetate illud fuisse confectum, confingi illud poterat,
nisi jam persuasum fuisset Recinetensibus, id verum esse, quod de sacra Nazarena aede
in eo traditur : dic pariter de ea narratione seu legenda, cujus piissimus Montanus auctorem
facit Petrum Minoritam Maceratensem episcopum : neque enim haec ipsa confingi poterat
(si confictam eam vis), nisi in populorum animis jampridem alte inhaesisset de ea translatione, de qua contendimus, persuasio et, ut millies dixi, vulgatissima fama."

CHAPTER IV

*The Translation of the Holy House represented in a Picture by Fra
Angelico—Other miraculous Translations across the Sea.*

THE Blessed John of Fiesole, the celebrated Florentine painter commonly
known as Fra Angelico, was born within a century of the Translation
of the Holy House, and represented the miracle in a picture which came
into the possession of the Confraternity of Our Lady of Loreto erected
in Rome. The Academy of S. Luke, by the written testimony of its
members, who were appointed to be art critics for the year 1733, declared
this painting to be in the best style of Fra Angelico. We reproduce the
documents in the foot-note.*

* " Noi infrascritti pittori aggregati nell' insigne accademia di S. Luca in Santa Martina
di Roma, e pubblici stimatori della medesima eletti, dichiariamo ed attestiamo co' la presente,
anche mediante il nostro giuramento a chiunque spetta, qualmente a richiesta di Monsignor
Illustrissimo e Reverendissimo Martorelli ci siamo portati nella chiesa detta la Madonna
di Loreto de' Fornari alla Colonna Traiana di questa città di Roma : ad effetto di riconoscere,
e referir, di qual tempo e di qual mano sia il quadro, che serve di tavola all' altar maggior
di detta chiesa ; qual quadro abbiamo trovato dipinto in legno all' uso antico, ed in qualche
parte lumeggiato d'oro, rappresentante la Santa Casa co' la Santissima Vergine sedente sopra
il tetto, e tenente il Santo Bambino in braccio ; sotto vi sono figure di putti, rappresentanti
angeli, che reggono la detta Casa, e nei lati son dipinti in uno S. Rocco, e nell'altro S.
Sebastiano : ed avendolo bene e con tutta l'attenzione considerato, l'abbiamo riconosciuto
per opera bellissima del celebre beato o venerabile Giovanni da Fiesole, detto comunemente
il Pittore Angelico, di cui ci è ben nota la maniera ; e per esser questa pittura di tutta
perfezione la giudichiamo fatta non nella vecchiaia di quell'insigne pittore, ma in quell'età
più vigorosa, nella quale suole chi dipinge haver lo spirito più vegeto, e la mano più franca,

No. XXIV. Our Lady of Good Counsel, whose miraculous Translation renders Genazzano "the Loreto of Latium."

No. XXV.—Ruins of the Church at Scutari whence the Translation took place.

(a) The niche which Our Lady of Good Counsel used to occupy. (See *Monsignor G. J. Dillon.*)

In 1500 the Guild of Bakers of Rome took as their patron the Blessed Virgin under the title of the Madonna of Loreto, a choice peculiarly appropriate, for is not the Holy House of the Incarnation the *Mystic Oven* from whence, by the operation of sacred fire of the Divine Spirit, came forth the Bread of Life ?   Over the high altar they placed the Translation of the Santa Casa by Fra Angelico ; and in 1507, when they built the present church of the Madonna of Loreto on the Forum of Trajan, they transferred this painting to it.*

The miracle of the transport of the Holy House by the ministry of angels is by no means the only case of the Translation of a sacred object across the sea. We may point, for example, to the miraculous picture of Our Lady of Good Counsel, which arrived at Genazzano from Scutari on April 25, 1467, whilst a great crowd was assembled in the public square, S. Mark's day being the chief festival of that locality.

A General of the Augustinians, Ambrose di Cori, who was Provincial of that province in the year of this Translation, writes thus with regard to it : " An image of the Blessed Virgin appeared miraculously on the walls of this church, and all Italy was moved to come and see it, so much so that

come ordinariamente anche nell'opere d'altri insigni autori si ravvisa da periti nella stessa professione. E per esser tale la verità così attestiamo, riferiamo, e deponiamo.   In fede, etc.
                        " In Roma questo di 6 Ottobre 1733.
                " Gio. Paolo Melchiorri, mano propria.
                "Domenico Maria Muradori, mano propria."

" Io infrascritto pittore aggregato nell'Insigne Accademia di San Luca in Santa Martina di Roma dichiaro co' la presente, anche per mezzo del mio giuramento qualmente essendomi portato a richiesta di Monsignor Illustrissimo e Reverendissimo Martorelli già Vescovo di Montefeltro, nella chiesa detta della Madonna di Loreto de' Fornari alla colonna Trajana in questa città di Roma, per vedere, e considerare il quadro, o tavola dell' altar maggiore, qual quadro dipinto in legno all'uso antico, e molto lumeggiato d' oro, rappresentante la Santa Casa di Loreto, portata e sostenuta in aria da angeli, e la Beatissima Vergine sedente sopra il tetto, che tiene in braccio il Bambino Gesù, ad effetto di riconoscere, e riferir di qual tempo e mano possa dirsi fatta quella pittura, ed avendola veduta bene d'appresso e attentamente considerata, dico, riferisco, attesto che la detta pittura e antichissima e una delle belle opere che abbia fatto il celebre pittor e venerabile, o beato Giovanni da Fiesole, quale viveva nel decimo quinto secolo, in cui pur fiorì Pietro Perugino, come si vede nel Vasari, ed altri, che hanno scritto le Vite de' Pittori ; e questo io lo so, e distinguo benissimo la maniera, e l'opere del detto Beato, da quelle degli altri pittori noti, per averne in più, e diversi occasioni vedute, e considerate altre della stessa mano ; e così attesto, depongo, e riferisco per la verità, secondo la mia perizia, e coscienza ed in causa di scienza.   In fede, etc.
                " Questo di 1 Novembre, 1733.
                        "Cavaliere Pietro Leone Ghezzi,
                                mano propria."

* The architect was the celebrated Antonio da San Gallo. It was on the high altar of this church that Muradori, Melchiorri and Ghezzi found the picture in 1733. Since that time a Translation of the school of Perugino has, it seems, taken its place.

whole cities and towns came in procession in the midst of signs and wonders." To register the miracles daily wrought before the picture, the public notary of Genazzano was officially employed. Two days after the Translation, he began his work ; and he relates all the particulars of one hundred and sixty-one miracles wrought between April 27 and August 14 of that year. The then reigning Pontiff, Paul II., ordered an investigation of this marvel ; and Michael Canesius, who wrote the Life of this Pope and was himself contemporary with the event, arrived at conclusions in favour of the Translation. *

The first migration of the inhabitants of Scutari, after the Turks had taken the town in 1478, was towards Latium. Senni and all the historians of this fact say that they went there to be near their beloved Madonna

At Scutari there is a copy of the sacred picture which is venerated at Genazzano ; and the Catholics of all the surrounding country have always shewn their devotion towards Our Lady of Good Counsel by regarding the festival as the chief feast of Albania, coming on pilgrimage to the ruins of the church, and prostrating themselves barefoot before the scene of the miracle.

In the wall of this church of the Annunciation at Scutari is to be seen the spot from which this fresco of the Blessed Virgin was miraculously detached ; and its dimensions correspond exactly with those of the picture venerated at Genazzano, which is not painted on canvas or wood, but on plaster. The marble chapel also at Genazzano is a monument of the event; for it remains just as it was when the blessed Petruccia erected it over the image in 1470, and it bears the inscription : DIVINITUS APPARUIT HÆC IMAGO A.D.N. MCCCCLXVII. XXV. APRILIS. ("This image divinely appeared April 25, 1467.")

When Urban VIII. made the pilgrimage to Genazzano, the secretary of the Duke of Paliano addressed the following words to the Pontiff : "Your Holiness, moved by your devotion, has undertaken this journey from a great desire to visit in person so celebrated an image of the Holy Virgin, which from far distant regions has been transported here by an evident miracle, *recalling the ever memorable Translation of the Holy House of Loreto from Sclavonia to Picenum by the ministry of angels.*"

Not a few other miraculous Translations are recorded in ecclesiastical history, forming together a cumulative mass of evidence that the ministry of angels has been so used by Divine Providence. For the moment, let us merely look at the case of the Greek Madonna venerated in the Basilica di Porto at Ravenna.

* No doubt the investigation ordered by Paul resulted favourably, for the Congregation of Rites has appointed a special mass and office, and the Popes from Benedict XIV. to Leo XIII. have been members of the confraternity.

Just before the rising of the sun on the morning of April 8, 1100, which was the octave of Easter (*Dominica in Albis*), a bright light shone on the shores of the Adriatic near Porto di Ravenna. The portentous event drew the attention of S. Peter degli Onesti and the small community that lived under his direction. On going out of the church upon the beach they saw coming over the sea, borne between two angels carrying lighted torches, a Greek icon of Mary sculptured in marble. When it drew near to the blessed Peter, he received it in his

No. XXVI.—The Vergine Greca of
Ravenna.

arms, carried it into the new church, and placed it with great joy upon the altar.

Among those present on the sea-shore at the moment of its arrival was Father Decabono, who became the successor of S. Peter degli Onesti, and left in the archives of the monastery an account of what he saw. A mosaic made in 1112 represents this miraculous passage over the Adriatic, and, in 1155, the Emperor Frederick Barbarossa presented to Archbishop Anselm a silver image of this Madonna escorted by two angels bearing torches.

Besides these three contemporaneous monuments of the event, S. Peter degli Onesti instituted a confraternity to which many of our Catholic ancestors belonged. The Church has confirmed the miracle by granting a special Mass and Office in honour of this Translation, and a brief of his Holiness Leo XIII. speaks of this ancient Greek icon being borne miraculously over the waves of the Adriatic sea. *

The Santa Casa of Loreto and the Vergine Greca of Ravenna both came across the same sea, from countries ruled by Mahomedans and by schismatics, into the centre of Christendom, bringing with them innumerable blessings.†

* See Pontifical Brief of May 2, 1891.

† See the periodical *Gloria della Vergine*, published by Canon Buzzi, Ravenna.

" Here will I dwell, for I have chosen it."—Ps. cxxxi. 14.

PART VII.

Guide to Loreto and its Environs.

VIEWS OF THE SANCTUARY SURROUNDING THE VENERABLE STATUE AS IT IS ON
HOLY THURSDAY WITHOUT ITS JEWELLED ROBES.

CHAPTER I

Sacred Objects contained in the Holy House—Its external Ornamentation.

SOME objects of great value in the estimation of the faithful have been preserved in the Holy House. Among these are three eating-vessels, called *Le Sante Scodelle.* "What touching memories these relics evoke!" exclaims a pious writer; "they were daily in the hands of Mary. S. Joseph used them to quench his thirst. The Child Jesus took His repasts from them. Oh what are the golden vessels used at the banquets of kings in comparison with these earthen vessels used by the Holy Family? Should not our eyes fill with tears while we press them to our lips?"

One evening, while the custodian of the Holy House took out the little vessel that had been used by the Child Jesus and poured a small bottle of water into it, at the request of a pious pilgrim, there remained a few drops at the bottom of the sacred vessel, after the water had been put back again into the pilgrim's phial. Now there stood by the superior of St. Sulpice, Paris, who bore the appearance of a man near death. The custodian presented to him the sacred vessel, and no sooner had he drunk the few remaining drops than he was restored to a perfect state of health.*

This *Santa Scodella* is kept in a receptacle in the east wall,† and the pilgrims put their rosaries and medals into it. The other two eating-vessels are kept in the holy cupboard ‡ of the Virgin of Nazareth, which is in the north wall and near where the Gospel is read. Fac-similes of the *Sante Scodelle* may be obtained in the town as a memorial of the pilgrimage. They should, of course, touch the relics and receive the seal of the *Santa Casa.* Additional value attaches to them owing to

* See *Mémoire sur M. de Brétonvilliers*, by the companion of his pilgrimage, M. Bourdon, A.D. 1871.

† This is the only one that was saved out of the pillage in 1797. Pius VII. succeeded in recovering the others, but they had been partly broken by the soldiers.

‡ This cupboard, called *il santo Armadio*, has a cedar-wood shelf in a perfect state of preservation, and built into the wall. Its height is 30½ inches, its width 23 inches, and its depth 13½ inches.

the earthenware being partly formed of dust that had collected on the walls of the Holy House.

In the north wall is also seen the ancient doorway with its cedar lintel. At Nazareth it opened into the Cave, which had the chief entrance close by this internal doorway.* It was walled up by the order of Clement VII., who had three† new doorways made on account of the great concourse of pilgrims, sometimes numbering forty thousand.

The ancient altar erected by S. Peter opposite the doorway was changed into its present position when the doorway was walled up. It is encased in a larger altar, but may be seen through an opening. Its length is only 4 ft. 5 in.; its material is the same limestone as the walls, and it is surmounted by a slab of dark grey stone. The identity of the *Santa Casa* with the Holy House of Nazareth is strikingly confirmed by the existence of this altar in it. The Divine Sacrifice is offered on it, by privilege, up to the end of Vespers; and it is always the Mass of the Blessed Virgin, except at nine o'clock on Thursdays, when the Mass of the Holy Ghost is sung.

In the west wall is seen the window which gave light to the whole House. Over it is placed an ancient figure of Jesus crucified, painted on canvas and stretched out upon a cross of cedar-wood. It arrived with the Holy House and is attributed by tradition to S. Luke. At one time it became very celebrated, on account of a great number of miracles; and Abraham Bzovius testifies that, when it was removed into the basilica to give it greater honour, it returned three times miraculously into the *Santa Casa* during the night when the doors were fastened.

The stone restored by the Bishop of Coimbra (as already related) is near the credence, and an authentic copy of his letter is kept in the holy cupboard. Above it is a cannon ball that fell harmless at the feet of Pope Julius II. during the siege of Mirandola in 1505.

The upper part of the walls is still covered, here and there, by "a fading fresco that demands a sigh." Cardinal Bartolini writes concerning them: "It is probable that the first paintings were executed on the walls by order of S. Helena; but I cannot decide the question. The existence of different layers of plaster, bearing traces of colour, shews that picture succeeded picture in successive epochs. It seems that they did not form a series of historical subjects, but rather a variety of compositions suggested by the piety of those who had them painted. Hence we see several representations of the Blessed Virgin surrounded by the patron saints of the pilgrims, who wished thus to perpetuate the memory of graces received by their intercession.

* This has been already illustrated by the plates in Part I. Chapter IV.
† The fourth doorway seen from the outside only leads up to the roof.

No. XXVII.—NORTH WALL, CONTAINING THE SANTO ARMADIO, THE WALLED-UP DOORWAY WITH WOODEN LINTEL, THE REMAINS OF A PARTITION BEAM, FRESCOES OF OUR LADY AND S. CATHERINE.

No. XXVIII.—WEST WALL WITH THE WINDOW, CRUCIFIX AND FRESCOES.

No. XXIX.—SOUTH WALL WITH FRESCOES OF THE BLESSED VIRGIN, S. GEORGE AND S. ANTHONY, THE REMAINS OF A BEAM SAWN OFF, A CLEMENTINE DOOR, AND THE STONE RESTORED BY THE BISHOP OF COIMBRA.

In the first rank among the saints represented in fresco are S. George, S. Anthony and S. Catharine, special patrons of the Greek Church, which had care of this sanctuary for several centuries. S. Louis, King of France, grateful to the Virgin for deliverance out of the hands of the Saracens, had painted, as an *ex voto* on the west wall, the venerable image of Mary together with his own portrait. He stood before her in a deferential attitude, vested in his regal robes and holding in his left hand a sceptre, whilst with his right he offered iron chains, in token of the captivity from which he had been set free.

The *Santa Casa* measures internally 31 feet 2 inches long, by 13½ feet wide and 14 feet high.

At the west end there is one of the beams of the Holy House let into the floor, and its perfect condition is worthy of note; for the feet of the pilgrims, which have worn out so many sets of pavement, have had no effect upon it.

The remains of another beam, which probably formed the top of a partition separating off the east end of the Holy House, are to be seen in the north and south walls. That portion which is in the north wall, between the holy cupboard and the ancient doorway, has become so loose, that it may be taken out to shew the exact thickness of the wall.

In the east wall behind the Altar is visited the *Santo Camino* (the Holy Hearth). At the time of the arrival of the Holy House, there was a simple recess in the wall blackened by smoke. The Nazarenes do not use chimneys for letting out smoke, and the cooking was probably done in the Cave.*

Immediately over the *Santo Camino* stands the miraculous statue of the Blessed Virgin, which came with the Holy House and is said to be the work of S. Luke the Evangelist. It is only three feet high, and the great length of the robe, which descends to the base of the pedestal, is in memory of a robe which the Blessed Virgin had worn during her life at Nazareth, and which the Christians of that town put upon the statue after her Assumption. This relic was still at Loreto in 1797, but was lost during the French Revolution. Fortunately, Peter Moscati, who afterwards became senator and consul at Milan, had detached a piece of this robe, and he gave a portion of it in 1804, together with

* The little Cave at Nazareth is commonly called the kitchen of the Virgin. We may point out that the present form of the *Santo Camino* only dates from 1534, when the floor of the east end of the Holy House was raised, and a fire-place, surmounted by a niche, was constructed out of the stones taken from the walls in making the Clementine doors. No ancient picture exists to shew us the original shape of the *Santo Camino*. Cardinal Bartolini, in his minute description of the houses of Nazareth, says with regard to the fire-place, "In one of the rooms is found the hearth, level with the floor."

a certificate, to the Canon of Monza, Angelo Bellini. This Canon sent the relic to Loreto in 1812, accompanied by an attestation in due form, and it is kept in a reliquary placed on the right hand side of the niche of the Madonna.

Not content with taking the robe of Mary and pillaging her sanctuary, the invaders carried away her venerable image to Paris. * This outrage deeply grieved the Sovereign Pontiff, and, at the urgent request of his Holiness Pius VII., the sacred image was restored to public veneration. The servants of Jesus and Mary in Paris felt the need of making reparation for the violation of the shrine of Loreto, the reduction of the Holy House to poverty like that at Nazareth, and the sacrilegious deportation of the sacred image into France. When, then, the Virgin of Loreto made her entry into Notre Dame, she stood amid thousands of throbbing hearts that came to testify their love; and in place of the gems that had been plundered, she found living jewels to adorn her crown.

As soon as the venerable statue reached Rome on its way to Loreto, Pius VII. received it in his private chapel at the Quirinal, where His Holiness crowned the heads of the Mother and Child with golden diadems set with pearls and emeralds. Her new robe was white and splendidly embroidered. Her necklace was of pearls with a rose of emeralds surrounding a Brazilian topaz.

Thus apparelled, the Madonna of Loreto was placed on the high altar of the Church of San Salvatore in Lauro, where, during the last three days of November, 1802, all the population of Rome flocked to venerate her.

Her return to the Holy House, where she had received the homage of the faithful during so many centuries, was a great cause of joy at Loreto. The Bishops of Recanati and of Nocera received her at the gate of Recanati and carried her in procession to the cathedral. The next day the clergy, magistrates and people of Loreto, headed by the Cardinal Archetti and the bishops of the province, came to meet her on the summit of Monte Reale. The fêtes lasted for three days, during which the Virgin of Loreto remained on the altar of the Annunciation. As a climax to the rejoicings, the Madonna was replaced in the niche of the Holy House, where she is to be seen to-day, attired in magnificent robes.

The jewels that cover her dress bear their testimony to the number of favours received. The custodians will point out the chief of the *ex votos*, among which will be seen the famous medallion adorned with ten large

* It was put in the National Library, in the department of Medals and Antiques, among other objects of art brought from different parts of Europe.

No. XXX.—THE CENTRAL NAVE OF THE BASILICA, SHEWING THE WEST END OF THE HOLY HOUSE
AND ITS WINDOW OVER THE EXTERNAL ALTAR OF THE ANNUNCIATION.

solitaires, the gift of his Majesty Anthony Clement, King of Saxony, in thanksgiving for having obtained, in 1828, for his brother Maximilian a male heir to succeed to the throne.

The entire statue of the Virgin of Loreto is resplendent with precious stones: rubies, sapphires, emeralds, turquoises, amethysts, diamonds glisten in rich profusion.

But the Madonna of the *Santa Casa* has her days of mourning. During the last three days of Holy Week, she lays aside her splendid robe and all her jewels, retaining no ornament save her crown, and covered from head to foot in a black gauze veil. * This veil is afterwards distributed among thousands of the members of the Confraternity of the Holy House, being cut up into small pieces and attached to pictures of the Virgin of Loreto with the seal of the *Santa Casa* and the signature of the custodian.

On Holy Thursday and Holy Saturday the sacred statue is placed on the altar of the *Santa Casa*. It is then seen to be of the Jewish-Egyptian school of sculpture, as it was described in the catalogue of the Bibliothèque Nationale of Paris. It is covered with plaster that bears traces of colour, and, where the plaster has been removed, the natural wood is visible. The sculptured robe of the Virgin is so long that only the fore-part of the feet is seen, and these are kissed by the pilgrims of Holy Week. The robe is gathered in at the waist by a girdle, and the back portion of it is covered by a long flowing veil. Both Mother and Child are cut out of one block, which has remained untouched by the worm; and, though the faces are dark, the wood is in reality light.

The Litany of Loreto † is recited every day after Vespers. It is then that the *Santa Casa* is closed until the morning, although the Basilica remains open till much later. The ceremonies used at the nightly closing of the Holy House should not be missed by any pilgrim. They commence by ringing the little bells which came with the sacred Dwelling. ‡ Most pilgrims obtain small models of these bells carried by the angels: they may be used in times of thunder. When the lightning flashes round the Holy House, the little bells ring out their loudest peal, as if to silence the artillery of heaven. A procession forms and marches round until the power of prayer prevails. It is a thrilling scene amid the darkness of a storm.

* The author of this book has been present at this touching ceremony.
† "Quisnam fuerit auctor seu primus inventor illius compertum non habeo."—Justinus Miechoviensis.
‡ " Non dixit historicus campanulas ibi positas ab Apostolis, sed cum eadem Domo, sive a Syria ad Dalmatas, sive a Dalmatis ad Picenos traductas, ibidem repertas."—Clypeus Lauretanus.

The exterior ornamentation of the *Santa Casa* is a great work of art, designed by Bramante and carried out by Sansovino, Lombardi, Tribulo and San Gallo. The celebrated sculptor Canova sent his pupils to study it, telling them that it contained *nearly everything*. And Vasari, the renowned painter and architect, called the bas-relief of the Annunciation *a divine work*. "You might cover this house with diamonds and pearls, but what would all these treasures be in comparison with such masterpieces?"

This marble casing of the *Santa Casa* is, in fact, one of the most remarkable productions of art and, in itself, quite a gallery of sculpture. Ten Prophets and ten Sybils, who foretold the Conception of the Virgin Mother, are grouped two and two around the holy Place of the Incarnation. Next to each seer is set forth a mystery:—The Birth of the Blessed Virgin, her Marriage, the Annunciation, the Visitation, the Nativity of the Son of God, and the Death of the Immaculate Mother of God.

At the left of the Annunciation, which is over the window, are placed the Prophet Jeremias and the Sibyl of Libya; on the right, Ezechiel and the Sibyl of Delphi.* On the north façade, Isaias and the Sibyl of Marpessa on the Hellespont; Daniel and the Sibyl of Ancyra in Phrygia; Amos and the Sibyl of Tivoli. On the south façade Malachias and the Sibyl of Persia;† David and the Sibyl of Cumæ in Italy; Zacharias and the Sibyl of Erythræa. On the east façade Moses and the Sibyl of Samos; Balaam and the Sibyl of Cumæ in Æolia.‡

We owe to the chisel of Sansovino (Contucci) the Annunciation, the Shepherds at the Nativity of Christ, and the Prophet Jeremias. He also commenced the Birth of the Blessed Virgin, her Marriage, and the Adoration of the Magi. The Prophets David, Malachias and Zacharias are by Jerome Lombardi, and so are also the four bronze doors.

The Translation of the Holy House is the work of the Florentine sculptor Nicholas Tribulo. The Death of the Blessed Virgin was finished by Dominic d'Aimo, called also the Varignano, but what sculptor began it is unknown.

The two scenes represented on the right and left of the window of the *Santa Casa* are by Francis da San Gallo: they are the Visitation of the Immaculate Virgin to S. Elizabeth and the Enrolment at Bethlehem.

It is due to the memory of these illustrious sculptors to record that for the most part they devoted their great talents to the honour of the Blessed Virgin without seeking any earthly recompense.

---

* Some say the Sibyl of Persia.   † Some say the Sibyl of Delphi.

‡ In the *Dies Iræ* the Church refers to the Sibyls: *Teste David cum Sibylla*. Great numbers of the early Christians were converted from paganism by the fulfilment of the prophecies of the Sibyls in Jesus of Nazareth.

No. XXXI.—THE FAÇADE OF THE BASILICA AND THE
APOSTOLIC PALACE.

No. XXXII.—THE MARBLE CASING OF THE SANTA CASA.

CHAPTER II

The Treasury, Basilica, Apostolical Palace, and Environs of Loreto.

THE votive offerings in testimony of graces received through her who "never meets with any refusal from God," * the rich gifts of monarchs, princes and nobles, the pectoral crosses of Popes, Cardinals and Bishops, the jewels and presents of all kinds offered by the pilgrims, have been well-nigh innumerable, so that a vast treasury was erected in 1612, and beautifully decorated by the masterly hand of Pomerancio. The size of this treasury, with its numberless compartments enclosed by glass doors, will give some idea of the confidence of Catholics in the miracle of the Translation of the Holy House, and how they prized the intercession of the Virgin of Loreto.

When S. Alphonsus de Liguori was shewn the treasures of the *Santa Casa*, and was told how this gift was made to the most holy Virgin by a certain prince, this by a certain sovereign, the saint shed tears of joy on seeing how the Mother of God had called forth the love and veneration of the great of the earth.

Up to the time of the French Revolution, the treasury surpassed all that the imagination can picture. The losses incurred in that sacrilegious depredation can be never fully repaired; but the pilgrim will, nevertheless, find much to admire.

We will not enter into details concerning all the precious stones, gold and silver vessels, chalices, monstrances, reliquaries, chandeliers, diadems, necklaces, ear-rings, bracelets, robes, decorations, rings, coral, amber and crystal presents made in profusion by the pilgrims. A complete enumeration is out of the question, but we may mention a chalice, given in 1838 by Maximilian, Duke of Leuchtenberg (Armoire no. 12); a flower formed of diamonds, the gift of Louise de Bourbon, Queen of Etruria, in 1815; also a chalice presented by Queen Amelia of Bavaria (no. 19); a gold reliquary enclosing part of the Blessed Virgin's robe (no. 26); a diamond given in 1816 by Marie Louise of Parma, Queen of Spain; a necklace and cross offered by Marian Caroline and Maria Christina, of the house of Savoy, who became respectively Empress of

* S. John of Damascus.

Austria and Queen of the two Sicilies (no. 27); a figure of Christ in gold attached to a cross with a crystal pedestal, given in 1816 by Charles IV., King of Spain (no. 28); a magnificent oriental pearl, which was celebrated in the treasury before its spoliation, and a string of forty-eight large oriental pearls offered, in 1817, by the Princess Mary of Wurtemberg (no. 31); a chalice given by Pius VII. on his return from Fontainebleau; two more chalices given by Pius VIII. and Pius IX. (no. 35); the Holy Name of Mary composed of diamonds and rubies (no. 39); two banners offered by Austria and Venice in thanksgiving for the victory of Lepanto and the taking of Belgrade from the Turks (no. 40); the Holy Name of Jesus formed out of gold rings (no. 66).

No. XXXIII.—THE TREASURY.

The sixty-nine walnut cupboards which are round the treasury, cost 65,000 lire. The magnificent frescoes painted on the ceiling are themselves quite a treasure, and the sacristy attached to it is adorned with pictures of great beauty.

The Basilica was completed under the pontificate of Paul III., 1538. In the list of architects, the first named * is Marino di Marco Cedrino,

* No document gives the name of any earlier architect; but we find by the testament of Gozio di Butolo, who left two measures of grain towards "the building of the Church of St. Mary of Loreto," that a church was contemplated, or in actual course of erection, in 1362. A controversy has arisen as to whether the original plan was of the same dimensions as the present Basilica. We refer the reader to *Loreto: Monografia Storico-Artistica compilata dal Prof. Eduardo Facco da Lagarda* (Roma, 1895.)

No. XXXIV.—A Portion of the Decoration of the Dome.

A.D. 1468. Then follow, Master Thomas in 1479, Julian da Majano, and his nephew, Master Benedict, in 1488. Then comes Julian da San Gallo in 1499. In 1509 Bramante made a wooden model of the marble casing of the *Santa Casa*. After this great master, there follow three architects less known, and, lastly in 1531, Anthony da San Gallo. In his time, the cupola, which had only been erected thirty-one years, threatening to fall in, he built the present solid pilasters to support it.

The painting of the interior of the dome, representing the titles of the Blessed Virgin drawn from the Litany of Loreto, is a stupendous work, and is due to the artistic talent of Professor Maccari of Siena.

The piety of the faithful has erected to S. Joseph a throne of honour on the right hand of his ancient dwelling. The decoration of the chapel has been designed by Count Sacconi; the statue of S. Joseph is by Don Barron, the rest of the sculpture by Eugene Maccagnani, and the tracery by Francis Prosperi; the stained glass windows are by Francis Moretti, the frescoes by Faustini; the bronze work comes from the establishment of Achilles Crescenzi; the gilding is by Hector Brandizzi, and the precious stones have been furnished by the house of Frenkle von Walsirck, of Baden.

The choir of the Basilica is being decorated by the offerings of German Catholics. The design is by Louis Seitz, and the style Gothic-Venetian. Leo XIII. has described it as "an epic poem of the life of the Virgin." There also is portrayed much of the symbolism of Mary, in which the Canticle of Canticles and the Fathers of the Church abound.

The large chapel on the left of the *Santa Casa* is in course of decoration by the French nation, in honour of S. Louis. The walls are to be adorned by representations of the sainted king venerating the Holy House of Nazareth, when first he came in sight of the Basilica containing it, and afterwards assisting at the offices of the feast of the Annunciation. In the windows will be portrayed the principal facts in the life of the saint, whose statue will surmount an altar in bronze and marble. St· Francis of Assisi and S. Dominic will be placed on the right and left hand of S. Louis.

The chapel adjoining is being decorated by the offerings of the Slavs. The design is by Count Sacconi and is being carried out by Professor Stella and Professor Cav. Moretti. The stained glass representing Slav saints is the work of the latter. Over the altar is depicted the Blessed Virgin with S. Cyril and S. Methodius, apostles of the Slavs, and the walls are adorned with a variety of coloured marbles.

In most of the chapels of the Basilica there are beautiful mosaics that come from the Vatican. Nine of these represent the Conception,

Birth,* Presentation, Childhood,† Marriage, Annunciation,‡ Visitation,§ Desolation and Assumption‖ of the Blessed Virgin. There are also mosaics of the Last Supper, S. Michael,¶ S. Francis of Assisi,** S. Benedict, S. Dominic, S. Ignatius of Loyola, S. Philip Neri, S. Charles Borromeo. S. Francis of Paul, and S. Emideo.

The richly decorated baptistry in bronze is the work of Tiburzio Verzelli and John Baptist Vitali.

The bronze bas-reliefs of the principal entrance of the Basilica are by the sons of Jerome Lombardi. Beginning from the top upon the right we have:—1. the Creation of Eve; 2. God blessing Adam, who is thanking the Lord for having made him ; 3. our first parents cast out of Eden ; 4. the Catholic Church, represented by a majestic woman, receives the homage of the faithful ; 5. the murder of Abel; beneath is Innocence, holding a palm, and being received lovingly by the Church.

On the left side are : 1. Eve giving the forbidden fruit to Adam ; 2, Heresy, symbolized by a serpent, who molests the Church, represented by a matron ; 3. the law of labour: Adam digs and Eve spins; 4. the Church, holding a lily, welcomes penitent sinners ; 5. Cain as a fugitive ; 6. Heresy flees from the Church, biting its hands.

The side door, on the north towards the Palace, is by Tiburzio Verzelli, pupil of Jerome Lombardi. On the right are :—1. the Creation of Adam—between the Annunciation and the Baptism of Christ ; 2. an angel comforting Agar in the desert—between Agar driven forth from the house and the angel shewing a spring to refresh her dying son ; 3. the Sacrifice of Isaac—between Jesus on His way to Calvary and Jesus on the Cross ; 4. the passage of the Red Sea—between Moses who announces the death of the first-born of the Egyptians, and Moses who lifts up his rod to re-unite the waters; 5. the Manna in the desert.

On the left side :—1. the Creation of Eve—between Jesus giving the keys to S. Peter and the Descent of the Holy Ghost ; 2. Eliezer and Rebecca—between Eliezer received by Bathuel and Laban, and Rebecca mother of Esau and Jacob; 3. Joseph governor of Egypt—between Christ amid the doctors and Christ entering in triumph into Jerusalem ; 4. the death of Holofernes—between Judith going to the Assyrian camp and Judith placing the head of Holofernes on the walls of Jerusalem. Then follow two medallions of Christ driving out the sellers from the Temple and rising from the dead ; and 5. Moses smiting the rock.

---

* After Caracci.
† Mary watering a lily, accompanied by her parents, after Angelica Kauffman.
‡ After Barocci.   § After Barocci.   ‖ After Fra Bartolomeo di San Marco.
¶ After Guido Reni.   ** After Domenichino.

The side door on the south is by Anthony Calcagni, assisted by Tarquin Jacometti and Sebastiani.   On the right :—1. the sacrifices offered by Cain and Abel—between the Nativity of the Blessed Virgin and her Presentation in the Temple ; 2. the sacrifice of Noah after the Deluge—between the entry into the Ark and the cursing of Cham ; 3. the translation of the Ark to Jerusalem—between the Visitation and the Birth of Christ ; 4. the Burning Bush—between Moses in a basket of bulrushes and his rod changed into a serpent—the two medallions represent the Circumcision of Jesus and the flight into Egypt ; 5. Abigail meeting David.

On the left :—1. the murder of Abel—between the Espousals of the Virgin and her Annunciation ; 2. Jacob's Ladder—between Jacob tending Laban's flock and Jacob wrestling with the Angel ; 3. the throne of Solomon—between Anna the Prophetess at the Presentation of Jesus and the Adoration of the Magi ; 4. the Brazen Serpent—between Joshue and Caleb returning from their exploration of the Promised Land and Nadab and Abiu destroyed by fire from the Lord ; 5. Queen Esther pleading with Assuerus.   The two medallions represent the Apostles at the tomb of the Virgin and the Coronation of Mary in Heaven.

The cost of these bronze doors amounted to £8,000.   They are the gift of Sixtus V.

Over the central doorway this same Pontiff placed a most beautiful bronze statue of the Blessed Virgin, the work of Jerome Lombardi.

The façade of the Basilica having also been terminated during the Pontificate of Sixtus V., that great Pope is represented seated on a throne in front of the entrance.   This statue is by Anthony Calcagni, and at the four angles there are symbolical figures of Justice, Charity, Religion and Peace.   Two inscriptions engraved over the side entrances record that it is to this Pontiff that the church owes the title of Cathedral, and Loreto the honour of being a city.

The arms of Gregory XIII. are placed over the chief entrance, because this Pontiff completed the first half of the façade.

The clock-tower was added during the pontificate of Benedict XIV. and was designed by Vanvitelli.   Its lower part is Doric, to which succeed Ionic, Corinthian and composite.   The stone is from Istria, and the height of the tower is about 200 feet.   The largest bell is named Lauretta ; it was cast in 1516 by Bernardin of Rimini, and weighs 22,000 lbs.

The bronze ornamentation of the fountain in the Piazza della Madonna is by Tarquin and Peter-Paul Jacometti.

The arcades of the Apostolical Palace enclose this piazza only

on the north and west sides, but, according to the design of
Bramante* and the intention of Julius II., the Palace ought to enclose
the whole square. On the west side is placed the balcony from
which the Sovereign Pontiffs were accustomed to give their benediction
to the faithful assembled in the Piazza.

The rooms shewn to visitors are hung with tapestry and paintings.
Among the former are copies of the cartoons of Raphael, which were
purchased by Charles I., and are now in the South Kensington
Museum. Of the paintings in the first room, the most remarkable
are the Last Supper, by Simon Vouet; the dead Christ in the arms
of God the Father, attributed to Guercino; † S. Clare, by Bartholomew
of Modena; the Circumcision, by Philip Bellini; the Madonna and
Holy Child, by Mazzuola; the Descent of the Holy Spirit, by Felix
Damiani da Gubbio; the Conception, by Joseph Crespi of Bologna; the
Woman taken in adultery, by Lotto; ‡ the Translation of the
Holy House, by Francis Foschi; S. Nicholas of Bari, by Conca.

In other rooms there are a Holy Family, attributed to Coreggio; the
Immaculate Conception, by Philip Bellini; the Nativity of the Blessed
Virgin, by Maratti; the Crib, by Hannibal Caracci. The ceilings
were painted by Francis Stagni of Bologna.

Opposite the Apostolical Palace is seen the former Illyrian College,
which has been secularized.

Let us now go down the street that leads to the back of the
Basilica : there is obtained the best idea of the massiveness of this vast
structure and the altitude of the battlements that protect it on the
east.

The Marine Gate (*Porta Marina*) is at the back of the cathedral, and
commands a very fine view. Thence is seen the battlefield of
Castelfidardo. " Sanctuary of Loreto," exclaims Monsignor Dupanloup,
" they beheld thee then while fighting ! Thou didst appear to them
as a refuge open to their souls, and towards thee were turned their
dying eyes in hope and consolation."

Still to the north, but further off, stands out in bold relief the
headland of Monte Conero. The town at its foot is Sirolo, the ancient
Humana, much visited by the pilgrims to Loreto on account of a
miraculous image of our Lord, known throughout the Catholic world
as the Crucifix of Sirolo.

On the left of the line of railway to Ancona there rises up the
ancient town of Osimo, where pilgrims visit the shrine of St. Joseph

* Some attribute the plans to Julian da San Gallo.
† Some say Peruzzini of Ancona.
‡ There is another of the same subject of the school of Titian.

No. XXXV.—THE VOTO NAZIONALE OF THE ITALIANS.
(See Pag 175.)

No. XXXVI.—THE PORTA MARINA AT THE BACK OF THE BASILICA

No. XXXVIII. Miraculous Picture of Our Lady of Seven Dolours at Campo-Cavallo, near Loreto.

No. XXXVII. The Statue in the Chapel of S. Joseph.

of Cupertino, whose body rests beneath the High Altar of the cathedral.

A still finer view is obtainable from the summit of Monreale, which is reached from the Porta Romana. The panorama is of indescribable beauty : the eye passes from peak to peak of the Apennines, and from hill to hill crowned with picturesque towns, whilst, on the east, there glistens in the sun the gilded statue of the Virgin of Loreto, which surmounts the stately dome covering her beloved Abode.

Every pilgrim ought, if possible, to visit the different spots sanctified by the temporary presence of the Holy House. First, the Banderola, where the sacred Dwelling alighted on its first arrival in Italy. This is where the Italians are preparing to erect a beautiful chapel as a *voto nazionale* in commemoration of the sixth centenary. The place is easily reached, as it is only a few hundred yards from the railway station, and on the left side of the road, adjoining a farm-house with *Santa Casa* over its entrance. *

Next in interest is the site it occupied for a time on the land of the two brothers. It will be found at the south-west corner of the Cathedral square. As soon as the projected chapel has been built upon the spot, it will be readily discovered, but, for the present, not being visible from the street, some help is requisite in looking for it. It is recognized by a bas-relief in *terra cotta*, placed against the side wall of the Apostolical Palace, and representing the Translation. It seemed that to form the Cathedral square the little valley between the hill of the two brothers and the summit on which the Holy House finally rested, was filled up and levelled.

The only remaining place memorable for a stay of the Holy House since its departure from Nazareth is, as the reader is aware, not at Loreto, but on the opposite shore of the Adriatic. It is, however, very easily reached by well appointed steamers from Ancona,† and, not to mention the surpassing loveliness of the gulf on which it stands, it is a perennial fount of Grace, as the title acquired by this Madonna testifies.

Ancona is about fifteen miles from Loreto. S. Cyriac, its bishop, visited the Holy House at Nazareth in the fourth century. His body was miraculously translated from Palestine, where this saint had died ; and his mortal remains continue to this day in a perfect state of incorruption. The cathedral of S. Cyriac is rich in relics ; and, on this spot where Venus once bore sway and vice prevailed, there reigns in spotless purity the Queen of all the Saints. On the feast of

---

* Plate XXXV. (See page 171.)

† The steamers sail at 10 p.m. from Ancona, and in about six hours enter the magnificent gulf of Quarnero, reaching Fiume by 8 a.m.

S. William, June 25, is usually commemorated the first occasion on which this Madonna of Ancona miraculously assumed the appearance of a living person.*

The Penitentiary of the *Santa Casa* being confided to conventuals, we may point out to the faithful that this year the seventh centenary of the birth of S. Anthony of Padua will be celebrated by that Order. Many Loreto pilgrims, without going much out of their way, might visit Padua. Ravenna would then lie on their route ; and they could visit also the celebrated Greek Madonna (*la Madonna Greca*), brought there miraculously by the holy angels.

The members of the Archconfraternity of S. Michael should endeavour to extend their pilgrimage to Monte Gargano ;† those of the Third Order of S. Francis to Assisi ; the clients of St. Nicholas to Bari ; and all, with few exceptions, to Rome.

* See the English translation of the *Official Memoirs of the Juridical Examination into the Authenticity of the Miraculous Events which happened in Rome in the Years* 1796-7. Published in England, 1801. Appendix on Ancona.

† S. Michael is the special protector of the Church. His appearance to the Bishop of Siponto on Mount Gargan in the year 493 is the origin of the festival of May 8. From Loreto there is train to Manfredonia, where the Monte Sant' Angelo is situated. The pilgrim has to change at Foggia.

" I rejoiced at the things that were said to me : We will go into the House of the Lord."—Ps. cxxi. 1.

PART VIII.

Sixth Centenary of the Translation into Italy.

Y

CHAPTER I

Thoughts on the Pilgrimage of the Holy House.

ECHOES of the Holy House resound in every Catholic Church throughout the world. The Litany of Loreto is sung before the Blessed Sacrament when the Saviour of the world comes to give His Benediction. This halo of glory surrounding the *Santa Casa* teaches the faithful to acknowledge in the lowly Dwelling venerated at Loreto the holy Place of the Incarnation, whence came forth the Divine Victim that we adore upon the altar. This aureole takes the place of the star to the Magi; it invites us to set out and follow on until we reach the blessed Abode.

It is in her divine maternity that the greatness of Mary consists; and it is her bond of maternal tenderness with Jesus of Nazareth that produces in our hearts confidence and love. Have we need of succour? This is the House of her who is the "help of Christians." Do we wish for consolation in this vale of tears? This is the House of her who is the "comfort of the afflicted." Have we infirmities of body or soul? This is the House of her who is the "health of the sick." Are we tormented by the remembrance of transgressions? This is the House of her who is the "refuge of sinners." Do we feel the need of Grace? This is the House of her who is the "Mother of Divine Grace." Here, where S. Gabriel proclaimed her to be full of grace, she distributes to the necessitous the abundance of God's grace.

Devotion towards Mary in her sacred Dwelling dates from the beginning of Christianity. During eighteen centuries the Holy House has been a great object of pilgrimage. At Nazareth, for twelve hundred years, it received the visits of saints, crusaders, and pilgrims of every nation. At Loreto, during six hundred years, the most eminent men, sovereign pontiffs, monarchs, princes of the Church and those of the world, philosophers and theologians, men of every rank and degree of attainment, from the master minds of each age down to the most illiterate, have gone to render homage to this marvellous Sanctuary. A pilgrimage to the Holy House is equivalent to one to Palestine. Its Translation into Europe was a partition of the Holy Places between the East and West: the East retains the Holy Caves at Nazareth and

Bethlehem ; God has given to the West the sacred Chamber of the Incarnation.   The East keeps the plot of ground sanctified by the Immaculate Conception and the Nativity of Mary ; God has conveyed into
the West the actual Room in which she was conceived and born.   The
East possesses the Holy Sepulchre, the abode of Christ when dead ;
God has granted to the West the possession of the House in which
He lived.

It is amid these few small stones quarried out of the rock at Nazareth
that He Who was the *Heir of all things** took up His earthly Dwelling.
He Who created the heavens by a word, here bent down daily over His
lowly task.   He Who by the breath of his mouth could uproot all the
cedars of Lebanon, here patiently forms into yokes † and ploughs this
wood of the forest.   Hard toil ! Abasement and grandeur ! The divine
Carpenter was constructing the coffin ‡ of paganism, whence man has
come forth risen and transformed.

Within these sacred Walls was inaugurated the true civilisation of
the nations.   This House is the central spot where the Church arose to
spread throughout the world.   It is the place whence first came forth
the grace and hope which now rejoice the hearts of Christians.

It is upon our knees and with a heart overflowing with gratitude
that we should contemplate this House in which the Redeemer prepared Himself as a Prophet for His mission and as a Victim for His
immolation ;—this House that He never quitted till the time when He
went forth to evangelize the people and bear His Cross to Calvary.

Angels' feet alone are worthy to pass across this threshold ; but the
voice of Mary reassures us, bidding us to come into her home.

On entering the sacred Dwelling the pilgrim seems to be at Nazareth·
The Divine Master is there and speaks to His blessed Mother, regarding her with a look of infinite love.

It is not a dream that we enter the House of Mary : it is a great
reality. You will see the humble Dwelling where the King of kings
passed His hidden days.   You will see the Walls that sheltered the
Founder of the Church which is built with eternal cement.   You will
see the Door through which He passed, Who alone can open to our
souls the gate of Heaven.

Is there a better means of preparing for eternal life than in going
to visit this earthly Paradise ? The pilgrimage will rekindle in our
hearts the fire of divine love that has been well-nigh extinguished by
the cares and the passions of this life ; it will strengthen us in our

* *Hebrews* i. 1.   † See S. Justin the Martyr's Dialogue with Trypho.
‡ When Libanius, a friend of Julian the Apostate, asked a Christian in irony what
the Nazarene was doing, he replied : "Making a coffin for Julian."

No. XXXIX.—His Holiness Pope Leo XIII.

temptations and our trials, and will procure for us the sublime con-solation of a happy death. For all the remaining days of our life on earth, the name of the Holy House will revive in us memories of inex-pressible joy, the foretaste of eternal bliss.

CHAPTER II

His Holiness Pope Leo XIII. calls on all the Faithful to celebrate the Sixth Centenary of the Translation of the Holy House into Italy.

IT is to a pilgrimage to this sacred Dwelling that the Vicar of Jesus of Nazareth convokes the Catholics of the entire world. It is His Holiness' hope "that God, by the intercession of His most holy Mother, will be pleased to send down more effectual succour to His Church under her afflictions." And He writes to the Bishop of Loreto, whose Church is so greatly ennobled by the presence of the dear Home of the Blessed Virgin, "that the divine token of the fulfilment of this hope shines more brightly from an approaching and signal event in the history of the Holy House, namely the close of the sixth century since our ances-tors were first favoured by the coming of so great a gift."

To foster this hope, His Holiness determined to exhort all Christian people by the following Apostolic Letter :

Brief of His Holiness Pope Leo XIII. respecting the Sixth Centenary of the Translation of the Holy House of Loreto.

LEO XIII. TO ALL THE FAITHFUL WHO SHALL SEE THE PRESENT LETTER, HEALTH AND APOSTOLIC BENEDICTION.

The happy House of Nazareth—where, at the salutation of the Angel addressed to the chosen Mother of God, *the Word was made Flesh*—is justly regarded and honoured as one of the most sacred monuments of the Christian Faith ; and this appears clear from the many diplomas and acts, gifts and privileges accorded by Our predecessors. No sooner was it, as the annals of the Church bear witness, brought over miraculously into Italy, in pursuance of a most benign counsel of God, and exposed to the veneration of the faithful on the hills of Loreto, in the March of Ancona, than it drew to itself the fervent devotion and pious aspiration of all, and, as the ages rolled on, it maintained this devotion ever ardent.

Suffice it to recall to mind how numerous and magnificent have been the pilgrimages made to this spot from every quarter ; how splendid the Basilica erected there, most remarkable for its artistic ornamentation together with the dignity of its sacred ritual ; and how auspiciously, under the patronage of the Blessed Virgin, there sprang up around it a new town, just as if *another Nazareth!*

Very many signal favours, public as well as private, ever welling up there as from a perennial fount, have increased the veneration for this place and nourished the faith of the pilgrims. By granting these favours, God has been wont to so exalt the Name of Mary, invoked as the Virgin of Loreto, that we may say that *there*, in all its grandeur, has been verified the prophecy—*All generations shall call me blessed.*

Let us behold with rejoicing how mindfulness of such great benefits, manifested by many ingenious marks of love on the part of the great of the earth and those of low degree, is daily flourishing, as a most beautiful crown of glory adorning the brow of Mary.

To Us who long since, while rendering Our homage to her dear Home, experienced within its walls the beneficence of the Divine Mother, it comes so much the more welcome that, chiefly at the initiative and by the great assiduity of Our Venerable Brother, the Bishop of Recanati and Loreto, there should have entered into the souls of the faithful far and wide an eager desire to prepare special solemnities for next December, when the sixth century terminates since this treasure was placed, as a good omen, in the bosom of the Church.

Perfectly well known to Us are the projects set forth, as well as the works begun and already far advanced, through munificent emulation, with the object of reinvesting the Basilica with more than its pristine splendour.

While engaged in paying the tribute of Our praise, so justly due, to the promoters of these undertakings, we gladly embrace this occasion to forcibly stir up the devotion of all the Faithful towards the earthly Home of the Holy Family and the Mysteries wrought within its walls.

May all people, and especially the Italians, understand what manner of gift from God this is; by how great an act of divine providence it was snatched from an unworthy domination; and with what a manifestation of love it was given to them. For in that most blessed House took place the beginnings of man's Salvation, by the great and admirable Mystery of God made Man, to reconcile to the Father the lost human race and restore all things—a Mystery of immense goodness and joy, which the Church, with motherly care, admonishes her children to call to mind three times a day. Amid the poverty of this retired dwelling, there lived those models of domestic life and harmony, a spectacle to angels, to which We Ourselves have more than once endeavoured to recall and conform all families, having even established for this end a special Association. From that august Sanctuary there has flowed into the Church a great abundance of divine grace and a great influence for holiness ; there also a considerable number of saints have either felt their hearts inflamed for the first time with the love of pre-eminent virtue or their desire after perfection quickened.

That which stood forth before the eyes of our devout forefathers as the glory and support of their faith, the desire and joy of their piety, and a most efficacious means of imploring the divine mercy, ought to remain so in our age, especially since everything in the world is in a state of degeneracy and disorganisation, and nowhere else than in religion can there be found a sure support and alleviation.

Accordingly it is Our desire that, during the solemn centenary fêtes at Loreto, which occur most opportunely, all the faithful throughout the world, giving heed to the inward call of their own piety and complying with Our exhortations, should strive to shew in the best possible way the grateful joy of their souls and the entire confidence that they have in Christ the Lord, in His most holy Mother and in His most provident Guardian. (It is most fitting that in this the Italians should surpass all other peoples.)

Thus will it come to pass that, in accordance with Our wish, they will receive as a reward for their eminent piety, signal blessings, as well for themselves as for those they love ; and, which is most to be desired, they will obtain them moreover for the Church, that is fought against to such a degree in these troublous times.

It has seemed good to Us for this reason, and on account of the great importance of the matter, to accede to the request of Our Venerable Brother, to the effect that We should increase and grace these centenary fêtes by the gift of holy indulgences.

Full of confidence, then, in the mercy of Almighty God, by the authority of the blessed Apostles Peter and Paul, confirming the privileges granted by Our Predecessors to the Basilica of Loreto, We grant, in the form of a *Jubilee*, a plenary indulgence and the remission of all their sins to all the faithful who, within the space of time that elapses between the first Sunday of the season of Advent, of the present year, and the Sunday of the most holy Trinity, of next year, inclusively, * shall fulfil the following conditions :

They shall visit the Basilica of Loreto three times, either on the same day or on different days, and there, for some time, they shall pour forth devout prayers to God, according to Our intention, for the liberty and exaltation of our holy Mother the Church, for the peace and unity of Christian peoples and for the conversion of sinners; they shall fast during one day, only using such articles of food as are permitted on fast days; moreover this fast shall be made on a day which is not

* The Jubilee has been prolonged till September 18, 1895.

z

already consecrated to a similar fast by a precept of the Church; they shall further receive the most holy Sacrament of the Eucharist, after duly confessing their sins; they shall also, under the title of almsgiving, contribute something towards a good work.

We accord also the faculty of applying this indulgence, by way of suffrage, to the souls that have departed this life united to God in charity.

In the case of the pilgrims who are not of the dioceses of Loreto and Recanati, we concede that the journey itself may take the place of the prescribed fast.

We give also to confessors the faculty of dispensing with the Communion in the case of children who have not yet been admitted to it.

Furthermore, during the whole of this time, and for gaining the Jubilee, We grant to all confessors, legally approved, but only in the two dioceses above mentioned, all those faculties that We conceded to them in the Apostolic Letters *Pontifices Maximi*, dated February 15, 1879; however, all those exceptions mentioned therein will remain as exceptions.

Lastly, for the spiritual good of all the faithful, We grant, for the same period of time, to each and everyone who shall devoutly recite the Litany of Loreto an indulgence of seven years, to be gained once a day, and a plenary indulgence to those who, having recited it every day for a month, shall approach the sacraments of Penance and the Holy Eucharist, and fulfil the other usual conditions: We permit also that these indulgences should be applied in suffrage for the souls in Purgatory.

We wish that to the present Letters, copied or printed, and signed by a public notary and confirmed by the seal of a person constituted in an ecclesiastical dignity, the same faith should be given as to the original, where it is presented.

Given at S. Peter's, Rome, under the seal of the Fisherman, January 23, 1894, in the sixteenth year of Our Pontificate.

L ✠ S   For the Lord Card. SERAFINI,

NICHOLAS MARINI, Substitute.

———

Letter of His Holiness to His Excellence Monsignor Thomas Gallucci, Bishop of Loreto and Recanati.

LEO XIII., POPE.

Venerable Brother, salutation and Apostolic Benediction.

Your welcome letter has recently come to Us, as the witness of a general rejoicing and as the joyful herald of a happy event.

It was specially pleasing to Us to see fully confirmed by you Our hope that God, by the intercession of His most holy Mother, will be pleased to send down more effectual succour to His Church under her afflictions. You, also, whose church is so greatly ennobled by the presence of the dear Home of the Blessed Virgin, say with reason that the divine token of the fulfilment of this hope shines more brightly from an approaching and signal event in the history of the Holy House, namely, the close of the sixth century since our ancestors were first favoured by the coming of so great a gift. With all Our heart We unite with you in this hope and joy ; and We desire to foster them by every means in Our power.

Wherefore, at your instance, We have determined to exhort the Christian people and to offer it incitements to more fruitful piety, by special Apostolic Letters.

And do you, Venerable Brother, recognise in this an evidence of the singular benevolence which we entertain in your regard, and also a recompense for your untiring zeal as the author and promoter of these solemnities ; hereafter, from the most beneficent Mother herself, you will receive rewards worthy of you.

And now, for a happy issue to your wishes and to implore an abundance of heavenly gifts, We very lovingly impart to yourself, your clergy and your people, the Apostolic Benediction.

Given at S. Peter's, Rome, January 25, 1894, in the sixteenth year of Our Pontificate.

LEO XIII., POPE.

CHAPTER III

The Response to be expected to His Holiness' Appeal.

THE readiness of the faithful to comply with such an appeal can scarcely be a matter of doubt. The Jubilee proclaimed in honour of the Holy House is calculated to arouse in the Catholic world a holy enthusiasm, similar to that of the exposition of the Holy Coat at Trèves, and of the blood-stained under-garment of Our Lord at Argenteuil.* If more than two millions of Catholics went to pay honour to the raiment that our dear Redeemer wore, may we not expect a vast concourse to visit the sacred Dwelling He inhabited ? Surely the rooms in which the Saviour and His Blessed Mother lived inspire a deep and ardent devotion in all who have a heart to feel ! The kingdom of Christ is

* See *Essai critique*, par R. P. Jacquemot. (Desclée, Lille.)

founded upon love; and all His loving people would wish to see with their eyes and touch with their hands that privileged Abode whose every stone has repeated by its echoes His gracious words, and still murmurs the *Ave* of S. Gabriel and the names of Jesus, Mary and Joseph—names ever blessed in Heaven and on earth.

The Catholics of the West know how to appreciate the possession of one of the most sacred and affecting Sanctuaries of the Holy Land. Not in vain will the voice of the venerable Pontiff call them to the Home of the Holy Family. They will come with that faith and that love of which they have given so many proofs! They will proclaim boldly in the face of a scoffing world their devotion towards that hallowed Dwelling that Heaven itself has loved to honour by the stupendous miracle of its Translation, that it delights to honour by its preservation through so many ages and by the prodigious graces bestowed upon its worthy Pilgrims.

What a touching scene to behold thousands of Christians come from every part of the world to bend the knee within that blessed Abode! With what love and joy they will cross the threshold of that kind Mother whom none of her children ever invoke in vain. Every heart will thrill with joy in union with the saints and all the angelic host; the incense of prayer will burn on the fire of heavenly love; ardent supplications will rise up to the throne of God, and the divine mercy will descend on the pilgrims of Loreto.

Worthy of the Ages of Faith has been the winter festival at Loreto; but magnificent as were the fêtes of December, they will be surpassed by those of the spring, summer and autumn. Throughout the Jubilee and the whole of the rest of the year, there is every reason to believe that the dioceses, parishes and zelators will continue to rival each other in zeal to marshal their Christian legions to Loreto, victors over the world by faith.

On their return to their native land, the pilgrims of every race and clime will propagate devotion towards the Holy Family, and entire populations will place themselves under its protecting care. This, as you have seen, is the will of the Vicar of Christ.

This pious pilgrimage has been a true joy to millions of Christians who have undertaken it. The soul of the pilgrim, when there, recalls how many of the saints have poured out in the Holy House all the tenderness of their hearts and drawn fresh graces from this heavenly source. He meets at every step with memorials of the visits of innumerable pilgrims, who now in the House above enjoy the glory of which they had a foretaste here.

In the Revelations of St. Bridget it is written: "Whosoever shall

visit the place where Mary was born and brought up will not only
be purified, but become a vessel of honour." *   Few can go to the Holy
Land, but many could go to Loreto; and the Sovereign Pontiffs declare
with no uncertain voice that in the *Santa Casa*, now in Italy, was born
and was brought up the holy Mother of God.

Every Christian to whom God has given the means should make the
pilgrimage of this Holy Place once, at least, during his life.   And if
the power to go is not given to all, everyone should endeavour to be
represented there, either by a relative, or by a friend or neighbour, to
whom they can entrust their offerings and perhaps even confide their
requests.

The Virgin of Loreto raised up the Hermit of Mount Orso to make the
faithful understand the greatness of the favour her divine Son had
bestowed upon them in the miraculous gift of His Holy House.   Let
each of us in our sphere preach this great gift of God as he did.

We have seen how many families from Tersatto and the surrounding
town and villages went to fix their dwelling beneath the shadow of the
Holy House.   If we have not zeal enough to quit for ever our country
and our home, let us go for a few days at least to worship our dear
Lord and to venerate His precious Mother and S. Joseph in their
beloved Abode.

We admire the courage of the thousands of pious pilgrims who, in spite
of the difficulties and dangers of travelling in former days, went through
Europe and Palestine without any other baggage than their cloak,
and without any other weapon save their staff to support them on their
toilsome way.   The bad state of the roads, the inclemency of the seasons,
did not appear to them sufficient excuse for not undertaking the
journey to the Holy House.

In our day, the fulfilment of this filial duty does not involve such a
length of time and toil and hardships.   The invention of railways
and steamers has made the journey to Loreto a very small matter.
At no time could pilgrimages be made so easily as now, and the
conductors of the pilgrims relieve them of all trouble and anxiety.   The
sum to be paid is reduced to a minimum, and, if the intending
pilgrim lays by a little week by week, he may soon be able to meet
the outlay.

Is there then any real obstacle to your going to Loreto?   Think
over it.   Pray over it.   Be ready to make some sacrifice.   Respond to
the invitation of Mary.   Resolve to do your part to "crown this
Sanctuary with fresh honours."

* "Qui ad locum ubi Maria nata est et educata fuit venerit, non solum mundabitur,
sed erit vas in honorem meum."—S. Brigid. *Revel.* lib. v.

An increase in the honour paid to the holy Mother of God in this her greatest sanctuary is so much the more opportune at the time of this sixth centenary, and in this age, when the Blessed Virgin has proclaimed in her sweetest accents: *I am the Immaculate Conception.* This privilege of Mary redounds to the honour of the sacred Place in which it was accomplished; and, not only have the Sovereign Pontiffs Paul II., Julius II., Pius IV., and Pius IX. affirmed that the Queen of Heaven was conceived in the *Santa Casa*, but the Immaculate Virgin herself has told us so by the lips of the Hermit of Mount Orso.

Who then can measure the blessings poured out upon the faithful in connection with this privileged House? If the Holy Virgin delights at all times in receiving the felicitations of her children with regard to this privilege which is so dear to her heart, how much greater must be her delight on receiving those felicitations within the Holy House itself? What special graces also will she not obtain for those who make this blessed mystery the object of their pilgrimage, coming from far distant lands to this immortal Shrine, sanctified by her Immaculate Conception? The sweet title of Mary Immaculate sounds still sweeter in the Holy House: and there, it would seem, she has always been invoked under this unique title which she alone can claim; for whether we read of her while her House was still at Nazareth, she is spoken of as the *Most Immaculate Mother of God,** or whether we read of her when she had brought her House to Loreto, we find Angelita habitually speaking of her as *Immaculate.* If there is a pestilence, and prayer is made to her in accordance with a decree of the magistrates of Recanati, it is to the *Immaculate Virgin* that the supplications are addressed; and if a golden crown set with precious stones is decreed in gratitude for the cessation of the plague, it is to the *Immaculate Virgin* that it is given.† We ask not for new crowns, but we ask for new honours befitting our Immaculate Queen. This centenary, which His Holiness calls on you to celebrate, is the first since the proclamation of the Immaculate Conception by the Holy See, and the first since Mary proclaimed herself Immaculate at the rock of Massabielle; let us then assemble round the Holy House, and in united chorus sing, "Immaculate! Immaculate!" This is the strain that evokes the most rapturous *Magnificat* of Mary, and in response to which are manifested her most miraculous powers. Let us shew, then, how feelingly we congratulate her on the great privilege of being exempt from the burden of sin, beneath which we groan.

* *Immaculatissima Dei Parens.* See *De Locis Sanctis* by the Greek monk John Phocas. (*Acta Sanctorum*, t. ii. Maii.)

† Such a pestilence, followed by the coronation of the Immaculate Virgin of Loreto, occurred in 1499.

Let us consecrate ourselves anew to the great daughter of S. Ann, within those sacred Walls where she was born, free from every spot and stain, the most perfect of the creatures that have come forth from the hands of the Creator! Let us go with the Archangel Gabriel to salute with heart and mouth the Mother of Christ, where Heaven proclaimed her *Blessed among women*. Let us recite our *Aves* where she tended Jesus as an Infant, as a Youth and as a Man; where she gave Him His daily food, and where she wove the seamless Robe empurpled with His Blood on the great day of His Passion. Come and listen to what these stones have to tell you. Everything in this Sanctuary speaks to us of the Author of our salvation and of His tender and compassionate Mother. Come and see where dwelt the Divine Son of Mary; whence *the Light of the world* shot out its beams to illuminate our souls, and whence *the Lamb of God* came forth to *take away the sins of the world*.

Rabbi, where dwellest thou? Come and see. *—Come and see where dwelt He Who *being rich became poor, that through His poverty we might be rich.* † Come and see that Cottage-home of the Lord of glory, that the angels who *ascend and descend upon the Son of Man* ‡ have translated, to bring it nearer to you and to uphold the arms of the Sovereign Pontiff. Come and honour that symbol of the indefectible unity that Christ has promised to the Christian Family. Come, and you shall find in the midst of glorious reminiscences, strength and life; you will bless the day when you went to the House of the Holy Family; you will return from this new Nazareth, as the shepherds from Bethlehem, glorifying and praising God for all the things that you have seen.

　　* *S. John* i. 38.　　　† 2 *Corinthians* viii. 9.　　　‡ *S. John* i. 51.

CHAPTER IV

Restoration of the Basilica.

THE veneration of Catholics for the Holy House has filled them with the desire of celebrating worthily the sixth centenary by embellishing the superb Basilica, beneath whose stately dome there stands that Edifice which is the most sacred that earth has ever seen.

The decoration of the dome having almost disappeared, Monsignor Gallucci has displayed most laudable zeal for its restoration, and by May 31 the whole of Professor Maccari's splendid frescoes will be completed.

The Sanctuary of Loreto belongs to the whole Catholic world, because it contains the Holy Place where the Word was made Flesh and where the Immaculate Virgin became His Mother. France has her chapel that she is decorating in commemoration of the centenary. The Germans and Slav Catholics have each their chapels that they are embellishing to the utmost of their powers. And Italy has her Chapel of S. Joseph, which surpasses every other chapel of the Head of the Holy Family to be seen in any part of Christendom.

As these centenary fêtes advance and pilgrimages arrive from every land, we shall find other countries asking to have a chapel that shall bear their name; and thus will all the chapels round the Holy House belong to different nations, like the chapels that surround the Holy Sepulchre.

Our holy Father the Pope gives his cordial support to the appeal of the Bishop of Loreto to the generosity of the faithful, and His Holiness adds the powerful stimulus of his example, by promising a contribution towards the erection of a new pontifical altar in the choir.

The successors of S. Peter have proclaimed to the faithful that Loreto is *worthy of all honour* * and its sanctuary *the most august and the most sacred,*† because it is *the first Tabernacle of God with men.*‡ After such testimony on the part of the Vicars of Christ, and more

---

* *Laureti civitas, magni quidem semper habita, omnique honore digna.*—Leo XII.
† Pius IX.   ‡ Innocent XII.

especially the recent Apostolical Letter of our Holy Father Leo XIII., in which His Holiness speaks with joy of "the works undertaken through munificent emulation with the object of reinvesting the Basilica with more than its pristine splendour"—after also the tribute of praise paid by the Sovereign Pontiff "to the promoters of these undertakings," and His forcible appeal written to "stir up the devotion of all the faithful towards the earthly Home of the Holy Family,"—it would be superfluous to add further reasons why Catholics should send their offerings to restore the Basilica privileged to contain within its hallowed precincts that blessed Place chosen by Heaven for the accomplishment of events destined to have the greatest and most lasting effects on the whole of humanity.

The Holy House is no longer in the lowly valley of Nazareth: Mary, "the valley of valleys, has been raised above all the mountains," * and the House of the Lord is *exalted above the hills, and all nations flow unto it.* †

The surpassing glory with which God has surrounded the Holy House demands that the Basilica containing it shall be adorned in a manner worthy of it. The Lord Jesus Christ by the miracle of its Translation has drawn the attention of His people towards this great monument of His Incarnation and His earthly life; and there is no question that so great a mark of the Saviour's love towards us as to send His sacred Dwelling "carried by the hands of Angels and accompanied by a heavenly escort,"‡ ought to fill us with an ardent desire to gather all the fruits of His divine munificence.

If we sincerely wish not to lose our share in the gifts distributed in this most holy Place, let us not fail to make our offering towards the restoration of the cathedral, rendered so sacred by the possession of those hallowed Walls which sheltered what was greatest upon earth —God Incarnate, His Immaculate Mother, His holy Foster-Father; and, before the Holy Family, SS. Anne and Joachim, whose destiny surpasses that of all other saints, in that they were chosen to be the father and mother of her who has given birth to God.

Loreto is, out of all Europe, pre-eminently the town of Mary: its first house was that of Mary brought there by angels; its first name, drawn from the House itself, was *Villa di Maria.*

The faithful seem to have ever regarded the register of the donors to the sanctuary of the Holy House as a book of life, and not for the future life alone; all Christendom has but one voice to thank Our Lady of the Holy House, who returns *good measure* for all that she receives:—*Give and it shall be given to you, good measure pressed down,*

---

* S. Bridget.   † *Isaias* ii. 2.   ‡ Paul II.

A A

shaken together and running over. *   "We see," says Pope Paul II., "multitudes of pilgrims come from the most distant parts of the world, on account of their having experienced the marvellous effects of the assistance of their sovereign Protectress."

Let us pay our tribute of love to the Mother of our Saviour by adorning by our gifts the humble but glorious Abode that she embellished by her virtues. Mary in return will cover us with her maternal protection.

Any sacrifice is light to gain the thanks of the Mother of God and of her adorable Son. "This lowly Dwelling," says the Venerable Mary d'Agreda, "has been rendered divine, consecrated as a new sanctuary of the Lord." Who of us, then, can tell how much the smallest offering made in honour of the Dwelling of the Lord may weigh in the balance of Heaven ?

* *S. Luke* vi. 38.

" Doth not Wisdom cry aloud, saying: ' Ye children hear me; hear instruction and be wise, refuse it not. Blessed is the man that heareth me, and that watcheth daily at my gates, and waiteth at the posts of my doors.' "—Proverbs viii. 32, 33, 34.

PART IX.

The House of Mary the Seat of Wisdom.

CHAPTER I

" Whosoever is a little one, let him come to me." * *" I enrich them that love me and fill their treasures."* † *" My fruit is better than gold and my blossoms than choice silver."* ‡ *" He that shall find me shall find life, and shall have salvation from the Lord."* §

THE Lord, Who has gone to prepare a place for us in the House of His Father, has given us while on earth the House of His Mother as the best place of preparation for that heavenly dwelling. The House of Mary is the way to heaven, while the house of sinners is the way to perdition. Here we learn to *say to wisdom, Thou art my sister, and to call prudence our friend.* ‖ Here we look daily into the Mirror of Justice, ¶ and, perceiving the blemishes that disfigure our countenance, seek to reflect in our life only the virtues of Mary. Here we sit at the feet of Wisdom and study in that book which was entrusted to S. Joseph—that living Book in which he read with so great profit that none among the saints are higher than he.

The Holy House is the school of faith and of every Christian virtue. " What happiness," exclaims S. Ambrose, " to be able to be instructed in this admirable school! If a celebrated teacher raises in us the desire to be taught by him, was there ever a preceptor more celebrated than the Mother of God ? "

Education for Heaven consists more in example than precept. The soul, like the body, requires a pure atmosphere in which to develop its moral beauty. This is precisely what the Confraternity of the Holy House aims at. Its members are admitted, so to speak, into a special intimacy with the Holy Family, the imitation of whose virtues is calculated to effect in their lives a great rise in the scale of holiness. Our Holy Father Leo XIII. wishes all Catholics to live in the presence of the Holy Family, and to have a picture of them hung up in their homes. The House forms the background of the picture, in which are represented Jesus, Mary and Joseph :—" Let us picture to ourselves the House of

---

* *Prov.* ix. 4.　† *Prov.* viii. 21.　‡ *Prov.* viii. 19.　§ *Prov.* viii. 35.
‖ *Prov.* vii. 4.　¶ Litany of Loreto.

Nazareth, that abode of sanctity at once earthly and divine. What a
beautiful model we shall find it for our daily life! What a spectacle
of perfect family concord! There reign simplicity and purity; perpetual
harmony, which naught ever comes to disturb; and mutual support and
love."

Our Lady of Loreto counselled Balthazar Alvarez to cultivate a special
devotion towards S. Joseph; and S. Francis of Sales and S. Theresa *
were specially raised up to spread devotion towards the Head of the
Holy Family. This incomparable master in the knowledge of Jesus and
Mary teaches us how to live truly united to the Lord and His
Immaculate Mother. It was for Jesus and Mary that S. Joseph laboured;
all that he did was done from a great desire to please them and to show
the unselfishness of his devoted love. In the school of the Holy House
all teaching has its starting-point at love; truths and duties are impregnated with love; we are instructed how to give true beauty to our
actions by consecrating them to the Sacred Heart of Jesus. It is living
teaching: truths that seem lifeless in mere books, are here full of vitality.
Not in vain would you inscribe your name among the pupils of this
school. No greater advantages can be offered than those of living in the
presence of such perfect teachers and models, and of passing your days
and nights beneath their roof and fostering care.

What an advantage again to have as preceptors those who brought
up Mary in her tender age! The House where Mary was born recalls
to us her infancy and early childhood, her father and her mother. The
maternity of S. Ann has nothing above it except the divine maternity;
after Mary, S. Ann is doubtless the greatest and most blest of women;
and Mary herself has often advised us to seek the patronage of her holy
mother. Jane of Matel, who founded the Order of the Incarnate Word,
tells us that the Lord Jesus in a vision taught her to invoke S. Joachim
and S. Ann as *prince and princess of all the saints;* and Holy Church, on
the festival of S. Joachim, puts into the mouths of her priests that
God was pleased to *choose him before all His saints* to be the father of
His Son's Mother.

In dwelling in thought on Mary brought up by her parents in this
House, we shall aid our preparation for the Kingdom of God; those who
become most like this little child will be greatest in the Kingdom of
Heaven.

Having produced every kind of good fruit in this blessed garden, Mary
may be compared to the remarkable tree seen by Pliny at Tivoli, and

---

* The Carmelite monasteries became to S. Joseph like his House at Nazareth, and the
Jesuit colleges like the place of his peaceful sojourn in Egypt. See *Life of S. Joseph,* by
Monsignor Ricard (Desclée, Lille).

No. XI.—S. Ann.

alluded to by S. Francis of Sales:—"On one branch were cherries, on another nuts, on others grapes, figs, apples; so that this single tree combined all the fruits of a cherry-tree, apple-tree, nut-tree, fig-tree and vine."

Similarly those who are planted in the garden of the Holy House will more readily produce the fruits of patience, gentleness, humility, purity, obedience and every other kind of fruit of the divine tree:—*They that are planted in the House of the Lord shall flourish in the courts of the House of our God.* *

Here was planted the Mystical Rose, that is in bloom throughout the year; whose perfume soothes the sad and heals the sick;—the Rose without a thorn, towards which the Divine Bee winged His gracious flight.

In this garden of the Holy House there grew that sweet flower which produced a remedy for the bites of the venomous serpent and for all the infirmities contracted by the sons of the first Eve,—a flower of immortality, which though cut down by death soon reappeared blooming and imperishable in the never-fading wreath of the glorious Assumption.

Mary is the most admirable production of the heavenly Gardener; in her the Fruit destroys not the flower, and, like the incorruptible cedar, she is free from the corruption of evil; like the palm, she is the most exalted of the trees in the forest of the Lord; like the olive, she is the symbol of peace; and like the laurel, she is the triumphant victor's meed. And how well a laurel crown will sit upon the head of a servant of the Laurel Queen! Let us, then, join our voices to the rapturous songs of the glorified pilgrims of Loreto. Let us strive to obtain, like them, the unfading garland that the *Virgo Lauretana* bestows upon her faithful clients.

The symbol of a crown contained in the title of the Virgin of Loreto (properly Laureto †), brings in its train a promise of grace sufficient to win it. Those who hope for crowns, must seek for grace; and Mary directs us to her House as a treasury of grace. "God has resolved," she tells us by the Hermit of Mount Orso, "to grant the petitions made by the faithful in my House, and to pour out upon them the treasures of His grace."

And how fully has the Holy House proved to be a treasury of grace! What but grace has filled with holy joy the hearts of myriads who have come here? What but favours received has led back again to this shrine the steps of countless pilgrims? Oh, how many signal graces have been bestowed in this House! How many hearts disenchanted

---

* *Psalm* xci. 14.

† In Italian a *Laureto* is a laurel-grove, derived from the Latin *Lauretum*, the ancient name of the district of Loreto.

of the world have found here an abode of love and peace! How many
who were as orphans have found this House a home with the tenderest
of mothers—the Mother given by Jesus from the Cross to console the
sad, the poor, the broken-hearted,—the sympathizing Mother, whose look
is full of sweetness and whose hand is prompt to succour! Yes, the
Virgin of Loreto may truly say: *I have ministered in the holy
Dwelling-place* *—ministered in the presence of my Son, to those whom
He has given to dwell with me as my adopted children.

It is the height of happiness to belong to the family of Mary. Let
us say, then, to the Virgin of the Holy House, as Ruth to Noemi:
Where thou dwellest, I will dwell. † And Mary will answer: "Since it
is thy choice to dwell with me on earth, I will house thee with me in
Heaven."

Happy shall we be at our last hour, if we live and die where Jesus
and Mary suported the head of dying Joseph. Thrice happy if we
can receive the Viaticum filled with a sweet desire of being united to
the Holy Family in the *House not made with hands eternal in Heaven.* ‡

When, then, we invoke the Virgin of Loreto under her title of *Gate of
Heaven*, let us ask her to obtain for us the grace to make her House a
passage to the other world; for this blessed Dwelling *is no other but the
House of God and the gate of Heaven.* § The holy angels hover over
this abode; they guard and console those who live beneath its roof; and,
when the hour of departure to a better world arrives, they bear them
in their arms, as formerly the Holy House, from a land ravaged by
the enemy to the celestial heritage of the children of the Church.

* *Ecclesiasticus* xxiv. 14.   † *Ruth* i. 16.   ‡ *2 Cor.* v. 1.   § *Gen.* xxviii. 17.

CHAPTER II

The Extension of Devotion towards Our Lady of Loreto by means of the Universal Congregation of the Holy House and by the Affiliation of Churches and Chapels.

DEVOTION towards the Holy House has recently greatly revived by the institution of the "Universal Congregation." Like a brilliant star, it sends forth the rays of its light. A million voices, in more than twenty different languages, daily invoke the Virgin of Loreto, and seven thousand propagators are continually spreading the knowledge of the Sanctuary.

This is the revival of a time-honoured devotion; for there exist churches erected in honour of the Holy House of Loreto in France,* Germany,† Austria,‡ Switzerland;§ in Italy,|| Belgium,** Spain and Portugal; in Mexico, Peru and Paraguay,†† and even in the Fiji Islands.‡‡

Emulating the piety of the faithful who built these churches, let us set up a spiritual Loreto in our hearts, offering our prayers as if bodily present in the Holy House. We shall find it thus much easier to raise our hearts and minds to the sublime mysteries of which this hallowed Dwelling was the chosen scene. And if, after the example of the Virgin of Nazareth, we cultivate a spirit of humility and prayer, the

* Paris, Issy, Rheims, Amiens, Saint Omer, Rennes, etc., also chapels at Roussines, Poulaines and many other places.

† Cologne, Holtum, Bühl, Burgau, Freiburg in Breisgau, Pfalz, Wurtemburg, Sossau near Straubing.

‡ Vienna, Prague, Waldei near Prague, Chrudim, Rumburg, Leipa in Bohemia, Nikolsburg, Brünn, Salsburg, Blafana and Ala in the Tyrol.

§ Achenberge, Biberegg, Ennenberge, Bürglen, Bisemberg, Lichtensteig, Pruntrut, Solothurn near S. Ursanne.

|| Rome, where there are three; Naples, Milan, Turin, Mantua, Cremona, Aversa, Spoleto, Vercelli, etc., and at Palermo and Messina in Sicily.

** In the cathedral at Bruges and the Church of the "Minimes" at Brussels there are chapels belonging to old Confraternities of the Holy House. There is also a chapel in the Ardennes, 8 miles from St. Hubert, and others elsewhere.

†† The Spanish Jesuits placed their missions to the aborigines of Paraguay under the patronage of Our Lady of Loreto.

‡‡ The most flourishing mission in Fiji is under the invocation of the Virgin of Loreto.

holy angels will come to visit us, and the Spirit of God descending
on us will form Jesus Christ in our souls. *

Great treasures are to be found in the House of the Holy Family,
if only we will use the lamp of Christian reflection. S. Vincent
Ferrer tells us that Mary herself used often to visit in thought the Holy
House of Nazareth when she was no longer able to be there; and he
points out the advantages that accrue to those who make such spiritual
pilgrimages. Everyone cannot go on so long a pilgrimage, and yet
we may say to the poorest and the most infirm: "To-day and whenever
you please, you can go to the Holy House of Nazareth, where the Son
of God became Incarnate. You have only to make your pilgrimage a
spiritual one." †

Blessed are they that dwell in Thy House, O Lord.‡ Blessed indeed:
for where else can there be found an abode so fit for those who have
received the *adoption of sons* and are *joint heirs with Christ?*§ The
knowledge and love of Jesus of Nazareth should be learnt in His House;
and this is the surest way of obtaining peace: *Learn of Me, because I
am meek and humble of heart: and you shall find rest to your souls.*‖

When we live in the presence of the Holy Family and as far as
possible participate in their daily life at Nazareth; when we see Mary
and Joseph entirely devoted to Jesus, and the Son of God shewing his
love towards His tender Mother and his affectionate foster-father, the
contemplation of such a perfect union of hearts enkindles in our souls
the ardent desire to love Jesus as much as they did, and to love them
as much as Jesus loved them.

These few words will suggest to a thoughtful Christian some of the
benefits to be derived from becoming a member of the Congregation of
the Holy House. The goodness of God has sent from the East to the
West this most precious gift, to draw our attention to what might other-
wise have escaped us; and *Blessed is the man that watcheth daily at my
gates and waiteth at the posts of my doors.***

*One thing have I asked of the Lord, this will I seek after; that I may
dwell in the House of the Lord all the days of my life.*†† *The sparrow
hath found herself a house and the turtle-dove a nest for herself.* ‡‡ Yes,
what the nest is to a bird, such is this Holy House to the soul: and
it is specially the place for those unfit to fly alone. It is piteous to see

* *Galatians* iv. 19

† "Vita B. Mariæ fuit contemplativa isto modo. Nam quolibet die visitabat Loca Sancta.
Primo Nazareth in Camera ubi Filium Dei conceperat. . . . Ideo spiritualiter fiat illa
peregrinatio: hodie et quolibet die potestis ire Nazareth ad Cameram ubi Filius Dei
fuit incarnatus."—Serm. I. *De Assumptione B.M.V.*, p. 220.

‡ *Psalm* lxxxiii. 5.   § *Romans* i. 15-17.   ‖ *S. Matthew* xi. 29.
** *Proverbs* viii. 34.   †† *Psalm* xxvi. 4.   ‡‡ *Psalm* lxxxiii. 4.

unfledged birds out of the nest! Let us seek a place in this nest, under the maternal wing of Mary and near her heart. No bird of prey can take this Mother: here shall we be safe and in repose.

The young heirs of immortality are best brought up in this room. "The Blessed Virgin," writes S. Anselm of Canterbury, "gives milk to famished infants, consoles us when we cry in our cradle, washes us from our uncleanness, wins our hearts by her caresses, cherishes us, warms us and nourishes us deliciously."

To obtain the fulness of blessing that flows from the Holy House, we should link ourselves with it by the special bond of the Confraternity. All its members are committed to the loving care of Mary under her favourite title of *Immaculate*, celebrating thus the accomplishment of that mystery, which is so glorious for Mary, so humiliating for the devil, so consoling for humanity, and so fruitful in graces for all those who invoke their heavenly Mother under this precious name.

As the Lord has manifested his desire of drawing His children to His Holy House, let us be *fellow-workers with the Lord*. If He Himself has drawn our hearts towards this great monument of His life on earth, let us draw the attention of our fellow-Catholics towards it. Let us shew a holy fervour, like that of the Prophet-King, who exclaimed: *The zeal of Thy house hath eaten me up.* *

If we feel this sacred flame and enkindle it in others, soon will all Catholics wish to be members of this Congregation, and the grand prophetic title given it under great Leo XIII. will be realised: it will be "the Universal Congregation of the Holy House"—*universal*, like the holy Scapular of Our Lady of Mount Carmel and the holy Rosary, that, as we all wear that sacred garment and wield that spiritual weapon, so we shall all live and die in this dear Home, having a place at the table of Mary in life and her sweet presence at our side in death.

This is our grand privilege: let us not lose any portion of it. We are members of the Holy Family that has increased from three to countless myriads, and the *Holy House is the paternal roof* where all the members of this vast Family may meet at the same board: where all may feel and know themselves to be children of one loving Mother, brethren of one dear Saviour, and sons and daughters of one tender-hearted Foster-father.

A place in this paternal home is now offered by the institution of the Universal Congregation. The *Door of the Holy House* has been *thrown wide open*. Our place in it is prepared for us. Let us not rest content until we occupy it. Let us be what our privileges entitle us to be—*members of the household* in which God placed His own Son. There is no more

* *Psalm* lxviii. 10.

privileged abode in the whole world, and Jesus, Mary and Joseph are waiting with open hearts and outstretched arms to welcome us into the household. Let us go, then, with childlike confidence; let us enter our paternal home; and may the *Alma Domus* deign to receive us.

———

CHAPTER III

" Wisdom hath built herself a House." *—A Spiritual Visit to this House of divine Wisdom.

LET us enter this mysterious House of Wisdom, every visible object in which is like a sacrament beneath whose veil God Incarnate dwells concealed. The veil has been so far drawn aside that we are allowed to pass the threshold of the sanctuary of the Incarnation, but never in this life shall we be able to penetrate fully into the hidden mysteries of this new Nazareth.

In the interest of our souls, the Holy Spirit Himself, speaking by the mouth of the Fathers and Doctors of the Church, has taken care that the things of Mary should be suggested to our minds by similitudes drawn from material objects, and Pius IX., in an Apostolic Letter quoted above, says: " It is with reason that all the faithful who come to visit this Sanctuary with a true faith do not seem so much to visit the Virgin's House as the Virgin herself." May we not, then, apply to the Holy House some of the metaphors which are the glory of Mary, who is styled by Holy Church the House which the Lord hath built ? †

The Holy House of Nazareth is more glorious than the house of gold built by Solomon; *the glory of this latter House is greater than that of the former;* ‡ for there is the nuptial Chamber in which the King of kings espoused humanity; there the throne which bore the Lord of Hosts, the throne of the Divinity, the throne of Grace and Mercy.

The Holy House is the place where He who is *clothed with light as with a garment,* § put on our flesh, and Mary is the royal and spotless robe, the

---

* All the faithful know that the Church applies to the holy Mother of God the Psalm, *Nisi Dominus ædificaverit domum.* We shall draw our metaphors for the most part from the writing of saints, of whom several are Fathers and Doctors of the Church : S. Ambrose, S. Amedeus, S. Anastasius, S. Andrew of Crete, S. Anselm, S. Bernard, S. Bonaventure, S. Catharine of Siena, S. Ephrem, S. Epiphanius, S. Francis of Sales, S. George of Nicomedia, S. Germanus of Constantinople, S. John Chrysostom, S. John of Damascus, S. Jerome, S. Methodius, S. Proclus, S. Thomas of Villanova, and the Blessed Albert the Great.

† *Prov.* ix. 1.   ‡ *Aggeus* ii. 10.   § *Psalm* ciii. 2.

purple mantle divinely prepared and worthy to cover the only Emperor, whose Kingdom shall have no end. In this sacred Vestiary saints are clothed with honour and glory, sinners with pardon and grace.

The door is the entry of hope for the afflicted, and hope for those seeking shelter and protection, hope for the guilty; for none ever knock at this door in vain.

The window is the inlet of light : by it the rays of the *Sun of Justice* shine into souls, and the light of Heaven reaches those who lie in dusky gloom.

The time-piece of the House of Wisdom is the Sun-dial over which the true Sun passed announcing the hour of salvation.

The genial heat from the Family Hearth warms those benumbed by the chilling blasts of an ice-bound world ; nor can any coldness in religion last when near that furnace of divine love, " the Virgin all of fire." *

Beside the Hearth is seen the crook of the Good Shepherd which has caught so many wandering sheep and brought them back to the fold. There too is the staff on which the aged, lame and blind may lean, and which upholds the weak lest he should fall.

Wisdom hath *sent forth her maids* to invite to her House; she has *mingled her wine and set forth her table*. Upon her board is placed the Bread which nourishes souls and unites them to God ; for here is the granary where the true Joseph kept the divine corn destined to feed the whole Church, and here is the mystic Oven, in which, by heavenly fire, the Holy Spirit prepared the Bread of Life Eternal.

The Banqueting-Hall lacks not ornament nor perfume, for Mary is the flower of beauty and a golden urn filled with celestial balm ;— she is the vase formed out of the treasures of the Temple of the Lord, and chosen of God to be placed on high to adorn the throne of honour in His Palace.

The ceiling is studded with stars, to represent the firmament, emblem of Mary, the new firmament in whom all virtues shine more brilliant than the stars and *shew forth the glory of God*. (*Ps.* xviii. i.)

Peculiar to this House is the seven-branched candelabrum, whose brilliant light, coming from the Most High, dispels the darkness of our souls, and whose oil supplies the lamps of all the faithful.

To inflame the Christian's courage, trophies are erected, which record the memories of conquests won. There is the victorious Banner that waved at the head of the Christian legions when they repulsed the enemies of the Church ; there are the sword and shield whose succour was implored by S. Pius V. before the triumph at Lepanto ; there is the arrow which slew Julian the Apostate and wounded the Dragon—the arrow that flies so

* St. Amedeus.

swiftly, so directly at the mark and penetrates so deeply that never has been found armour that could resist it. *Ave, Sagitta electa!*

Hark, the trumpet sounds! Not now to battle does it call: it is a Jubilee that it proclaims! A Herald promulgates an amnesty! The King of kings has remembered mercy! The Queen, with crown-encircled brow and hand that bears the royal signet, brings us a reprieve, breaks our chains, pays our debts and invites us to her Palace: *Come*, is her gracious word; *come, eat my bread and drink the wine that I have mingled for you!* In this Banquet there is found refreshment for the weary, and strength for the weak; the Harp of David also is there to soothe those troubled by an evil spirit, * an instrument of joy from whence proceeds enchanting melody, changing the harsh sounds of malediction into the sweet harmonies of blessing!

No more palace of an earthly monarch this: it is the Temple-palace of the *Prince of the kings of the earth*, the *King of kings and Lord of lords.* † In this Temple the great Virgin herself is the *Living Altar* on which the Divine Lamb is mystically offered, as she was the altar of holocaust in the Passion of her Son. Mary is the *Monstrance*, in which the Body of Jesus is exhibited at Benediction; and she is the *Tabernacle* even where no eucharistic urn reposes on her knees. ‡ Mary gives us her Son in the sacrament in which He is concealed, as formerly at Nazareth she visibly held forth the Divine Child in this same hallowed Dwelling. Mary also is the Altar of our oblations, § as it is written: *They shall be offered upon My acceptable Altar, and I will glorify the House of My Majesty.* ‖

* 1 *Kings* xvi. 23.   † *Apocalypse* i. 5, xix. 16.
‡ To represent this idea, the Abbot de Rancé, founder of the monastery of La Trappe, had the tabernacle made in the form of an urn, which rested on the knees of a statue of the Virgin Mother.
§ See Blessed Albert the Great on *S. Matthew* v.
‖ *Isaias* lx. 7.   See Richard de S. Lauren. *De Laude Virg.* lib. ii.

No. XLa.—Monsignor Gallucci, Canon Andrenelli, Father da Malaga.

p. 203

CHAPTER IV

Canonical Erection of the Universal Congregation of the Holy House of Loreto.

Decree of Monsignor Thomas Gallucci, Bishop of Loreto and Recanati.

ALTHOUGH it may not be possible for us mortals, because of our weakness and frailty as earthen vessels, either to see or understand the depths of the riches of the wisdom and providence of the Most High, Whose judgments are incomprehensible and Whose ways are unsearchable, nevertheless, if with humble and devout discernment we consider the high and wonderful works wrought by God before our eyes on this earth, where we are pilgrims, not only is our soul filled with admiration, but it also feels the most lively sense of gratitude towards the supreme Author thereof, exalting and magnifying Him in His sublime works.

Amongst these works, if we turn our mind to the mystic Ark of the Covenant that is preserved and venerated within the walls of the most august temple of Loreto, who can disapprove if we, moved by the greatest admiration and equal devotion, exclaim in a transport of exultation that God hath not done in like manner to every nation—*non fecit taliter omni nationi*—as to Italy, and in a special manner to the Province of Ancona, having ordained that in a part of the territory of Recanati, now called Loreto, six centuries ago there should appear by Divine Will the sacred Chamber of Nazareth, so celebrated through the memory of the sublimest Mysteries, and venerated by the daily visits and devotion of the faithful ?

Wherefore we—considering and pondering in our heart how much already has been done in the Catholic Church, and how much more is being done to-day for the greater glory of God and the procuring the salvation of souls by means of the institution of several pious Congregations of Christians, who, with great earnestness, give themselves to the promoting of devotion towards the most blessed Virgin Mary, Mother of God, and our most beloved Mother, under various glorious titles attributed deservedly to her—we ourselves, as much as lies in our power, have resolved to

C C

procure the greatest possible increase of veneration and devotion towards the Mother of God in this her most Holy House of Loreto.

Now, therefore, in order that, with the divine favour and the help of the same Virgin, this may be put into effect, and that this same worship, that can already be called universal, may every day extend and increase more and more, we, by the present Decree, found and erect a pious society and pious union, or, better, a Universal Congregation of the Holy House of Loreto ; and the same we declare canonically erected and instituted : to which whoever of the Christian peoples shall here and elsewhere concur, may give their own name as a token of their devotion to the Mysteries that had their fulfilment in this heaven-praised Dwelling. And, truly, in it the Queen of Virgins was hailed by the celestial messenger as Mother of the Saviour of the world, and here *the Word was made Flesh.* In this sacred Abode she lived with her most pure spouse St. Joseph, and with Jesus, the true Life, Who, from the maternal dwelling-place, was called the Nazarene.

Hence we propose some pious practices to be observed by the members of this new Congregation, so that spiritual advantages may be enjoyed. Therefore, that to the indulgences already annexed may be added more abundant fruits and spiritual favours, it will be our office to implore with humble reverence that the Holy See will impart to us more ample powers.

Above all we exhort all the faithful to inscribe their names with devout and happy feelings in the catalogue that they will find open and in the charge of the Reverend Capuchin Fathers, who are employed in the service of this Holy House.

Finally, let it be noticed by all that the appointment of the Director-General of the new Congregation is reserved to us and our successors. To-day, then, we declare and nominate as Director-General the Reverend Father Fr. Pietro Maria da Malaga, priest of the Holy Order of the Capuchins of St. Francis.

We decree all this with our ordinary authority, placing great faith in the Divine help, and in the special protection of the Immaculate Virgin and of her spouse St. Joseph.

Given at Loreto on May 27, 1883.

✠ THOMAS,
Bishop of Loreto and Recanati.

PRACTICAL DEVOTIONS.

1. The members will recite according to the custom of pious Catholics at morning, mid-day and evening the Angelus Domini in

honour of the Incarnation of the Word in the chaste womb of the Virgin, accomplished in the Holy House of Nazareth, now in Loreto. In case the Angelus cannot be recited, five Hail Maries may be said with the same intention.

2. They will receive the holy sacraments of Penance and the Eucharist on March 25, the feast of the Annunciation, and also, in honour of the Translation of the Holy House, on December 10. If not able to do so on these specified days, they will choose some other day either during the novena which precedes these feasts, or during their Octaves.

3. They will pray the Immaculate Virgin for the Pope, the exaltation of the Catholic Church, and the prosperity of the Congregation and its members.

4. They will make an offering for the restoration and embellishment of the Basilica. This will be once for all at the time of their enrolment, and need not be an obstacle to persons of humble position. In America five cents in postage stamps, or even less, is received, though larger offerings are welcome.

SPIRITUAL FAVOURS.
Plenary Indulgences.

On the day of admission ; at the hour of death, on invoking the holy Name of Jesus, if unable to receive the Sacraments ; on December 10, being the anniversary of the Translation into Italy ; on the feasts of the Annunciation, the Immaculate Conception, the Maternity of the Blessed Virgin, and her Assumption ; on Christmas day and Ascension day ; on the festival of the titular saint of the Congregation, if it have another patron besides the Immaculate Virgin Mary and her holy Spouse the blessed St. Joseph ; on visiting a church of the Congregation during the Forty Hours ; and twice a year on any days not both in the same week, on visiting and receiving the Blessed Sacrament after making a general confession, or at least a general one since the last general confession ; those of the Stations of the churches of Rome on saying seven Paters and seven Aves in a church on the days fixed for those Stations ; those accorded to the Prima Primaria at Rome ; and those attached to the Holy House. If hindered by circumstances from keeping more than five or six days out of the eight of a Retreat with the Spiritual Exercises, a member shall gain the whole indulgence.

Priests who are Zelators, having obtained permission from their respective ordinaries, whenever they visit the members of the Confraternity in sickness, exhorting them to suffer with patience, and to accept death with pious resignation, should it come from the hand of the Lord, can apply the plenary indulgence to them, provided they recite three Paters and three Aves before the image of Jesus Crucified, according to the intention of the Sovereign Pontiff, having confessed and received Holy Communion.

If the Confraternity have another titular or another patron, besides the Blessed Virgin, a plenary indulgence is granted on the day on which the festival is celebrated, subject to the conditions named above.

If, with the approbation of the ordinary, the feast of the Blessed Virgin or of the titular saint be transferred to another day of the year, the plenary indulgence may be gained on that day, and if it coincide with a double feast, it will suffice to celebrate one votive mass of the festival transferred.

Indulgences of Seven Years " Toties Quoties."

On hearing Mass on days that are not of obligation ; on praying for one in agony or dead, and on accompanying to the tomb one who has died in communion with Holy Church ; on visiting the sick or prisoners ; on reconciling enemies ; and on making an examination of conscience on retiring to rest.

Other Indulgences and Privileges.

Fifty days, once a day, on kissing the medal, and saying, " Virgin of Loreto, pray for us." Participation in a Mass offered every month in the Holy House, and in all the good works practised in the Order of the Capuchins.

Indulgences for the Dead.

All the above indulgences are applicable to the departed. Also the Congregation enjoys a privileged altar for all priests saying Mass for deceased members ; and any altar is privileged at which Mass is said for a deceased member by any priest.

Masses said at Loreto.

The faithful may have Masses said at two francs in the Holy House and at one franc and a half in the Basilica. Post office orders should be sent to the *R. P. Custode, Santa Casa, Loreto, Ancona.*

RULES
for the Promoters of the Devotion to the Holy House of Loreto.

Devout persons who think they can spread the devotion to the Holy House by gaining members for the Universal Confraternity, which is now spreading rapidly throughout the whole Catholic world, are requested to apply to the Director for the required authorization, in conformity with the following rules laid down.

Communications should be addressed to the R. P. Fr. Pietro Ma. da Malaga, *Direttore-Generale, Santa Casa, Loreto, Ancona, Italy.*

The Director-General, on receiving the application, will immediately send everything requisite for the establishment of such branches.

The applicant will find in the packet addressed to him the number of tickets applied for, an equal number of medals of various sizes, and

No. XLI.   DECORATIONS GIVEN TO LADIES OF HONOUR OF THE HOLY HOUSE.

a printed form, on which the names of members are to be very legibly written; also a circular letter declaring the applicant a promoter of the devotion; the Decree of Canonical Erection of the said Congregation; and lastly, a list of the privileges enjoyed by the Honorary Chaplains of the Holy House, by virtue of a diploma which *(with the consent in writing of the ordinary)* is sent to priests who have displayed much zeal in establishing branches of the Universal Congregation of Loreto.

RULE 1. The Promoters, in filling up the list of members, will give the surname, Christian name and nationality of each.

2. The Promoters, when they fill up the printed forms, will continue the order of the numbers marked at the beginning, and not exceed the number given at the foot of each form, and give each member a ticket bearing the number attached to his name on the form.

3. The printed form containing the names of members, together with their offerings, is to be returned to the Director of the Congregation in the course of the year during which the Promoters received it, no matter in what condition the list is. This rule must be strictly carried out to avoid disorder.

4. The amount of the offering made at the time of enrolment is not fixed, in order that the poor may be able to join the Congregation and participate in the spiritual blessings attached to it.

5. The expenses of postage, etc., may be deducted from the offerings collected by each Promoter; but this deduction is to be mentioned in a letter to the Director of the Congregation, and is not to be entered on the printed form containing the names and offerings.

6. The blessed medals are to be distributed to members only, since the indulgences have been applied to the said medals for them alone, and by them alone can be gained. But, although each member has a right to a medal, since the medals vary in size and value, the distribution is left to the prudence and equity of the Promoters.

7. The Zelators and members of the Confraternity of the Holy House are earnestly requested to communicate to the Director all the graces and blessings which they may receive through the intercession of Our Lady of Loreto, in order that they may be immediately published, but not necessarily with the names.

Affiliation to Our Lady of Loreto.

Pius IX., by a Bull dated August 26, 1852, conferred on the Holy House the power of affiliating churches and chapels. This affiliation to the Basilica of Loreto carries with it a participation in its spiritual treasures, and confers rightful claims upon the heritage of their Mother. Pius IX. tells us that he was inwardly moved to accord this faculty, that devotion towards Our Lady of Loreto and the House of the immaculate Virgin might *flourish from one end of the world to the other.*

Conditions of Affiliation.

Application must be made to the Congregation of Loreto at *Rome*, which grants the Diploma without charge. The Bishop of the Diocese must authorise the request, and there can only exist one church, oratory or altar of Our Lady of Loreto in each town: but to this rule there are exceptions. Neither churches already affiliated to a Basilica or Archconfraternity, nor yet the churches of Regulars can be affiliated.

PRAYERS.

Indulgenced Prayer appointed to be said on making a Spiritual Visit to the Holy House.

Most Holy Virgin, who wast chosen from amongst all creatures as being the fairest like the rose of Jericho, and the most exalted like the cedar of Lebanon, to give to the world the Incarnate Word Who came down from heaven to redeem man, to deliver him from the slavery of the devil, to open to him the gates of the kingdom of heaven, and to shew him the way that leads to eternal glory; O thou, who by a wondrous prodigy didst place in the very centre of God's Church that sacred House sanctified by the presence of the Son of God made man; O thou, most tender Mother, vouchsafe in thy goodness to accept the prayers and supplications of thy child. Assist me, O great Queen, in all my necessities, by thy powerful and efficacious intercession; obtain for me, from thy divine Son Jesus, the grace I implore (*here mention it*), with the pardon of my sins, final perseverance, and a holy and happy death.

I revere thee in thy Holy House, O Virgin, who wast pure and immaculate even before thy birth; assist me, intercede and pray for me, O Our Lady of Loreto, whom in company with the Archangel Gabriel I praise and salute.

Ave Maria.

I revere thee in thy Holy House, O Virgin, who wast pure and immaculate at the moment of thy birth; assist me, intercede and pray for me, O Our Lady of Loreto, whom, with the celestial Paranymph, I praise and salute.

Ave Maria.

I revere thee in thy Holy House, O Virgin most pure and Immaculate after thy birth; assist me, intercede and pray for me, O my Mother, Virgin of Loreto, whom, with the celestial messenger, I glorify, saying with my whole heart:

Hail Mary, etc. Glory be to Father, etc.

V. The Angel of the Lord declared unto Mary.

R. And she conceived by the Holy Ghost.

Let us pray.

O God, Who in Thy mercy didst hallow the House of the Blessed Virgin Mary by the Mystery of the Incarnation, and in a wonderful manner didst place it in the midst of Thy Church; grant that we, keeping ourselves aloof from the dwellings of the wicked, may be made worthy inhabitants of Thy Holy House. Through the same Our Lord Jesus Christ Thy Son, Who liveth and reigneth with Thee in the unity of the Holy Ghost God world without end. Amen.*

Ejaculatory Prayers.

Blessed be the Holy and Immaculate Conception of the Blessed Virgin Mary, Mother of God.

(400 days' indulgence.)

O Mary, conceived without sin, pray for us who have recourse to thee.

(300 days' indulgence.)

Invocation of the Blessed Virgin, her holy Spouse and Parents, together with the Saints who have visited her Holy House.

O Immaculate Virgin, Tabernacle of the Most High that He hath sanctified, habitation worthy of the Only-begotten of the Father, mansion, pure from all stain, that God prepared for His Son, blessed are the Walls wherein thou first didst draw thy breath, blessed is that privileged Chamber where first was heard thy name of Mary, "melody in the ear, joy in the heart, and honey in the mouth." We felicitate thee, and

An Indulgence of 40 days is attached to the above spiritual visit.

magnify the Lord with thee, *for He that is mighty hath done great things unto thee* in this Holy House. By the ineffable grace thou didst receive within these sacred Walls, by the great joy that thou didst feel when thou didst know that thou wast found worthy to be the Mother of Christ, deign to rejoice the hearts of all who honour thee in thy Holy House. O Blessed Virgin of Loreto, who dost *dispense the treasures of heaven*, aid us in our spiritual visits to thy House, that our hearts may be visited by an abundance of heavenly gifts. O thou who dost *ravish hearts* make us love thee ardently, and fill our souls with a tender devotion towards thy Holy House for love of Jesus and of thee. O thou, *our powerful defence*, may our confidence in thy protection ever increase, and do thou defend all the inscribed members of thy Household of Loreto. Thou thyself art *the miracle of miracles;* help us to unceasingly admire the miracles that God has wrought for thy Holy House, and to become ardent propagators of devotion towards thee in it. We feel ourselves unworthy to put forth our hands to touch this sacred Ark,* and our eyes are too impure to look within it; yet may the gracious Lord of the House not be angry with His servants, and may our work for His Holy Habitation be rendered acceptable by thy kind intercession, O *Virgin most merciful,* and be offered up by thy immaculate hands on the golden salver of thy merits; and may we ourselves be presented to thy Son by thee, and sing eternally His praise and thine in the *house not made with hands eternal in heaven.*†

Holy Joseph, most worthy head of the Holy Family in the House at Nazareth, remembering thy power over the Heart of Jesus, we humbly crave thy intercession for ourselves and other members of the Congregation of the Holy House, which was formerly thy dwelling.

Holy Ann, whose maternity is next in greatness after the Divine Maternity, *all generations shall call blessed* the Immaculate to whom thou didst give birth within the Holy House: holy Joachim, possessor of the Holy House, through whom Jesus is *of the seed of David according to the Flesh;* holy Gabriel, Archangel of the Annunciation, and all ye holy angels who bore this sacred burden across land and sea; holy Peter, Prince of the Apostles, who didst set up its altar; holy James, who didst come to it from Spain just before thy martyrdom; and all ye holy Apostles; S. Mary of Magdala and ye holy women, who loved the Holy House; S. John Baptist and S. Catharine, whose knights protected pilgrims to its sacred walls; S. Helen, who didst raise a temple in its honour; S. Jerome, who lovedst Nazareth, *the Flower of Galilee;* S. Paula, who on the wings of faith *didst speed to Nazareth the Nursery of the Lord;* S. Francis of Assisi, who didst bedew its sacred

---

* 1 *Kings* vi. 19; 2 *Kings* vi. 6.   † 2 *Cor.* v. 1.

No. XLII.—Mgr. Podaliri, Bishop-Auxiliary of Loreto and Recanati.

p. 216

No. XLIV.—St. Francis Xavier preaching to the Indians.

No. XLIII.—St. Francis Xavier and St. Ignatius, on the departure of the former for the Indies.

floor with tears ; S. Louis, who didst offer thy life in sacrifice to defend the Holy House ; S. Nicholas of Myra and Bari, who didst visit it at Nazareth, and S. Nicholas of Tolentino, who didst foretell its coming into Italy ; S. Catharine of Siena, who hast a post of honour among the Virgins in the dome that crowns the Holy House ; S. Ignatius of Loyola, who didst go to Loreto to place the Society of Jesus under the protection of His Virgin Mother ; S. Francis Xavier, who within those sacred walls didst feel thyself called to evangelize the East ; S. Francis of Sales, who while young didst there bind thyself with a vow, and eight years after didst return to give thanks for the conversion of so many heretics ; S. Alphonsus Liguori, who wast there replenished with such grace that thy countenance became seraphic ; and all ye sainted pilgrims who are indebted to Our Lady of Loreto—pray ye one and all for the Zelators and Members of the Confraternity and for the spread of the Universal Congregation of the Holy House. Amen.

" Blessed is the man that heareth me, and that watcheth daily at my gates, and waiteth at the posts of my doors."—*Prov.* viii. 34.

LIST OF ILLUSTRATIONS,

This Statue stands behind the altar of the Holy House. The reredos
in gilt bronze and crystal is to be erected in honour of the sixth
centenary. The design is by Count Sacconi, and may be seen in its
entirety in Plate IV.

To the Labarum was attached the promise of victory. The medal is
a facsimile of that given to S. Geneviève by S. Germain and S. Loup.

The Marine Gate, *Porta Marina*, on the right of which is seen the
railway station. The promontory of Monte Conero, or the Mount of
Ancona, extends to about the same length as Mount Carmel. Between
Loreto and this headland may be discerned the monument erected in
commemoration of the battle of Castelfidardo. The town of Loreto
contains about 8,500 inhabitants. The Salesians, invited there by the
zealous Archdeacon Monsignor Ridolfi, have opened a college since 1891,
and their work deserves the encouragement of all Catholics. Sisters of
the Holy Family conduct a school for girls, and Sisters of Our Lady of
Charity have a Refuge for female penitents ; the Bishop of Loreto has
laid the foundation-stone of a new Refuge, and the devoted Sisters are
striving to raise funds to build it.

In Part VII. will be found details of the sculpture round the *Santa
Casa* and of the frescoes in the dome.

On the left of the Altar is seen the cupboard, called *Il Santo Armadio*,
and between it and the modern door may be traced the form of the
ancient door used by the Holy Family. The fire-place, called *Il Santo*

Camino, is behind the Altar. The present roof does not rest upon the walls of the Holy House, but on the outer walls built up to enclose the sacred edifice without touching or supporting it. The roof with which it arrived in Italy was taken down in the sixteenth century and placed beneath the altar, which at that time was being removed from opposite the doorway into its actual position. Some of the gilt stars which formerly adorned the roof are shewn to pilgrims in the *Santo Armadio.* When the *Santa Casa* arrived, the upper part of the walls was ornamented with semicircles of gilt wood, in the midst of which were cups, plates and other vessels sealed with great care. The statue of the Madonna was originally in a recess in the south wall ; the upper portion of this recess is still to be seen above the Clementine door, which leads from the south transept of the Basilica into the part of the Holy House situated behind the Altar.

A Capuchin is represented in the engraving, as the Holy House is entrusted to that Order, which attends to the lighting of the lamps and the cleaning of the floor. And, as the conventuals hold the office of Penitentiaries in the Basilica, so also the Capuchins hold the office of directing the *Universal Congregation of the Holy House.* Their present monastery was given them by Cardinal Barberini in 1630, but they had already served in the Holy House for half a century. Other details of the *Santa Casa* are given in Part VII., and of the Confraternity in Part IX.

Plate V.—THE CHURCH OF THE ANNUNCIATION AND FRANCISCAN MONASTERY
AT NAZARETH   -   -   -   -   -   -   -   *Page* 18

This stands on the site of the Holy House. S. Antoninus the Martyr, who visited the Holy Land in the sixth century, when it was still under the rule of the Christian emperors residing at Constantinople, saw the original Basilica in all its splendour, and has left us an enchanting description of the fertility of Galilee.

"On visiting," writes Lamartine, "places consecrated by those mysterious events which have changed the face of the world, one experiences much the same feeling as a traveller going up a vast stream, such as the Nile or the Ganges, to discover and look upon its hidden and unknown source. It seemed to me while climbing the last hills that separated me from Nazareth, that I was about to behold at its mysterious source that vast and productive religion which for the last two thousand years has made its bed in the universe from the top of the hills of Galilee, and with its pure and life-giving waters has quenched the thirst of so many generations ! There was the source, thence flowed Christianity ; an obscure source, a drop of water unperceived in a hollow of the rock of Nazareth, where two sparrows could not drink, that a ray of the sun might dry up, but which to-day, like a great ocean, has filled all the abysses of human wisdom and bathed with its inexhaustible floods the present, the past and the future. . . . As I made these reflections, I perceived at my feet, at the bottom of a valley in the form of a basin, the white and prettily grouped houses of Nazareth. . . . God alone knows what passed within my heart at that moment; with a spontaneous and, so to speak, involuntary movement, I found myself upon my knees in the dust!" *

Built in 1730. Its architecture is Arabic. Beneath the high altar is seen the *Chapel of the Angel*, built on the former site of the Holy House, whose foundations surround it. Fifteen marble steps led from the nave of the Chapel of the Annunciation to this Chapel, which has an altar dedicated to S. Gabriel and another to SS. Ann and Joachim. It is twenty-six feet long by ten feet wide, and stands in front of the sacred caves. The lower cave measures eighteen feet each way and is divided by a wall † into two chapels, dedicated to the Annunciation and to S. Joseph, especially commemorating the Flight into Egypt. The upper cave is twelve feet each way, but very irregular; on its east side there is a walled-up doorway. The staircase is tunnelled in the solid rock, and more winding than could be conveniently shewn in a sectional drawing. When the Holy House stood in the position now occupied by the Chapel of the Angel, it had no entrance on the south side, but only through the cave; and this sheltered situation contributed towards its preservation. The present Church of the Annunciation has been built on the site of the transept and a portion of the choir of the ancient cathedral, so that it lies north and south instead of east and west. (See Plate X.) The foundations of the Holy House are just outside the walls of the Chapel of the Angel, which is shorter and narrower, and has not been erected on the sacred foundations, as being

* *Voyage en Orient.*

† In the ground plan given by Quaresmius, who was commissary in the Holy Land, there is no wall dividing the large cave, and the altar of S. Joseph is at the back of the cave (which is to the north) and the altar of the Annunciation in the centre of the east side of the cave. (In Plate VII. the observer is looking towards the east.) Since the publication of this plan at Antwerp in 1639, the two altars have been placed back to back, abutting against a wall built to suit this new arrangement. The same plan by Quaresmius shews that the altar of S. Gabriel was at the east end of the Chapel of the Angel, and that of SS. Joachim and Anne on the south side. Hence all four altars have been changed.

relics too holy to put to such a purpose. They possess, it seems, a miraculous virtue, by which the sick are healed on touching a broken column represented near them in Plate VII. Bedouins from the other side of the Jordan broke this column in 1638, in the hope of finding treasure at its base; the idea is widely spread in Palestine that the Crusaders buried great quantities of treasure. Another column, which has remained unbroken, is built into the wall behind S. Gabriel's altar. We shall have occasion later on to speak more fully about these columns. *

Plate VIII.—INTERIOR OF THE HOLY HOUSE OF NAZARETH WHEN INHABITED
    BY THE HOLY FAMILY - - - - - - - *Page* 25

The small cave on the extreme left is commonly called the Kitchen of Mary, but whether it served this purpose is open to doubt. † Such caves are often used as granaries and cellars, and Cardinal Bartolini points out that if a family at Nazareth have a horse, a cow or an ass, they put them into a cave of this kind opening out upon the road by a secondary door. We shall postpone details as to the internal arrangement of the *Santa Casa* when at Nazareth until we arrive at Plate XVIII.

Plate IX.—EXTERIOR OF THE HOLY HOUSE IN THE TIME OF THE HOLY
    FAMILY - - - - - - - - - - *Page* 28

View shewing the entrance by the west door through the lower cave, in front of which the dwelling was erected. ‡

The House is represented without a terrace on the roof, because it was not in the middle of the town, but near the bottom of the hill. All the town was situated above it, so that other houses do not come into the picture. The building on the left is placed to illustrate the supposition of some writers that the Holy House contained other rooms, which, not being the most sacred portion of the dwelling, were not preserved or translated. It is usual in Palestine to cover the walls and the roof with

    * See the explanation of Plate XVIII., which represents the Annunciation in the Holy House. The note referring to the columns is at the end of the article.

    † There are those that think that this was originally a cistern and supplied the Holy Family with rain water. If so, it is equally a relic that has ministered to the bodily wants of God in the Flesh.

    ‡ See *Guide de Terre Sainte*, by Liévin de Hamme, third edition. The space existing between the foundations and the cave at its south-west corner has led to this important discovery, now brought forward for the first time in a history of the Holy House. Monsieur Capelle, in his full-sized model of the dwelling of the Holy Family, has placed a door in this position, as may be seen at Morslède, Belgium. Before this discovery, what is said of the Cave at Bethlehem by l'Abbé Le Camus might have been applied with the necessary changes to the Cave at Nazareth :—"The pilgrims are satisfied with praying before the hollow in the rock which contained the Manger, without asking themselves how the animals got in there to eat. Gladly would our faith strip off the marble to see and shew to everyone this indispensable attestation of authenticity, the entrance." (*Notre Voyage en Pays Bibliques.*)

plaster on account of the heavy rains, and frequently a verandah made of rushes is placed over the door to mitigate the heat of the sun.

Plate X.—THE HOLY HOUSE AS THE CRYPT OF THE CATHEDRAL ERECTED
    BY S. HELENA AT NAZARETH   -   -   -   -   - *Page* 31

On the north side, which lies to the right, there is seen a doorway, by which we reach the staircase represented in two former illustrations. "By it, if you enter the Cave and descend a few steps," writes Phocas, "your eyes behold the ancient dwelling of Joseph, in which the Arch- angel announced the good tidings to the Virgin."

On the south side, we see the entrance from the Cave into the Holy House standing in front of its mouth. In the south-west corner of the Cave may be observed the west door, of which we saw the outside in the preceding plate. At the approach of the army of Saladin in 1187, it was probably closed; for while it is mentioned by a pilgrim in 1114, * nothing is said about it at a later period, and we find that Phocas entered by the secondary door at the top of the staircase tunnelled in the rock.

The form of the Basilica is still able to be traced out; and, by the study of the sister Basilica at Bethlehem, we have succeeded in placing before the reader a fairly correct representation of the ancient Sanctuary at Nazareth. The Holy House was situated exactly like the Sacred Cave of the Nativity, and was neither under the High Altar nor beneath the transept, but under the space between them. The modern church of the Annunciation lies north and south; but, as it is fifty-five feet wide, while the transept of the ancient one, like that at Bethlehem, was only thirty-three and a half feet, it is not constructed on the site of the transept alone, but also on a portion of the choir.

We know from Quaresmius that there were only two rows of columns at Nazareth, whereas at Bethlehem there are four; but in other respects the two Basilicas were similar. The columns were mostly of red stone from the neighbourhood of Jerusalem, but some were of Egyptian granite. Up to the present day, the bases of two columns continue to occupy their original positions, and at several places there may be seen remains of the walls built of large blocks of stone cut similarly to those at Bethlehem. Another plate representing this Basilica will be seen in Part II. Chapter I., and also a ground plan of the choir and transept will be given when explaining a picture of the Annunciation, which is in Part III. Chapter II.

Plate XI.—ENTRANCE OF THE BASILICA ENCLOSING THE HOLY HOUSE AT
    LORETO - - - - - - - - - - *Page* 37

The former Illyrian Seminary is on the right.

* See Part V. Chapter I.

In Part VII. Chapter II. will be found a description of the interior of
this superb edifice.

It is probable that the Sovereign Pontiffs have wished to render evident
the idea of the Sanctuary of Loreto being a Temple-Palace by the erection
of this Palace.   To those to whom the term is new, we may explain
that a Christian Temple-Palace is an edifice erected in honour of Our
Lord as *King*.   Constantine built one at Byzantium ; Charlemagne at Aix-
la-Chapelle; St. Edward the Confessor at Westminster ; Philip II. of Spain
at the Escurial ; John I. of Portugal at Batalha ; Vladimir of Russia at
the Kremlin ; the Sovereign Pontiffs in the constructions at the Vatican.
If then we fall in with the title Palazzo Regio, instead of Palazzo
Apostolico, we do so in the sense of its being the Palace of Christ, Who is
the *true reigning King*.

This plate represents another view of the Basilica, already shewn in
Plate X. S. Louis had, of course, to descend into the crypt before he
could see the Holy House. Those who have visited oriental or Russian
churches will understand immediately that the High Altar is supposed
to be concealed behind the Iconostase, on which are painted icons of
saints and angels.   It is true that the crusaders, being accustomed to
the liturgy of S. Peter instead of that of S. James (abbreviated by
S. Basil and S. Chrysostom), may have removed the Iconostase when they
took the churches from the Greeks, but the one rite is quite as Catholic
as the other, * and they may well have been content with leaving open
the three doors in the Iconostase, which the orientals close during the
sacrifice of the Mass.

The Holy Family often went to pray on Mount Carmel, and the
Blessed Virgin is called "Decor Carmeli." The Holy House was
entrusted to the Carmelites of Galilee for a thousand years, according
to the opinion of Papebrock, which is confirmed by Apostolic Letters
written by Sixtus IV. and Innocent VIII. in favour of that illustrious Order.

* See Bulls of Leo XIII. on this subject.

S. Louis stayed several days at this monastery, and brought six of the monks with him to France to spread the Order in his country. Marraccio thus relates the occasion of this visit:—Shortly after night-fall a violent tempest arose and rent the sails and broke the masts of the ship in which S. Louis sailed, and he was in imminent danger of shipwreck. But the Mother of God appeared to him and said: "Fear not; I will deliver thee from this great peril; but, in acknowledgment of this succour, thou shalt take with thee into thy kingdom Brothers dedicated to me, who live upon Mount Carmel; for I ardently desire to see them spread throughout Europe." The Virgin Mother of God then disappeared, leaving S. Louis filled with sweet and heavenly consolation. Meanwhile the storm had ceased, and a gentle breeze had brought the ships to the foot of Mount Carmel, where the monks were singing their morning office. The holy king related the vision to his attendants, and ascended the hill to render thanks for the signal favour he had received.

Beneath the high altar of the monastery seen in the picture, is situated the cave of the Prophet Elias, * who is venerated as the founder of the Order, having directed there a school of prophets, of whom the Carmelites are the worthy successsors. At Loreto the Holy House was under the charge of the Carmelites from 1489 to 1499, and it is to their superior, the Blessed Baptist of Mantua, that we are indebted for one of the most valuable documents on the identity of the *Santa Casa*.

Plate XV.—THE TOWN OF FIUME AND THE BEAUTIFUL GULF OF QUARNERO SEEN FROM THE HILL OF TERSATTO   *Page* 69

Charlemagne destroyed an ancient Liburnian town of Croatia called Tersatica and situated on this gulf, *Sinus Flanaticus;* it is thought that the present town stands upon its site. Its modern name is taken from the stream *(flumen)* that flows past Tersatto in a lovely gorge. For a long time it was called Vitopolis (city of .Vitus), in honour of its patron, S. Vitus.

Plate XVI.—TRANSLATION OF THE HOLY HOUSE INTO ITALY   - *Page* 77

This is a reproduction from an old engraving presented to the author at Loreto, accompanied by a request to have it engraved. Differing entirely from the other illustrations, which are realistic, this has no claim to being more than the fancy of an artist.

Plate XVII.—THE ANNUNCIATION IN THE HOLY HOUSE AT NAZARETH   - *Page* 94

* Rabbi Benjamin of Tudela, who visited Carmel between 1160 and 1193, writes:— "You may still trace the site of the altar, which was rebuilt by Elias, and its circumference is about four yards. Christians have built a place of worship near the cavern of Elias."

This is the first picture ever made with the intention of representing the Blessed Virgin in the real House of Nazareth, seated at work, as tradition states that the Archangel found her, and at the exact distance from S. Gabriel that the same tradition assigns.

Let us commence by reconstructing the interior of the Holy House of Nazareth. It stood in front of a cave,* so that what we see through the door straight before us in the picture, is a cool grotto with a flight of steps tunnelled in the solid rock, leading up to another small cave, called at Nazareth "the Virgin's Kitchen." Through the door on our right is seen a cupboard hollowed out in the wall, after the manner of the Nazarenes, and called at Loreto *il Santo Armadio*. The stone walls are covered with plaster, of which very little remains in the *Santa Casa*.† The chests are such as are used in the Holy Land for containing clothing, and anciently, among the Jews, held the rolls of the Psalms and of the Prophets. No beds are represented, because they were mere mattresses rolled up and put away till night.

As S. Antoninus the Martyr tells us that he saw the seat on which Mary was sitting at the moment of the arrival of the heavenly messenger, ‡ and as Phocas and Daniel § both relate the tradition that the Immaculate Virgin was engaged in wool-work when the Archangel came in, we have, of course, not placed her in a kneeling position.

A window is placed in the west wall and near it the Angel. This part of the picture is based upon the following data : The Chapel of the Angel at Nazareth, which, as we have seen, was falling into ruins in 1620, had in its west wall a window called the Window of the Angel. Now this chapel may well be the same that was built by the Franciscans, who went there in 1300, and which was seen by Sanutus Torsellus in 1306. Being built in front of the cave in place of the Holy House, the mention of a Window of the Angel ‖ in its west wall is a confirmation of the existence

* The proofs of this are given in Part I. Chapter IV., and it has already been illustrated in Plates VII., VIII., IX.

† The greater part has been picked off by pilgrims, and the chastisements justly inflicted on them (see Part III. Chapter I.), tend to show that it has been sanctified by God Incarnate having taken up His abode within these walls.

‡ It may well have been preserved till A.D. 570. This saint saw also at Sephoris Mary's basket and spindle.

§ Greek and Russian pilgrims to the Holy House while still at Nazareth in the twelfth century. The latter says the wool was purple and the former gives the following description ; — "The mouth of the cave is adorned with a bas-relief, excelling in beauty a picture. An angel, who has flown down to this Mother who remains a Virgin, offers her his joyous salutation, while she is calmly and modestly engaged in wool-work. Startled at this unexpected apparition, the Virgin turns and almost lets the work fall from her hands."

‖ See Quaresmius, *Elucidatio Terræ Sanctæ*, lib. vii. cap. iv., F. M. Benvenuti, *Relazione istorica* (Perugia, 1634), and *El devoto Peregrino*, by Fra Antonio del Castillo, who visited Nazareth between 1600 and 1650.

of a window in that part of the House of the Holy Family. It is further a
confirmation of the antiquity of the tradition with regard to the spot
where the Archangel appeared, as a window of the Angel exists in the
Santa Casa, and one seems to have been constructed at Nazareth in imitation of it nine years after the Translation. Being a spirit, S. Gabriel
probably passed through the wall at a spot near the window.

The houses at Nazareth, which are often built in front of caves, are
generally divided by movable partitions into two or three rooms, according
to the requirements of the family; and Phocas speaks of having seen the
rooms of Our Lord, of our Blessed Lady, and of the Incarnation. These
are the three which we have endeavoured to represent in the picture.

The part of the large cave which has since been called the Chapel of
S. Joseph, was probably his private room. It was not separated
off from the rest of the cave by a stone wall, as at present,* but by a
light open screen, covered with matting or curtains. Phocas rightly
calls the entire dwelling "the ancient House of Joseph," because after
his marriage the paternal House of Mary became his. S. Thomas Aquinas
thus beautifully speaks of this matrimonial union: "The marriage of
Joseph is a sacred veil that covers the mystery of the Incarnation. In the
ancient law a cloud enveloped the Tabernacle before the Lord filled it
with His glory: thus the glory of the Lord would not have descended
into the immaculate womb of Mary, unless the marriage of Joseph had first
covered her with its shadow; he is the mysterious cloud that hides from
the eyes of man the miracles contained in the mystery of the Incarnation."

Shortly after the Ascension of Our Lord, the portion of the Holy
House in which the Incarnation took place was changed into a chapel
by the erection of an altar on the spot where the holy Mother of God
was at that supreme moment. We ask you then to imagine an altar facing
the door, by which Phocas entered the House from the cave. He tells us
that he saw the room of the Blessed Virgin on *the right of the Altar of the
Annunciation*, and the room of Our Lord *on the left of the place of the
Annunciation*.

This Greek pilgrim tells us two things with regard to the room occupied
by Our Lord:—that it was dark, and on the left hand side of the place
of the Annunciation. Both these conditions are satisfied, if we place it
at the east end of the *Santa Casa* that stood in front of the sacred Cave.
They are satisfied at Nazareth, because a partition forming a room on the
left-hand side of the Altar in the *Santa Casa* would have cut off the
light from the window of the Angel, which, as we have seen, was in the
west wall. And they are satisfied at Loreto, for the architect Nerucci

---

* There was no wall in the time of Quaresmius, as we have pointed out.

observed on the left-hand side of the Apostolic Altar, which then stood opposite the doorway, traces of a partition separating off the east end, and we find in the walls to this day two ends of a cross-beam, as if they had been sawn off. This partition must have shut out the light coming from the very small and only window.

According to Phocas' account, the Blessed Virgin was not in her own private chamber at the time of the Annunciation ; for he describes her room as situated on the right hand of the Altar of the Incarnation. We have placed a second partition, because the existence of a room distinct from the place of the Incarnation, and situated at Phocas' right hand on entering, seems to point to the existence of some kind of partition on the west side of the door in the middle of the north wall. Thus Monsieur Capelle of Morslède, Belgium, in his model of the House of the Holy Family has put in this position a light open partition, with a curtain to represent the partition shutting off the Blessed Virgin's room, which had the window. Such is the custom in Palestine, so that the air may pass freely through the rooms, by merely drawing back the curtains. As partitions of this kind are often movable, it is no wonder that we do not find traces of this one in the *Santa Casa*, nor of that in the Cave, which separated off S. Joseph's sleeping apartment. Partitions in the Holy Land are commonly of matting, or curtains drawn over upright laths of wood with a space between each lath. It must also be remembered that two new doorways now open into this part of the *Santa Casa*, and their stone lintels may take the places of the two ends of a cross beam, or even the plaster of the frescoes may cover the traces.

Before proceeding further, we must call to mind the changes made in the door, altar and window of the *Santa Casa* of Loreto during the sixteenth century :—

(*a*) Clement VII. walled up the original doorway and made new ones.

(*b*) The altar which faced the original doorway was made to face the east.

(*c*) Until the exterior ornamentation of the *Santa Casa*, the window was such as it is represented in the plate—smaller and nearer the corner.

To shew these changes at a glance, we insert three ground plans.

The distance between the Blessed Virgin and the Archangel is said by the Russian pilgrim, Daniel, to have been three sagenes, that is about twenty feet. Now, if S. Gabriel appeared near the window that bears his name, and if the Blessed Virgin was in the centre of the Holy House nearly opposite the door into the Cave and close to the south wall, we obtain in the *Santa Casa* the twenty feet which Daniel was told at Nazareth to have been the distance between them.

Thus, up to the time when the change was made in the position of the Altar in the *Santa Casa* of Loreto, the space between the north-west corner near the Window of the Angel, and the Gospel side of the Apostolic Altar was just the same as the space between the Blessed Virgin and S. Gabriel, according to the account given by Daniel, the pilgrim.

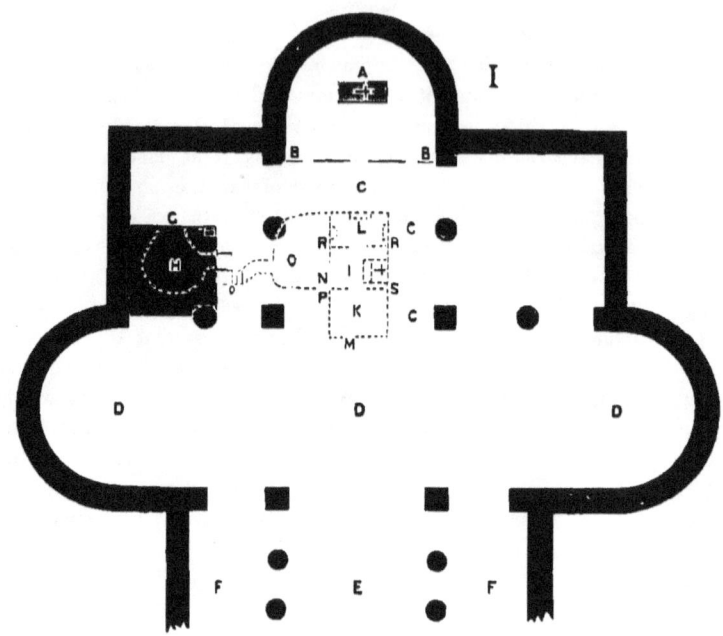

PLAN I.—BASILICA ERECTED OVER THE HOLY HOUSE AT NAZARETH.*

What we have said with regard to the positions occupied by the Mother of God and the Archangel is confirmed by the history quoted in the text. There we have related how a French lady, out of whom were cast seven devils, pointed to the Gospel side of the Altar of the *Santa Casa* (at that time opposite the door) as the spot where Mary was, and to a point near the corner of the *Santa Casa* on the right-hand side of the

* Plan I.—A—High Altar; BB—Iconostase; CCC—space over the Holy House; DDD—Transept; E—central Nave; FF—Aisles; G—Entrance to the little Cave; H—Erection over the little Cave, after the manner of that over the Holy Sepulchre; I—Room containing the altar placed in the *Santa Casa*; K—private Room of the Blessed Virgin; L—dark Room on the left of the Altar; M—Window of the Angel; N—Door from the *Santa Casa* into the Cave; O—Large Cave; P—West Entrance to the whole habitation; Q—Staircase leading to the little Cave; RR—Partition separating off the eastern portion of the *Santa Casa*; SS—Partition forming the Blessed Virgin's private room.

altar in a transverse direction, close to the Window of the Angel, as the

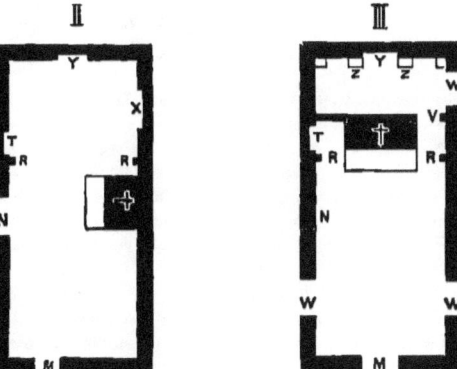

PLAN II.—THE SANTA CASA AS IT ARRIVED IN ITALY.* PLAN III.—THE SANTA CASA AFTER THE INTERIOR CHANGES MADE BY ORDER OF CLEMENT VII.†

position of S. Gabriel. These are the positions represented in our picture of the Annunciation. ‡

* Plan II. —The altar occupies its original position opposite the door ; RR—remains in the walls of the cross-beam which formed the top of a partition ; T—the *Santo Armadio*, or cupboard let into the wall ; X—the niche in which the Statue of Mary was found ; Y—the *Santo Camino*.

† Plan III.—The Altar is removed into an eastward position ; the ancient door (N) is walled up ; WWW—three new doors called *Clementine* are made in the walls ; ZZ—the *Santo Camino* is built up into the shape of a European fire-place ; on the Epistle side of the Altar there is an internal doorway (V) leading from one part of the *Santa Casa* to the other. To simplify this plan we have not added the external walls erected around the *Santa Casa*.

‡ There are some who think that the altar of the Annunciation was in the cave and at the spot where there is an altar now, but (1) the altar was placed where it is at a date subsequent to the plan of the Cave published by Quaresmius in 1639 ; (2) Phocas does not say that the private room of the Blessed Virgin was in front of the altar : on the contrary, he says that it was on the right of the altar, and that Our Lord's room was on the left. But the right and left of the present altar are both in the Cave ; and, if our Lord and His blessed Mother had their rooms in the Cave, who had rooms in the House ? Besides, on the left hand side of the altar, placed where it is in the seventeenth century, there is no space for a room, as the Gospel side of the altar, which is turned towards the north, nearly touches the west side of the Cave. True, the altar may have had an eastward position ; we will next consider how the question would then stand. (3) Phocas calls the Blessed Virgin's room very small (mikros oikistos, μικρὸς οἰκίστος); it was then not the whole, but only a part of the building whose foundations are in front of the Cave at Nazareth and measure the same as the *Santa Casa*, which would be a very large room for one person. Now, if the altar had been in the Cave and turned towards the east, the entire building erected in front of the Cave would have been on its right-hand side ; and, if Mary had it all as her private room, her chamber could not have been called small. (4) If the altar had been in the Cave and had had an eastward position, the room

Plate XVIII.—CHAPEL COMMEMORATIVE OF THE STAY OF THE HOLY
HOUSE IN TERSATTO -   -   -   -   -   -   *Page* 105

An open screen in iron-work separates this chapel from the central nave
of the church, of which it forms the sanctuary. Having no west wall,

on the left of it, once occupied by Our Lord, would have been merely the back part of the
Cave, and, on entering by the west door, a pilgrim would have had Our Lord's room
on his left hand. Now Daniel says : "On entering by the west door, one sees on one's
left the Sepulchre of S. Joseph, where his body was laid by the sacred hands of Jesus
Christ Himself." But the back part of the Cave could hardly have been at one and the
same time the Sepulchre of S. Joseph and the private room of Our Lord. Daniel could
not have meant this : therefore the altar he saw could not have been standing in such a
position.

(5) We have shewn just above in the text that the darkness of Our Lord's room by
no means proves that it was in the Cave instead of the House. But even if Our Lord
had lived in the Cave, it would not follow that the altar was erected in the Cave ;
because if Phocas, standing in the doorway of the *Santa Casa*, saw the room of the
Blessed Virgin on his right and the altar straight before him without any room on the
left of it, he might have called a room in the Cave the left of the *place* of the
Annunciation *(in lava parte vero Annuntiationis)*, although not the left of the altar.

(6) As soon as Daniel entered by the west door (P), the lamps of the altar in the
Santa Casa drew his attention (through the opening N) to the sacred spot of the
Incarnation, and on his "right-hand" he saw the "cell of the Blessed Virgin."

If Daniel, on going down into this ancient crypt, partly rock and partly masonry
covered with cement, did not notice exactly the difference and speaks of the whole as a
vault, or a cavern, because it was all equally underground, most of us would do the same, if
we were taken deep down underground to visit any similar crypt formed of rock and
masonry.   The writings of this Russian abbot have also been so mutilated by copyists
during the period of 780 years that there are a great many different readings, and, the
Russian national Church having become schismatic, its ecclesiastics are opposed to the
Translation of the Holy House into the territory of the Roman Pontiffs, as supporting the
claims of the See of S. Peter and condemning their separation from it.

(7) If the altar was at the spot in the Cave that these people imagine, where could
the Archangel have stood so as to be at twenty feet (three sagenes) from the Blessed
Virgin ? If they say that he might have been near the south wall of the House and
opposite the door leading into the Cave, we reply first that S. Ann, and not S.
Gabriel, had an altar at that spot in the plan made by Quaresmius, and secondly, that the
name given to the window implies that S. Gabriel appeared at a spot near the window
and not opposite the door.

For the above reasons, and on account of the Bulls of the Popes, we do not think that the
altar mentioned by Phocas and Daniel was in the Cave. But even if it were, the *Santa
Casa* would have a right to the title of Chamber of the Angelic Salutation.   For
supposing these pilgrims found the Altar of the Annunciation in the Cave, they found
also the Apostolic Altar in the *Santa Casa* and at about the distance mentioned by
Daniel as the space between the Blessed Virgin and the Archangel. And as we are told
that the Altar of the Annunciation represented the position of Mary, we should
naturally conclude that the other altar represented the position of S. Gabriel : so that,
even if Mary were in the Cave, the Archangel none the less delivered his message in the
Santa Casa.

There is still another theory that does not seem to rest on any firm basis : namely,
that two granite columns shew the positions of the Blessed Virgin and S. Gabriel.

there is, of course, no imitation of the window of the Angel; but in the east wall behind the altar * there is a fireplace like the *Santo Camino* of the Holy House of Loreto.

Ruins of the castle which was for 448 years the stronghold of the Counts Frangipani. In its donjon is the mausoleum of an English general who had purchased this historic fastness. Just below it is the Parish Church of S. George, a portion of which dates from before the Translation of the Holy House.

Tersatto is in Austrian Croatia, the ancient Liburnia, which formed part of the vast region of Illyria. The Emperor Tiberius divided Illyria into three districts, in which judicial courts were held (three *conventus*), and in the official language of the Roman Empire the whole of Roman Illyria began to be called Dalmatia. At this time Liburnia became the northern portion of the newly formed political—but not geographical— district of Dalmatia. This has led to confounding the Liburnians (and afterwards the Croatians) with the Dalmatians; but the Liburnians inhabited the territory extending from the Arsia to the Titius (modern Kerka), and the Dalmatians that from the Titius to the Drilo (modern Drino). In the sixth century colonies of Slavs were set up in Liburnia, and it ended in becoming the kingdom of Croatia; so that Tersatto has been in Croatia ever since that epoch. Nor has Croatia ever been ruled

The very height of these columns appears to contradict the idea that they were made for the places that they occupy. Luigi Vulcana della Padula, in his description of the Holy Land in 1563, says: "These columns rise up above the Cameretta (that is the Chapel of the Angel) and above the ruins of the church about the height of a man." Stefano Mondegazza, whose travels in Palestine were printed at Milan in 1616, says exactly the same thing (see Martorelli.) Since that time all that rose up above the Cave and chapel has been removed; but the top of the column has a hole for the clamp that fixed the upper block, which was taken off to make it level with the floor; the circumference as well as their original height points to their having been in the nave of the Basilica and not in its crypt. Besides the position of Mary was said by pilgrims (as we have seen) to have been indicated by an altar and not by a column, and, so far from there being twenty feet between the two columns, there are only three. Whatever opinion we may form as to the object of these columns, this is certain—that the one to the south stands *within the foundations of the Holy House*, so that even if this column shows the spot where S. Gabriel stood, the Archangel was none the less in that part of the Holy House of Nazareth which was translated to Loreto, and which is rightly called the Chamber of the Angelic Salutation. In conclusion, we may observe that these suppositions leave intact the truth of the Translation, and the eminent sanctity of the Habitation snatched out of the hands of the Mahomedans.

* When the Holy House stood on this spot, the Apostolic Altar was not at the east end, but in the centre of the south wall. The chapel erected by Count Frangipani about 1295 had to be rebuilt in 1614, and the altar was placed like that at Loreto, which under the pontificate of Paul III. had been removed from the south side to the east. No plan of the original chapel exists.

F F

by Dalmatia: the two countries were united from 1052 to 1088, but it was a Croate, Peter Crescimir, and not a Dalmate, who was king of both countries. We may add that the mainland of Dalmatia never extended further than 44° 25' north latitude and that Tersatto is at 45° 40'. The explanation of its having been called Dalmatia in histories of the Holy House appears to be that the first historians wrote in Latin, and retained the political nomenclature of the *conventus* set up by Tiberius.

The Dalmatians as well as the Croatians have shewn great zeal for the honour of the Holy House, and the festival of the Translation from Nazareth to Tersatto is celebrated by both peoples. The Slavs of Illyria were converted by SS. Cyril and Methodius, and have preserved for the most part the Catholic faith. The ancient confraternity for the conversion of the schismatic Slavs of Russia, Roumania, Servia, Bulgaria and Bosnia seems about to be re-established at Tersatto.

The Church of S. George on the left hand in our picture is of great interest. It is remarkable that the Holy House which contains an ancient fresco of S. George should have been conveyed into a parish placed under his patronage, and that the rector of his church should have been miraculously healed. As heretics have written against the existence of this church and the reality of the appearance of the Mother of God to its rector, it may be well to add a word on both these subjects. Some readers of this work may have elsewhere come across the assertion that there is no church of S. George within 400 miles of Tersatto. Let them be reassured; the picture of this church is made out of a photograph purchased by the author on the spot; he has assisted at Mass and Benediction at S. George's, Tersatto, during six weeks, and the existence of this church can be traced back to more than a hundred years before the date of the Translation. This is all of a piece with the ridiculous assertion that Catholics believe the Holy House to have come out of the mouth of the Cave at Nazareth, which was smaller than itself: whereas in fact its foundations remain in front of the Cave and not within it.

After ignorantly denying the existence of the Church of S. George, which has stood close to the castle for at least seven centuries, they falsely state that the whole story of a miraculous translation of the House is only based on a pretended vision, said to have been seen by the rector of this church. No such thing. The vision is not brought forward as proof, but as leading up to proof: it had the effect of causing delegates to be sent to Nazareth, who returned thoroughly convinced that the building was the same that had been in that holy place.

That the Blessed Virgin may have manifested herself and spoken to the rector of S. George's is by no means incredible. The appearances of the Immaculate Mother of God are too numerous and too well authenticated to allow us to doubt her having shewn herself upon earth since her removal from it. The Blessed Virgin appeared to SS. Catharine of Alexandria, of Siena and of Bologna; to S. Martina of Rome and to S. Martin of Tours; to SS. Nicholas of Myra and of Tolentino; to S. Dunstan, S. Ildefonsus, S. Alberic, S. Julian of Cuença on his deathbed, S. Andrew Corsini, foretelling him the day of his death, S. Clara of Rimini, advising her to take the veil, S. Thomas Aquinas, reassuring him as to the purity of his soul, S. Thomas of Canterbury, S. Ignatius of Loyola, S. Philip Neri, S. Elizabeth of Hungary, Thomas à Kempis, the seven Founders of the Order of the Servites, S. Simon Stock, S. Theresa, with a mantle covering her nuns, S. Norbert, pointing out the place (*Prémontré*, foreshewn) where the monastery of the Premonstratensians should be built and the habit of the Order, S. Germain of Montfort, S. Alphonsus Rodriguez, S. Stanislaus Kostka, holding the Infant Jesus in her arms. She appeared publicly to S. Alphonsus de Liguori and to many others, too numerous to name. And who in presence of the continuous miracles at Lourdes can doubt that the Immaculate Virgin appeared to Bernadette Soubirous in that grotto?

Whatever be the weight that we may personally attach to the testimony of the Blessed Virgin, spoken in an appearance to Don Alexander, whom she vouchsafed to heal as a proof of the reality of the vision, the identity of the Holy House rests upon intrinsic and extrinsic proofs entirely independent of visions and miracles.

Plate XX.—OUR LADY OF GRACE - - - - - - - *Page* 108
Sent to Tersatto by the Blessed Urban V.

Plate XXI.—THE FOUNTAIN OF MARY AT NAZARETH (From a photograph by Bonfils) - - - - - - - - - - *Page* 122
In the cool of the evening the women come to draw water at this well and the pilgrims bathe their heads with it.

Plate XXII.—CHURCH OF THE ARCHANGEL GABRIEL - - *Page* 122
Erected over the spring which supplies the water of the public well represented in the previous picture and seen in the left hand corner of this. It is 600 yards from the site of the Holy House; so that it is the more touching to see Mary carrying the pitcher on her head all the way from this spring to her home, and the Child Jesus walking by her side. "As soon as you have entered the city gate," says Phocas, "you find the church of the Archangel Gabriel, and in a small cave on the left of the altar a clear spring sends forth its waters, which the most Immaculate Mother of God used to come daily to draw." The walls here spoken of exist no longer, and the church is in the hands of the

Greek schismatics, but the spring in its little cave still occupies its former place at the left of the altar. The accuracy of this description by Phocas enhances the value of his account of what he saw in the Holy House.

Plate XXIII.—THE CHAPEL OF THE ANGEL AT NAZARETH - *Page* 127
This is merely a front view of the same chapel, seen in section in Plate VII., and already explained.

Plate XXIV.—OUR LADY OF GOOD COUNSEL - - - *Page* 144
Miraculously brought to Genazzano, called for that reason the *Loreto of Latium.*

Plate XXV.—RUINS OF THE CHAPEL AT SCUTARI - - *Page* 144
(a) The niche which Our Lady of Good Counsel used to occupy.

Plate XXVI.—THE VERGINE GRECA OF RAVENNA - - *Page* 147
A marble bas-relief carried by angels from the East to Ravenna, and representing the Mother of God holding up her hands in prayer. We have called it a "Holy Icon," because no other word fitly denotes such sacred images in veneration among the Greeks.

MADONNA OF LORETO, WITHOUT HER CUSTOMARY ROBES AND SURROUNDED BY VIEWS OF THE SANCTUARY - - - - - - *Page* 150

Plate XXVII.—THE NORTH WALL OF THE HOLY HOUSE - *Page* 154
Shewing its ancient walled-up doorway, the *Santo Armadio* (the holy cupboard), frescoes of the Blessed Virgin, S. Catharine, etc., and a portion of a cross-beam sawn off level with the wall.

Plate XXVIII.—WEST WALL OF THE HOLY HOUSE - - *Page* 154
With its only window and the remains of frescoes. In Serragli's description of the frescoes, written more than 250 years ago, the saint with a book under his arm is said to be S. Anthony, patriarch of monks; and Serragli is probably right in placing S. Louis in this west wall; but if so, his fresco has disappeared. Some think it is S. Louis and not S. George in the south wall.

Plate XXIX.—SOUTH WALL OF THE HOLY HOUSE - - *Page* 154
The door only dates from Clement VII. The frescoes are said by Serragli to represent S. George, S. Anthony, S. Bartholomew, Our Blessed Lady and S. Francis of Assisi.

Plate XXX.—NAVE OF THE BASILICA - - - *Page* 157
Shewing the west end of the Holy House with its only window and the Altar of the Annunciation. The tribunes on the right and left are for the Choir, which is one of the best in Italy.

Plate XXXI.—THE FAÇADE OF THE BASILICA - - - *Page* 161

Being octagonal, the following eight titles of the Blessed Virgin, which form the end of the Litany of Loreto, are represented in grand tableaux of the Patriarchs, Prophets, Apostles, Martyrs, Confessors, Virgins, All Saints and the Holy Rosary. Our plate gives the tableau of All Saints, with part of the Patriarchs and of the Procession of the Holy Rosary. Above is seen the Queen of Angels, the Mirror of Justice, the Towers of David and of Ivory. The titles House of Gold, Ark of the Covenant, Mystical Rose, Seat of Wisdom follow round the dome, and between them angels hold up scrolls of music, as if singing:—Cause of our Joy, Comfort of the Afflicted, Health of the Sick, Refuge of Sinners, Mother of divine Grace, Virgin most merciful, Virgin most powerful, Virgin most faithful.

On this spot it remained from December 10, 1294, to August, 1295. At that time there was a laurel grove (*laureto*), which is there no longer. The site is five minutes from the railway station. The design of the chapel is by Count Sacconi, and it is known as the *Voto Nazionale*.

Bastion at the east end of the town. Back part of the Basilica, flanked by castellated towers corresponding to the internal chapels.

It was not till after the fall of Constantinople that the Popes surrounded Loreto with walls; so that it cannot be the *Castellum de Laureto* mentioned in the text of the donation of Gualferio in 1062. Besides, that fortified place was situated in the parish of S. Elpidio, eighteen miles south of our pilgrimage. Again it cannot be the Loreto named in the donation of the Countess Gaeta in 1089, for that also was near S. Elpidio, as Umbremano is named in the text of both these donations. *

The town (*Oppidum*) of Loreto, in which Bishop Ulrich bought a property in 1088, to endow his church with it, must have been in his own diocese of Fermo, a city twenty-three miles south of the Loreto which contains the *Santa Casa*.

In the earldom of Sinigaglia there existed at a distance thirty-six miles north-west of the present site of the Holy House and before its

_____

* The estate of the Countess was situated between the sea and the rivers Aso and Potenza : "*Fines erant mare, flumina Aso et Potentia.*" The Aso is twenty-six miles south of the Aspido, as may be seen in the map of the March of Ancona, by J. Jansonius, and even on any good map of Italy. It is therefore ignorance to confound the Aso with the Aspido.

coming, two villages of Loreto near the river Esino, called Loreto the Greater, Loreto the Less, and the Hill of Loreto.* This *Castrum Laureti* was situated near Rocca-Contrata. †

In Amati's Geographical Dictionary of Italy no less than twenty-three places are called Loreto, Loretto, Loreta. In the middle ages the name was very common and was derived from laurel woods in which there were temples in pagan times. All the historians of the Sanctuary of Loreto speak of a wood of laurels in which the Holy House first remained. And it seems that not only this wood but quite a large district was called Loreto, and that a long time before the building of the town of Loreto. For example, in 1177, Gislain speaks of a Church of St. John of Loreto, or of Monte-Ciotto—*Ecclesia Sancti Joannis de Loreto, sive de Monte-Ciotto.* The hill of Loreto is distinct from the higher hill called Monte-Ciotto, which is on the road to Recanati and beyond the town : so that by Loreto Gislain denotes a district and not a town.

The Bishop of Humana gave, January 4, 1194, the Camalduli of Fonte Avellana a church called "Sancta Maria in fundo Loreti." This church must not be mistaken for the church of Our Lady of Loreto containing the *Santa Casa* for the reasons given in the note. ‡

The inhabitants of the district of Loreto in the middle ages were always very devout towards the Blessed Virgin. The church of S.

* " In comitatu Senegalliæ juxta flumen Esinum . . . fundum Laureti Majoris et Minoris et montem Laureti."—*Annales Camaldulenses,* t. iii. 326. (This inventory of the property of the Camalduli of S. Severus near Ravenna was drawn up in 1128.)

† "Castrum Laureti nunc appellatum Loretellum, in agro Rocchæ Contratæ diocesis Senegalliensis." See *Annales Camaldulenses,* t. ix. p. 35.

‡ 1. Nowhere in the annals of the Camalduli is it stated that the order ever had charge over the *Santa Casa.* 2. The church given to the Camalduli ceased to exist more than forty-five years before the date of the Translation of the Holy House into Italy, for the list of churches given in a Bull of Innocent IV. in 1249 does not mention it. 3. The land on which the Holy House stood belonged to the Commune of Recanati, whereas that on which this church was situated was the property of the Bishop of Humana. The act of donation was not signed by the authorities of Recanati, but only by Monsignor Giordano, the chapter and the rector of Gardetto. 4. Among the property of the church given over by the Bishop of Humana are enumerated water-mills. The land must then have been by the side of a river, and the church not on the top of a hill but in the plain of the Musone. 5. A lawsuit against Ghibellines who plundered the *Santa Casa* in 1315, exists still in the archives of Macerata. We learn from this document that the Sanctuary was served by a chaplain; which shews that it was quite distinct from the parish church given to the Camalduli. 6. The different kind of property of the one and of the other. That of the church given to the Camalduli was land, vines, olive-trees, water-mills, fields, pasturage, etc., while that of the *Santa Casa* in 1315 consisted of the offerings of pilgrims :—" The robbers took money out of an alms-box, wax-candles, images in wax and silver ; they took from the statue garlands with pearls, veils and scarfs of silk and other materials."

Mary in Fundo Loreti having disappeared, it seems, before the year 1249, we find, in 1285, another church called this time Sancta Maria de Laureto. This again must not be mistaken for the *Santa Casa*; for the Bishop had possessions joining this church,* while the hill on which the Holy House is situated was the property of the town of Recanati. The Bishop possessed in the fifteenth century lands in the plain of the Musone, joining the forests of the town, called the forests of Loreto (act of 1447). If we place the church in that direction, it will satisfy all the indications of the act of 1285.†

Plate XXXVII.—THE STATUE OF S. JOSEPH - - - *Page* 174

This is on the altar in the beautiful chapel dedicated to the Head of the Holy Family.

Plate XXXVIII.—OUR LADY OF SEVEN DOLOURS VENERATED AT CAMPO-CAVALLO, NEAR LORETO - - - - - - - *Page* 174

As near Nazareth there is the site of an ancient chapel commemorating Our Lady's trembling, so also near this new Nazareth the Mother of Sorrows seeks the sympathy of her children.

Not far from the hill of the Precipitation at Nazareth S. Helena erected the *Capella del Tremore*. The sympathetic soul of this great saint compassionated the pang of anguish that rent the heart of Mary while the Nazarenes were dragging her Son towards the precipice. S. Helena realised vividly what it was for the Mother of Jesus to hasten out of her house and try to prevent this terrible deed. Mary's love was stronger than the hatred of the Jews. She thought she could prevail if only she could reach the hill in time. But how could she do so? She feels her strength fast failing her. The fear comes over her that she will arrive too late! The thought is more than she can bear. She cannot take another step. Riveted to the spot, she trembles! O great S. Helena, well wast thou inspired to raise a monument to the anguish of the Mother of Sorrows. Obtain for us to sympathise like thee with Mary's woes.

We pass now to the New Nazareth: what do we find there? "In the little chapel of Campo-Cavallo the picture of Our Lady of Seven Dolours commenced weeping in the month of June, 1892, and still continues to open its eyes like a living person, in the presence of thousands of the faithful. Miraculous graces are accorded there: healings, conversions, etc.; faith is awakened, and blasphemies cease among the people since the Holy Image makes these manifestations."‡

* "Item habet in fundo Laureti, juxta ecclesiam Sanctæ Mariæ de Laureto et viam modiola iii. et staria vii."

† Anyone who wishes to enter further into details may consult *Authenticité de la Sainte Maison de Lorette* by the Abbé A. Milochau.

‡ See *La Madone de Campo-Cavallo*, by Rev. A. Mortier (Paillart, Abbeville).

APPENDIX

LATIN AND ITALIAN DOCUMENTS REFERRED TO IN THIS WORK, BUT NOT YET GIVEN IN THE ORIGINAL LANGUAGES.

Inscription placed on the Holy House by Clement VIII.

(Page 6.)

CHRISTIANE hospes, qui pietatis votivæ causâ huc advenisti, sacram Lauretanam Domum vides divinis mysteriis et miraculorum gloriâ toto orbe terrarum venerabilem. Hîc sanctissima Dei Genitrix Maria in lucem edita, hîc ab Angelo salutata; hîc æternum Dei Verbum caro factum est; hanc angeli primùm è Palestinâ in Illyricum advexêre ad Tersactum oppidum anno Salutis MCCLXXXXI, Nicolao IV summo Pontifice; triennio post, initio pontificatûs Bonifacii VIII, * in Picenum translata, propè Recinetum urbem, in hujus collis nemore eâdem angelorum operâ collocata est, ubi, loco intra anni spatium ter commutato, hîc postremo sedem divinitùs fixit anno abhinc CCC. Ex eo tempore tàm stupendæ rei novitate vicinis populis in admiratione commotis, tùm deinceps miraculorum famâ longè latèque propagatâ, sancta hæc Domus magnam apud omnes gentes venerationem habuit, cujus parietes nullis fundamentis subnixi, post tot sæculorum ætates integri stabilesque permanent. Clemens Papa VII illam marmoreo ornatu circumquaque convestivit, anno MDXXV. † Clemens VIII Pont. Max. brevem admirandæ Translationis historiam in hoc lapide inscribi jussit, anno MDXCV. Antonius Maria Gallus, S. R. E. presb. card. et episcopus Auximi, sanctæ Domûs protector, faciendum curavit. Tu hîc, hospes, Reginam Angelorum et Matrem gratiarum religiosè venerare, ut hujus meritis et precibus dulcissimo Filio, vitæ auctori, et peccatorum veniam, et corporis salutem, et æterna gaudia consequaris.

* Celestine V. abdicated three days after the Translation into Italy.

† "Paulus III. Pont. celeberrimum illud Pontificalis magnificenciæ monumentum ab Iulio destinatum, inchoatum a Leone, effectum à Clemente, ipse non quidem omni ex parte perfectum (deerant quippe statuarum pleræque et æneæ valvæ omnes), sed tamen eo perductum, ut absolutum videre posset, aperuit anno huius sæculi XXXVIII opus enimvero egregium ac mirabile, cui nova hæc operum magnificencia quicquam adhuc in pari mole adæquare non potuit."—Vide *Lauret. Histor.* Torsell. lib. III. cap. 6.

G G

Official Report of Architects.
(Page 16.)

NEL processo autentico che se ne fece, quegli architetti deposero con giuramento così: "Noi sottoscritti architetti e capomastri, secondo la nostra arte e perizia e coscienza, mediante il nostro giudizio, riferiamo, che le sacre mura di questa santa Casa, da noi bene riconosciute dal piano del primo scalino dell' altare a tutta la parte verso l'altare esteriore della Santissima Annunziata, non hanno veruna sorta di fondamento, trovandosi sotto di esse sacre mura terra smossa, ed in alcune parti polvere con brecette, e tufo naturale, come suol essere nei luoghi montuosi ; e in fede di ciò sottoscriviamo la presente di nostra propria mano." Questa deposizione si trova nell' archivio Lauretano, e si lege stampata nella Lettera Pastorale del vescovo di Recanati monsignor Felice Paoli dell'anno 1802.

See Antonio Riccardi, *Storia dei Sanctuari piu celebri de Maria SS.*

Comparison of the Sanctuaries of Loreto and Nazareth.
(Page 24.)

PATER Frater Jacobus a Vandosma, vir in rebus agendis apprime expertus, qui ab anno Dom. 1620, usque ad praesentem 1626, sacrae hujus Nazarethae domus regimen tenet, post multam indaginem et considerationem ad difficultatem respondit, Lauretanam domum fuisse e sancto Nazareth loco, ubi nunc est capella Angeli superaedificata, translatam.

Nec obstat, quod ista non recentior Lauretana appareat ; quia id accedit, quod non ut illa custodita sit, ut antea dictum fuit : nec quod ista illa augustior sit ; quoniam non adaequate supra vetera fundamenta fuit superaedificata, sed infra super ipsum pavimentum praeexistentis domus : et ex eo probat, quod inferius in meridionali et occidentali parte juxta portam recenter factam, e muro ablatis et lapidibus, deprehensum fuit vetus pavimentum, cui dicti lapides haerebant : quare cubiculum proximum antro quod superfuit, et nunc in Nazareth invisitur, ablatum fuit ministerio Angelorum, et in situ illius, etsi non ei adaequetur, quod nunc est sacellum Angeli superaedificatum : et illud mihi postea ostendit.

Quam responsionem oculatus inspector P. Frater Thomas à Novaria amplexus, pluribus explicuit in relatione à se edita de recuperatione sacrae domus Annuntiationis apud Nazaretham, sic enim ait : *Praedictus Frater Jacobus monasterii custos, cum eam sanctae domus partem, quae ad occidentem erat sub fenestra Angeli et ad meridiem prope domus januam ruinae proximam restaurare vellet, ad fundamenta usque solvit vetustatem : quippe quae diligenter et attente considerata sanctae lauretanae domus* *fundamentum duobus palmis crassum seorsum ab alio adinventum est: quod quidem ad substentandam fabricam, et exornandam interius domum, duobus item palmis latum ex positis lapidibus compactum a priscis illis Christifidelibus ex interiore parte adiectum reperimus. Hoc igitur dimisso, a vetusto ac vero incipientes fundamento, lineamque mensurationis rectam ab ipso ducentes, summa omnium exultatione plantæ sanctæ lauretanæ domus per omnia æqualis inventus est Nazareth locus, et fundamenta muris, et domus fundamentis, locusque loco, situs situi, spatiumque spatio, Nazareth inquam et Laureti, dempto quod dixi omnino convenire, ac commensurari, divina opulante gratia, veraciter invenimus.**

Bulls of Paul II.
(Page 34.)

QUAMVIS pro magnitudine gratiarum, quas divina Maiestas, ad intercessionem gloriosæ Virginis Mariæ, fidelibus ad eam pia vota dirigentibus quotidie facit, sanctæque ecclesiæ in honorem nominis sui dedicatæ, sint summa devotione venerandæ, etc. Manifestat autem rei experientia ad Ecclesiam Sanctæ MARLE de Laureto Recanatensis Diœcesis, UBI EST DOMUS ET IMAGO BEATÆ MARIÆ VIRGINIS ob magna, stupenda, et infinita miracula, quæ ibidem ejusdem Almæ Virginis opera apparent et NOS IN PERSONA NOSTRA EXPERTI SUMUS, ex diversis mundi partibus confluere, etc. *(Ex Bulla data Nov. 1464.)*

Cum ad Ecclesiam Beatæ MARIÆ de Laureto extra muros Recanatensis Civitatis fundatam, in qua, sicut fide dignorum habet assertio, ipsius VIRGINIS GLORIOSÆ DOMUS, ET IMAGO ANGELICO COMITATU ET CŒTU MIRA DEI CLEMENTIA COLLOCATA EXTITIT, et ad quam propter crebra et stupenda miracula, quæ ejusdem Gloriosæ Virginis meritis et intercessione pro singulis ad Eam recurrentibus, et ejus auxilium implorantibus cum humilitate, Altissimus operatur indies, et ex diversis mundi partibus ETIAM REMOTISSIMIS, ejusdem Virginis Gloriosæ liberati præsidiis populi confluat multitudo, etc. *(Ex Bulla data Feb. 1471.)*

Bull of Julius II.
(Page 35.)

CUM nuper Hieronymus Episcopus debitum naturæ persolverit, Nos attendentes, quod nedum in præfata Ecclesia de Laureto Imago Ipsius Beatæ Virginis MARIÆ sed etiam, ut piè creditur et fama est, CAMERA, SIVE THALAMUS, UBI IPSA BEATISSIMA VIRGO CONCEPTA, UBI

---

* Opus Fr. Francisci Quaresmii cui titulus *Terræ Sanctæ Elucidatio*, tom. II. lib 7, cap. 4, page 837.

EDUCATA, UBI AB ANGELO SALUTATA SALVATOREM SÆCULORUM VERBO CON-
CEPIT, UBI IPSUM SUUM PRIMOGENITUM SUIS CASTISSIMIS UBERIBUS, LACTE
DE CŒLO PLENIS, LACTAVIT ET EDUCAVIT, ubi quando de hoc sœculo nequam
ad sublimia assumpta extitit, orando quiescebat, quamque Apostoli Sancti
primam Ecclesiam in honorem Dei, et ejusdem Beatœ Virginis consecrarunt,
ubi prima Missa celebrata extitit, ex Nazareth Angelicis manibus ad partes
Sclavoniœ, et locum Flumen nuncupatum primo portata, et deinde per
eosdem Angelos ad nemus Lauretœ mulieris, ipsius Beatissimæ Virginis
MARIÆ devotissimæ, et successive ex dicto nemore propter homicidia, et
alia facinora, quæ inibi patrabantur, in collem duorum fratrum, et postremo
ob rixas, et contentiones inter eos exortas, in viam publicam territorii
Recanatensis translata extitit : cupientesque Ipsam, ad quam non minorem
devotionis affectum gerimus quam Paulus, et qui secundum carnem Avun-
culus Sixtus, in spiritualibus, et temporalibus in dies melius gubernari,
de motu proprio, ac de Apostolicæ Auctoritatis plenitudine UNIONEM,
ANNEXIONEM, ET INCORPORATIONEM dissolventes, decernimus, ipsam Ecclesiam
sanctæ MARIÆ de Laureto ab omni alia, preterquam Sedis Apostolicæ
subjectione debere esse immunem, eamque sub Nostra, ac Beati Petri, et
Sedis Apostolicæ protectione PERPETUO suscipimus, Nobisque, et Successoribus Nostris Romanis Pontificibus pro tempore existentibus, Sedi prefatæ,
Gubernatorique per Nos, seu Sedem prefatam inibi deputato subjicimus, et
subesse volumus, ipsamque Ecclesiam Beatæ MARIÆ in Nostram, ac Sedis
Apostolicæ Capellam perpetuo recipimus, etc.

Bull of Leo X.
(Page 35.)

GLORIOSISSIMÆ Virginis Matris DEI MARIÆ, a cujus laudibus sicut
neminem cessare fas est, ita ad illas explendas neminem sufficere
arbitramur. Cum siquidem nullum promptius miseris, aut efficacius pecca-
toribus refugium apud Deum inveniatur, merito totius animi, mentisque
affectibus recolentes Illam in Cœlis primum adorandam, deinde ubique in
Terris venerandam, et loca ejus Nomini dicata omni studio ornanda esse
censemus, et illa maximè, quœ ipsa Beata Virgo sibi ipsi Angelicis
comitata Cœtibus eligit, et assiduè in eis, in Christifidelium auxilium, et
sublevationem, miracula ferè innumera operatur, inter quœ omnium consensu, testimonio, ac devotione Locus ille Lauretanus fama celebris, ac
devotorum frequentia cultissimus, merito habetur primus.

Cum enim Beatissima Virgo, ut fide dignorum comprobatum est testimonio, E NAZARETH IMAGINEM, ET CUBICULUM SUUM DIVINO NUTU TRANS-
FERENS, postquam apud Flumen Dalmatiœ Oppidum primò, et deinde in

agro Recanatensi in loco nemoroso, ac rursus quodam in colle ejusdem
agri particularibus personis addicto posuit : demum in via publica, ubi
modo consistit, ILLUC ANGELICIS MANIBUS COLLOCANDA, SIBI ELEGIT, et in
eo assiduè miracula innumera illis meritis operatur Altissimus. OB
QUOD COMPLURES ROMANI PONTIFICES Prædecessores Nostri, et precipuè
fel. record. Paulus II., Sixtus IV., et Julius II., Sacratissimæ Virgini
merito devotissimi, ut populum Christianum, Omnipotenti Deo, et ejus
Virgini Matri redderent acceptabilem, Ecclesiam Lauretanam, quæ tanto
miraculo creverat, et augetur in dies, variis et præcipue spiritualibus
decorarunt muneribus, indulgentiis scilicet, et peccatorum remissionibus,
domosque, agros, bona, ministros, et personas ipsius ecclesiæ ac vicum ubi
illa consistit, variis donariis, muneribus, indultis, privilegiis, gratiis et
immunitatibus, etc. *(Augusto, 1518.)*

Bull of Sixtus V.
(Page 35.)

CONSIDERANS oppidum Lauretanum in provincia Piceni situm nullius
diœcesis Sedi apostolicæ immediate subjectum in toto orbe celeberri-
mum, et in eo unam insignem Collegiatam Ecclesiam sub invocatione
Beatæ MARIÆ Virginis fundatam excellere, IN CUJUS MEDIO INEST ILLUD
SACRUM CUBICULUM DIVINIS MYSTERIIS CONSECRATUM, IN QUO VIRGO MARIA
NATA FUIT, ET IBIDEM IPSA AB ANGELO SALUTATA SALVATOREM MUNDI DE
SPIRITU SANCTO CONCEPIT, MINISTERIO ANGELORUM ILLUC TRANSLATAM, et
ad d. Ecclesiam ob miracula, quæ indies Omnipotens Dominus intercessione ac meritis ejusdem Beatæ MARIÆ in eodem Cubiculo operari dignatur,
Christifideles ex omnibus Mundi regionibus, devotionis et peregrinationis
causa confluere, et propterea cupiens oppidum, et Ecclesiam hujusmodi
dignioribus titulis et nominibus decorare, etc. *(Ex Bulla data Mar. 1586.)*
Summa aurea de B. V. Maria, tom. X. cap. xc.

The Jubilee in the year 1300.
(Page 54.)

IPSO anno post Christum natum MCCC., qui primus Jubilæi celebritate
insignis fuit novi Pontificalis beneficii fama in omnes orbis Christiani
regiones perlata incredibilem omnium gentium, totiusque occidentis exivit
sedibus suis molem. . . Nullus pene dies abibat, quin Urbs ducenta pere-
grinorum millia hospitio exciperet, præter innumerabilem multitudinem
quæ erat in via. Horum igitur plurimi præsertim quibus Recinetum minimè

devium erat, miraculorum fama exciti ad Ædem Lauretanam utique diver-
terunt, testes ac nuncii suis quisque popularibus futuri eorum, quæ de
tam inusitato, inauditoque miraculo, non tam aliorum sermonibus accepissent,
quam suis ipsimet oculis hausissent. *Lauret Hist.* Torsell. lib I. cap. xv.

Clericus quidam, *Jubilæi tempore*, vidit per quietem sanctissimam Virginem, cum Filio in ulnis, in *quodam thalamo residentem.* Eam cum
clericus genu flexo adorasset, ita ipsa ad eum: " OMNIBUS MISERANS
INDULSIT DEUS." Eo autem subjiciente, *Num et mihi?* subticuit Deipara: rursumque post morulam interjectam, repetiit idem: " OMNIBUS
MISERANS INDULSIT DEUS, VIVIS ET MORTUIS." Prostratus iterum ille,
Num et mihi? Cui nec tum dato responso, at paulo post ait: " INDULSIT
OMNIBUS MORTUIS ET VIVIS MISERANS DEUS, ATQUE ETIAM TIBI." Ut de
vivis sileam, certe tunc temporis dæmones per energumenos publice
clamabunt omnes animas purgatorii æternam gloriam consecutas.

Vide *Pontifices Maximi Mariani,* A. P. Hippolyto Marraccio, cap. LIX.

Letter of the Bishop of Coimbra.
(Page 88.)

JOANNES episcopus Conimbricensis Præsidi Lauretano S. D. Pro meâ
erga Lauretanam Virginem religione, ejus lapidem (quod te non fugit),
summâ ope, operâque curaveram. Ac demùm interdicti Pontificii religione
solutus, à Pontifice Maximo impetrâram, Cardinali Carpensi Laureti patrono
non invito. Sed Deus ac Dei Parens haud obscuris argumentis mihi
denunciârunt, ut ablatum lapidem Lauretum remitterem. Quippè et
inusitatus morbus prosperam meam valetudinem divinitùs afflixit: et piorum
Deoque acceptorum hominum monitu hanc morbi causam esse perspexi.
Itaque ego nullâ interpositâ morâ, veniam pacemque precatus à Deo, ejusque
sanctissimâ Parente, sacrum lapidem per eumdem Franciscum Stellam
Aretinum sacerdotem meum, qui istinc eum abstulerat, referendum curavi.
Quæso obtestorque ut remissum, quâ par est religione cæremoniâque
recipias ac suo reponas loco, unâ cum calce quæ pariter remittitur. Unum
oro, ut arculas argenteas, quibus ea continentur, velut testes miraculi asser-
ves ad posteritatis memoriam sempiternam. Gratissimum quoque mihi
feceris, si Cardinalem Patronum ipsumque Pontificem Maximum de
totâ re feceris certiores, ut post hâc Censuras Ecclesiasticas in Ædis
Lauretanæ violatores ratas esse, ac sanctas velint; ne quid omninò
illinc in posterùm auferatur. Orabis etiam cum istis sanctis sacerdoti-
bus Beatam Virginem, ut hoc, quidquid est, sive erroris, sive culpæ, cle-
menter mihi condonet. Datæ Tridenti, VI. Id. Aprilis, Anno MDLXII.

Lauret. Histor. Torsell. lib. IV. cap. 4.

Testimony of Novidius to the Miracle of the Flames.
(Page 90.)

TENET fama anniversarium hoc spectaculum ad Pauli III. Pontif. Max. tempora durasse. Nec ferme ex Lauretanis rebus res est alia nobilior. Itaque id non tantum historici memoriæ providere, sed etiam Novidius Poëta minime obscurus in egregio carmine, quod dicavit Paulo III. Pont. Max., mandavit versibus, quos huic historiæ intexere pretium operæ duximus. Is igitur B. Virginem laudibus efferens ita cauit:

Evenére igitur, tot stant tibi templa, quot astra,
Quotque sibi gentes maximus orbis habet.
Stent licet, illa placent quibus est hæc orta, juvatque
Dicere: In hoc ingens est Dea nata loco.
Scilicet illius, visu mirabile, in auras
Parthum exosa domus vulsa recessit humo;
Cumque locis diversa foret, titulosque referret,
Ultima Piceni nomina gentis habet.
Neve sequens ætas mendacia credat, olympi
Hâc in nocte illam lambit ab axe jubar.

Lauret. Histor. Torsell. lib. I. cap. 17. Novid. *Fast.* lib. IX.

Indulgence granted after the Miracle of the Flames.
(Page 90.)

URBANUS VI. Pont. Max., quamvis schismate et schismaticorum principum armis atque insidiis exercitus agitatusque, tamen in tanto curarum et negotiorum mole ad Lauretanam Virginem ornandam curæ aliquid derivavit. Nam de *cœlestibus flammis*, V. Idus Septembris, supra ædem Lauretanam spectari solitis, certior factus, cœlesti Reginæ honestandæ animum adjecit, Natalemque Virginis lucem, cœlestibus a Deo prodigiis decoratam, pontificiis a Dei Vicario muneribus decorandam existimavit. Lauretanam igitur domum, ipso Natalis Virginis die, visentibus, cumulatissimam delictorum omnium indulgentiam impertivit.

Vide *Pontifices Maximi Mariani.* A. P. Hippolyto Marraccio, cap. LXVI. *Lauret. Histor.* Torsell. lib. I. cap. 21.

Text of Jerome of Radiolo, A.D. 1473.
(Page 128.)

Unde, et quomodo Ædes S. MARIÆ de Loreto initium sumpserit.

PRIMUM omnium Dei Genitricis Mariæ Templorum, quæ hac nostra tempestate opimis spoliis, coronisque aureis, argenteis, cereisve *

* Legit Martorell. : *cereisve.*

Imaginibus, et compedibus, catenis, aliisque instrumentis ferreis, quibus corpora mortalium excruciantur, ornatur ; quibus Virginis MARIE prodigia mira, et portenta Christianis devotè conspiciuntur, illud, quod vulgato nomine Sancta MARIA de Loreto dicitur, cunctorum assertionibus celeberrimum habetur.   Cujus egregii Templi priusquam initium expediam, pauca supra * repetam, ut omnia magis in aperto sint.   Hanc esse Cameram, seu rectius dicam Thalamum, in quem in Nazareth Galilææ Angelus Gabriel ad Virginem MARIAM de supernis Sedibus missus sit, omnes uno ore autumant, qui Hierusalem Civitatem devotionis gratia adeunt : ceterum voluisse nefanda Barbarorum facinora devitare.   Quæ quidem nutu divino per aerem primum in Pannoniam regionem, quam vernacula lingua Sclavoniam dicunt, mirè delata est. Inde aliquot annos post pari modo, id peccatis eorum exigentibus, in Italiam delata est, eamque Italiæ provinciam tenuit, quæ Ager Picenus dicitur, juxta Urbem, quam accolæ Recanatum dicunt.   Verum cum contines cujusdam agri duorum Fratrum occupasset, ex quo inter illos discordia oborta, quia uterque ad se de jure obligari diceret, ne ex hoc ad conflictum procederent, in iter publicum, ubi nunc ostenditur, sese contulit.   Cujus unde nomen, fama ubique non in Italia tantum, verum in aliis regionibus percrebruit, et si anteà ab ipsà Virgine Maria eo in loco plurima, et egregia prodigia demonstrata sint, tamen quam paucissimis absolverimus. . . †

Hinc itaque templum istud ante celebre, celeberrimum et excelsum prodigiis cœlestibus et regum ac principum donis et muneribus, qui non solùm ex Italia, verum ex universa plaga cœli, ubi Christi Jesu nomen glorificatur et extollitur, multis passim agminibus per omnes vias illuc cum devotione et pompâ favorabili advolant, redditum est.   Additur et miraculum aliud huic ; quod omnibus aspicientibus et stupori est, et admirationi.   Nam cum camera illa, quam suprà diximus, præter naturam per aerem delata, humilis sit et angusta, viri qui illi ædi devotissimè præsunt, eam miram et latam dimetientes hujus cameræ, seu capellæ parietibus hærere voluerunt.   Cæterum quidquid fundamenti, seu murorum jaciebatur, primo mane sequentis diei conspiciebatur dirutum, constratum et æquatum solo.   Cum enim hujus rei fama per urbem, et regiones finitimas manaret, admiratio omnes repentè incessit. Demum secum consultantes utile visum est, procul a thalamo illo gloriosæ Virginis Mariæ parietes et muros latos, et ingentes ædificare. Ad id assensere omnes, et Virgini Mariæ conspicuam, et egregiam ædem dedicaverunt.

Summa aurea de B. V. Maria, t. II. 817.

* Martorell. : *solum.*
† Here follows the account of the Hungarian knight related at page 99, note §.

Testimony of Pilgrims to the Holy Land.
(*Page* 128.)

(1) ANSELM OF POLAND, OBSERVANTINE.—De Zophor ad duas leucas contra austrum est illa gloriosa civitas Nazareth, ubi Flos florum de radice Jesse pullulavit. Hic est locus, ubi Angelus Gabriel nunciavit B. V. Incarnationem Filii Dei: sed illa capella, ut fertur, de illo loco translata est ad Loretum per angelos.

Descriptio Terrae Sanctae, Cracoviae, 1514. Martorell. tom. I. p. 573.

(2) SIR JOHN ZUALLARD.—Poco lontano di li è la Chiesa dell' Annunciazione, che è nel più basso, si discende per 12 scalini etc. li sono i fondamenti della Casa di Gioseffo, nella quale, come si è detto, il Salvatore essendo Fanciullo è stato allevato, e nutrito, e della quale il restante miracolosamente per gl'Angeli è stato trasportato in Christianità, ed al presente in Italia nella città chiamata S. Maria di Loreto, luogo veramente devotissimo, illustre, e risplendente, che merita (siccome in effetto è) di essere visitato da tutte le parti del mondo.

Viaggio a Gerusalemme, Roma, 1586. Vide Martorell. tom. I. p. 584.

(3) ANDRICOMIUS.—Porro quod ad sacrum angelicae salutationis domicilium attinet, id cum multo tempore hic frequentatum et in honore habitum fuisset, Palaestina Christianam religionem repudiante, ab angelis admiranda ratione Flumen, quod Illyrii oppidum fuit, delatum est. Verum cum incolae nullam pretiosissimi thesauri rationem duxissent, tanquam indignis possessoribus ereptum est, ac eorumdem angelorum opera, trans mare per aera vectum, in nobilis cujusdam feminae (a qua nomen Lauretanum hodieque retinet) silva in agro Piceno, seu, ut Itali vocant, Recanatensi collocatum est. . . . . Quapropter inde jam quarto in viam publicam Recanati translatum est, ac ibi sedem stabilem et quietam recepit. Quam vero admiranda, quamque multa beneficia homines ibi consequantur, declarant locus ipse et templum, quo quatuor tantum muris sine fundamento admirabiliter consistentem aediculam cinxerunt etc.

Theatrum Terrae Sanctae. In tribu Zabulon, num. 73.

Summa aurea de B. V. Maria tom. II. 780.

(4) STEFANO MONDEGAZZA.—In quel luogo dove abbiamo accennato esservi le due Colonne, e dove altre volte era la Casa del S. Patriarca Giosef, (avanti, che dalli Angeli fosse trasportata dove al presente si ritrova) sono i fondamenti di detta Casa, che già tant'anni sono a Loreto si trova.

Relazione tripartita del Viaggio di Gerusalemme, lib. 2, cap. 65. Vide Martorelli, tom. I. 572.

(5) JOHN OF CARTHAGE, COMMISSARY OF THE HOLY LAND.—Hoc sacellum a Nazareth civitate, relictis fundamentis, avulsum et elevatum, eo jubente, qui solus facit mirabilia magna, in cujus potestate cuncta sunt posita, Angelorum ministerio ad Dalmatiam, seu ad Illyricos propè oppidum

H H

Tersactum, et propè oppidum Flumen delatum fuit, suo, ut olim, cæmento, lapideaque structura cohærens, quatuorque adhuc parietibus constans, deindè illinc abreptum miro modo super æquora eodem angelico ministerio, primum in nemore, mox in colle fratrum, et tandem in via publica collocatum est in agro Piceno, sive, ut Itali loquuntur, Recanatensi, etc.

Homil. 3, lib. 5. Roma, 1611. Martorelli, tom. I. 575.

(6) QUARESMIUS, COMMISSARY OF THE HOLY LAND.—In poenam iniquissimorum hominum desolatum hoc illutrissimum templum Annuntiationis B. Virginis, et sacra aedes indè mirabiliter sublata est, et ad oras fidelium translata.

Elucidatio Terrae Sanctae, tom. II. cap. 3. Anv. 1639.

Text of Il Teramano.
(Page 131.)

ECCLESIA Beatæ Mariæ de Loreto fuit camera domus Beatæ Virginis Mariæ Matris Domini nostri Jesu Christi: quæ domus fuit in partibus Hierusalem Judaeæ et in civitate Galilææ, cui nomen Nazareth. Et in dicta camera fuit Beata Virgo Maria nata, et ibi educata, et postea ab angelo Gabriele salutata: et postea in dicta camera nutrivit Filium suum Jesum Christum usque quo pervenit ad ætatem duodecim annorum. Demùm post ascensionem Domini nostri Jesu Christi in cœlum, remansit Beata Virgo Maria in terrâ cum apostolis, et aliis discipulis Christi: qui videntes multa misteria divina fuisse facta in dicta camera decreverunt de communi consensu omnium, de dicta camera facere unam Ecclesiam in honorem et memoriam B. Virginis Mariæ: et ità factum fuit. Et deindè apostoli, et discipuli illam cameram consecraverunt in Ecclesiam, et ibi celebraverunt divina Officia. Et Beatus Lucas Evangelista cum suis manibus fecit ibi unam Imaginem ad similitudinem Beatæ Virginis Mariæ: quæ ibi est usque hodiè. Demùm dicta Ecclesia fuit habitata, et honorata cum magna devotione, et reverentia ab illo populo christiano, qui erat in illis partibus, in quibus stetit dicta Ecclesia, quousque ille populus fuit christianus; sed postquam ille populus dimisit fidem Christi, et recepit fidem Mahumeti, tunc Angeli Dei abstulerunt prælibatam Ecclesiam, et portaverunt illam in partes Sclavoniæ, et posuerunt eam ad quoddam castrum, quod vocatur *Flumen,* et ibi minimè honorabatur, ut decebat B. Virginem. Iterum de eodem loco Angeli abstulerunt illam, et portaverunt eam supra mare in partibus territorii Recanati: et posuerunt eam in quamdam silvam, quæ erat cujusdam nobilis Dominæ civitatis Recanatensis, quæ vocabatur Loreta: ex illo tunc accepit ista Ecclesia nomen a Domina, quæ erat illius silvæ domina, et patrona, Sancta Maria de Loreto. In illo tempore, quo ipsa Ecclesia permansit in dicta silva, propter gentium nimium concursum, in ea maxima latrocinia, et innumerabilia mala committebantur. Quapropter per Angelorum manus rursùs assumpta est et portata in montem duorum fratrum, et in eodem monte per Angelorum manus sita est. Qui fratres ob maximum denariorum, et aliarum rerum introitum, et lucrum, simul atque ad invicem ad maximas discordias, et lites venerunt; propter quas pari modo Angeli abstulerunt eam de eodem montis loco, et portaverunt in viam communem, et in eandem illam posuerunt, et firmaverunt eam, ubi est nunc, cum magnis signis, et innumerabilibus gratiis, et miraculis collocata fuit in eadem via ista alma Ecclesia. Tunc igitur totus populus Recanati fuit ad videndam dictam Ecclesiam, quæ erat supra terram sine aliquo fundamento. Propter quod dictus populus considerans tam magnum miraculum, et dubitans ne Ecclesia veniret ad ruinam, fecerunt dictam Ecclesiam circumdari alio muro bono grosso, et optimo fundamento, prout hodiè videtur manifestè. Tamen nullus sciebat undè ista Ecclesia originaliter venerit, nec unde recessisset.

Nota quomodo supradicta sunt scita in anno Domini MCCLXXXXVI., quia Beata Virgo apparuit in somnis cuidam sancto viro ei devoto, cui ipsa supradicta revelavit. Et ipse statim omnia divulgavit quibusdam bonis viris istius provinciæ, et ipsi immediate deliberaverunt velle scire veritatem hujus rei, et sic communicato consilio decreverunt, quod essent sexdecim homines notabiles et boni, qui simul irent ad Sanctum Sepulchrum, et demum ad illas partes de Hierusalem Judææ, et in civitatem Nazareth ad investigandum supradicta inventa: et ita factum est: nam ipsi secum portaverunt mensuram dictæ Ecclesiæ, et ibi vestigia fundamentorum d. Ecclesiæ invenerunt et illam mensuram ad unguem sicut est ista. Et in una pariete ibi prope est scriptum, et sculptum in muro, quomodo ista Ecclesia fuit ibi, et postea recessit. Demum quippe dicti sexdecim viri reversi ad istam provinciam, notificaverunt supradicta inventa per eos esse vera. Et ex tunc fuit scitum, quod dicta Ecclesia fuit camera S. Mariæ Virginis. Et exinde populus Christianus habuit magnam devotionem, et habet: nam omni die ibi Beata Virgo Maria fecit, et facit infinita miracula: prout experientia docet.

Hic fuit unus eremita, qui vocabatur Frater Paulus de Silva: qui habitabat in uno tugurio in silva prope istam Ecclesiam: qui omni mane erat in ista Ecclesia ad officium divinum: et fuit homo magnæ abstinentiæ, et vitæ sanctæ, qui dixit: Jam sunt anni decem, vel circa, quod in die Nativitatis Mariæ, quæ est octava die septembris ante diem per duas horas, stante aeris serenitate, et dicto Fratre Paulo exeunte de suo tugurio, et veniente versus Ecclesiam vidit unum lumen

descendere, de cœlo supra dictam Ecclesiam: quod in longitudine vide-
batur ferè duodecim pedum, et in latitudine fere sex pedum: et cum fuit
illud lumen suprà dictam Ecclesiam, disparuit. Ipse ob eam rem dicebat,
quod fuit Beata Virgo, quæ ibi apparuit in die nativitatis suæ: et hoc
vidit ille sanctus homo.

In quorum omnium fidem, et testimonium, mihi Præposito Teremano, et Gubernatori prænominatæ Ecclesiæ, quidam duo boni viri
prætaxatæ civitatis, hujus villæ inhabitatores retulerunt ac denuncia-
verunt, et pluribus vicibus dixerunt, quorum unus vocabatur Paulus
Renalducii, et alius Franciscus aliàs Prior. Et dictus Paulus dixit
mihi, quod Avus Avi ejus vidit quando Angeli duxerunt prædictam
Ecclesiam per mare et posuerunt illam in dicta silva, et pluribus
vicibus ipse cum ceteris personis ipsam Ecclesiam in prælibata silva
visitavit. Item dictus Franciscus, qui erat centum viginti annorum, dixit
ei, * quod pluribus vicibus visitavit dictam Ecclesiam in eadem silva.
Et pari modo ipse Franciscus retulit, atque dixit mihi per plures vices.
Item hujus rei credulitatem atque certitudinem approbamus: quomodo
ista alma Ecclesia fuit et stetit in dicta silva et pluribus probis personis
dictus Franciscus dixit quod Avus ejus habuit domum, et habitavit
ibi et ejus domus erat penes prædictam ecclesiam et in suo tempore
elevata fuit per Angelos a loco silvæ, et portata in montem dictorum
duorum fratrum, et ibi sita, et collocata fuit, ut dictum est superius.
Deo gratias.

V. Martorelli, *Teatro Istorico*, tom. 1. p. 506.

Text of the Blessed Baptist of Mantua.
(Page 132.)
Redemptoris mundi Matris Ecclesiæ Lauretanæ historia.

CUM nuper venissem ad sanctissimæ Virginis Mariæ sanctum domicilium, vidissemque qualia et quanta Deus ostendit in eo loco miracula, et suæ virtutis, atque clementiæ signa manifestissima, me subito
horror invasit et visus sum audire vocem Domini loquentis ad Mosen:
Non appropinques huc, solve calceamentum de pedibus tuis, locus enim in
quo stas terra sancta est. Sed mox quasi expergefactus, et reminiscens,
Christum in hac mortali vita peccatorum non abhorruisse consortia
quoniam Ipse cognovit figmentum nostrum, et scit, quod pulvis sumus,

* Franciscus autem Prior, *avum suum, cxx. annos natum*, integrisque adhuc
utentem sensibus non semel audierat (ut ipse pro testimonio dixit) cum referret, ab
ꞁe frequenter ad sacram Ædem in sylvam cum aliis itum: eamque sua memoria in
collem duorum fratrum esse translatam. V. *Lauret. Histor.* Torsell. lib. I. cap. 2, 8.

cœpi singula oculis perlustrare ; molem ingentem suscipere, et vota
parietibus affixa perlegere. Et ecce sese mihi offert tabella situ et
vetustate corrosa, in qua, unde et quonam pacto locus ille tantam sibi
vindicasset auctoritatem, conscripta erat historia. Tum fervore pietatis
accensus, ne propter hominum incuriam, quæ præclara omnia solet
obscurare, tam admirabilis rei memoria aboleretur, volui de tabella illa
carie et pulvere jam pene consumpta, rei gestæ seriem colligere. Nec
dubito quin ipsa Dei Genitrix, cui meus peculiariter dedicatus est
ordo, affectum magis, quam effectum inspiciens, studeat apud Filium
mihi veniam impetrare, cum annitar apud homines ejus laudem et
gloriam promulgare. Historia igitur in tabella continebatur hujusmodi ; Templum B. Dei Genitricis Lauretanæ quondam ipsius Virginis cubiculum fuit, in quo nata, nutrita, ab Angelo Gabriele salutata
et Spiritu Sancto fuit obumbrata. In eo Christus conceptus et usque
ad fugam in Ægyptum semper educatus. Erat autem hoc Venerabile,
Sanctumque Cubiculum, cum hæc in eo gesta sunt, in Nazareth
Galilææ civitate vicina Carmelo Heliæ Prophetæ. Post Ascensionem
Christi, Beatissima Virgo præsentia Filii destituta, quoad potuit cum
Apostolis et Christi Discipulis vitam duxit, et cum Joanne præsertim,
cui ob sanguinis conjunctionem, et similitudinem virginitatis specia-
liter fuerat a Christo commendata. Quo tempore Apostoli Cubiculum
ejus, quod in eo fuissent tot consummata mysteria solemni more conse-
crantes, in Domum verterunt orationis, et eam, quæ adhuc superstes
est, Crucem ligneam in Passionis Dominicæ memoriam suis manibus
fabrefactam intulerunt. Imago autem illa, cui tantus honor adhuc exhi-
betur, facta est instar Beatissimæ Virginis artificio Lucæ Evangelistæ
qui fuit ipsæ Virgini familiarissimus, et ab ea magnam eorum partem,
quæ scripsit in Evangelio diligenter intellecta fideliter explicavit. Fuit
Sacellum hoc in summa semper apud Christianos habitum reverentia
usque ad eam tempestatem, qua frigescente jam charitate multorum, et
generis nostri sanctimonia declinante, Terræ Sanctæ loca in Agare-
norum potestatem devenere. Sub Eraclio enim Romanorum Imperatore Cosdras Persarum rex immanissimus terram omnem Promissionis
invasit, et Hierosolyma vastata Lignum S. Crucis in prædam tulit, et
odio Christiani nominis longe lateque debacchatus, Ecclesiam Orientalem
valde debilitavit.

Tunc autem Mahumete invalescente, cœpit Dei Cultus et fides Ortho-
doxa ab Oriente in Occidentem transmigrare, tunc quoque fuit ipsum
Cubiculum Angelorum ministerio relictis fundamentis elevatum, et
ad Illyricos prope Castellum, cui nomen est Flumen, divino judicio
transportatum. Ubi cum forsan ob gentis illius incuriam, vel inscitiam
religiose minus haberetur, cum aliquandiu permansisset iterum trans

Adriaticum Sinum in Agrum Recanatensium, qui olim, ut opinor,
Recinenses appellabantur, divina virtute translatum est et in sylva
nobilis mulieris, cui nomen erat Lauretæ (unde et Sacello cognomen
inditum) est collocatum. Verum cum in ea sylva crebre fierent latrocinia, et plerique eorum qui ad locum illum Religionis gratia conflue-
bant, sicariorum insidiis trucidarentur, ne quod venerat ad salutem
fieret perditionis occasio, Cubiculum idem miro modo de sylva migravit
in vicinum collem duorum fratrum, qui lucrum de Religione sectantes,
cum cœpissent de quæstu Sacelli hujus inter se contendere, causa
fuere, ut Cubiculum de colle prædicto in viam publicam, ubi adhuc
sedit, Angelorum obsequio transferretur. Crescente in dies hujusmodi
transmigrationis (quæ nulla ope humana fieri potuit) et miraculorum
fama celebriore versi erant in stuporem vicini populi, et Recanatenses
præcipue, quos Recinenses, vel Recinates olim appellatos antediximus.
Nam in horum agro situm est Templum, vix tribus passuum millibus
distans a mari. Facto igitur Recanatenses magno hominum conventu,
ut Sacellum sine fundamentis repererunt, his, quæ vulgo de ejus trans-
missione ferebantur, fidem adhibuere et ne unquam collabi posset, muro
firmissimo jactis alte fundamentis circumdedere, qui tamen nunquam,
cum id maxime conarentur ædificantes, antiquo potuit ædificio cohæ-
rere, ne divinæ virtutis opus admirabile mortali observaretur industria.

Anno Christianæ Salutis MCCLXXXXVI., cuidam vitæ innocentissimæ
et puritatis immaculatæ viro, qui in Sacellum hoc studio pietatis assi-
due, die noctuque veniebat, Beatissima Virgo in somnis apparens,
prædicta omnia revelavit, et ut omnibus palam faceret imperavit, quem
ubi nova hæc, et vix auditu credibilia prædicantem audivissent, finitimæ
Urbes, primo deridere, mox ut eadem sæpius affirmantem, et sententia
firmum, nec ulla irrisione commoveri de proposito vident, ad altiorem
inquisitionem veri constantia vehementer animati, sexdecim cordatos viros
dirigunt, qui communibus circum adjacentium regionum impensis mari
longa navigatione transmisso, post Dominici Sepulchri visitationem per-
venerunt in Nazareth, ubi summa cum diligentia, et propter Barbarorum
sævitiam non sine vitæ periculo, fundamentis Cubiculi tandem inventis,
et parietum crassitudine, intercapedine, figura, et structuræ similitudine
manifeste deprenderunt vera esse, quæ de loco sacratissimo per virum
sanctum divulgabantur in patria. Reversi igitur, omnibus quæ solerter
invenerant explicatis, Deo verba eorum credibilia faciente, populos in ea
opinione et fide facile confirmarunt. Hinc factum est, ut non finitimas
tantum, verum etiam longe positas, transmarinas etiam ac transalpinas
nationes ad visendum locum fama perduxerit.

Nemo est enim tam obstinatæ nequitiæ, tam feris moribus, tam indo-
mitis cervicibus, qui si putet fuisse Virginis Immaculatæ Cubiculum ad

ipsum visendum, venerandumque summo non accedat ardore. Ipsa quoque Dei Genitrix, quae suapte natura semper mitissima fuit, et in favorem hominum inclinatissima, facere non potest quin ob Nativitatis quoque suae, et Incarnationis Christi jucundam, dulcemque memoriam digne supplicantibus postulata concedat, cum praesertim ad benefaciendum humano generi amplissimam a Filio potestatem acceperit.

Prope Sacellum istud, dum adhuc erat in sylva Lauretae vir quidem Paulus nomine solitarius mirabilis abstinentiae, orationis assiduae, puritatis angelicae, sub quodam tuguriolo dicitur habitasse, qui dum circa Virginis Nativitatem, sicut quotidie solebat, orationis gratia antelucano tempore veniret ad locum, quotannis decennio vidit lumen instar cometae clarissimae duodecim longitudinis, et sex latitudinis, ut a longe poterat aestimari, pedes habens, è coelo versus Ecclesiam descendere, quod mox ut pervenisset ad Ecclesiam, subtractum ab oculis evanescebat. Quamobrem dicere solitus erat, se putare beatam Virginem, vel Angelum ab ea missum ad Nativitatis suae solemnia quotannis adventare, qui venientes ad Ecclesiam protegeret, et confluentium ea die turbarum preces, et vota Deo praesentaret.

Paulus Rinaldutius Racanatensis perfectae fidei, et singularis prudentiae vir, propinqui vici tunc habitator, Teremano Sacelli hujus Rectori, juramento astrictus constantissimè saepius affirmavit, avum suum dicere solitum, se ab avo suo saepius audivisse, quod oculis ipse suis vidisset Ecclesiam hanc transfretare, et super fluctus marinos in modum navis allabi, ac in terram descendere, et in sylva ipsa se collocare. Eidem rectori Teremano Franciscus Racanatensis cognomento Prior jurejurando adactus retulit se audivisse avum suum, qui centum et viginti annorum erat, dicentem, se pluries d. Ecclesiam in sylva vidisse, introisse, et adorasse, et suo tempore loco mutato in duorum fratrum collem ascendisse, et avum suum praeterea villam habuisse vicinam Ecclesiae dum erat in sylva.

Haec quae suprà diximus omnia, exceptis admodum paucis, quae illustrant et nulla ex parte vitiant historiam ex praedictae tabulae exemplari authentico, cui fidem adhibere necesse est, decimo kal. octobris anno MCCCCLXXXIX., servata scripturae veritate transsumpta sunt.

Bapt. Mant. Vide Martorelli, tom. I. p. 510.

DE DOMO LAURETANA CARMEN. *(Bapt. Mant.)*

Vastus ab Arcturi plaustro decurrit ad austrum
Adria: et aggeribus dextra levaque superbis
Cingitur etc.
Ora levans circumque ferens Antonius altos
Per maria et montes oculos, in colle supino

Prospicit albentes muros, turrimque minantem
Pyramide in Cœlum, missoque in Sydera Cono.
Atque ait, o Rector, quænam hæc in collibus altis
Italiæ moles aspectu læta decoro ?
Quidquid id est, præclari aliquid promittit Imago.
Tunc Rector, quod cernis, ait, Picentia juxtà
Littora, delubrum est illud venerabile magnæ
Matris, ab Assyriis, quod Dii super æquora quondam
Hùc manibus vexere suis : visa ire per undas
Hæc (res mira) Domus, visi ire per æquora Divi.
Nam Divum Regina Arabiæ offensa Tyrannis,
Qui temere Assyriam sese effudere per omnem,
Jussit,* et huc voluit secum migrare penates,
Quotquot ab Assyriis hæc usque ad littora pontum
Juxta habitant, fecere fidem, Pamphylia jurat
Se vidisse, Cilix, Lycius, Minoja tellus :
Tænarus affirmat : Delphino, et Arione vecto
Tænarus insignis : facti meminisse fatentur
Arcades, Ætoli : scopulis Epirus ab altis
Ad mare tota ruit : thalamo fuit hospita sancto
Illyris. Illyricos primum divertit in agros,
Sed pertæsa locos parvo post tempore rursum
Prodigio grandi volitans de Littore in undas
Italiam versus gressum aspirantibus curis
Vertit, et ut tetigit terras, sublimis in auram
Exsiliens (vidit Picens miracula, et Umber)
Hos tenuit Colles, illaque resedit in arce,
Et quia transvectam mulier Laureta recepit
Virginis Ædiculam, præbens ubi sisteret agrum,
Lauretæ delubra vocant. Neu crede superbam
Hanc ædem venisse fretis : superaddidit ista
Templa Sacerdotum Princeps ingentia Paulus,
At breve sublimi latet hac sub mole Sacellum,
Quod fugat infernos manes, quod discutit omne
Morborum genus : extremis venit unde periclis
Auxilium, seu sors terra, seu sæviat alto.
Huc Itali, Siculique ferunt solemnia vota.
Huc fluit Epirus, fluit Illyris, accola Rheni,
Accola Danubii. Venit usque a littore Narbo
Galliæ, et Isthmiacæ Spartanus ab æquore terræ :

* Legit Trombell. : *Fugit.*

Tanta fides nunquàm Delphis : et Jupiter Hammon,
Et Claros, et Delos longe minor : omnia vincit
Quotquot erant olim veterum delubra Deorum.
Diva Parens magnum partu connixa Tonantem
Virgineo, quæ sceptra tenes fulgentis Olympi,
Audieram : nam Terrarum fama amplior Orbe est.
His tibi sacra locis immania surgere Templa
Quæ veneror : quæ si dederis me ad nostra reverti
Littora cum Sociis multo cum munere visam.
Audieram, voluique aliquando accedere motus
Majestate loci. Verum in discrimine rerum
Magno incertarum posito vota irrita fecit
Aspera sors, quæ me in ventos, et in æquora misit.
Salve Sancta Domus lactenti conscia Christo,
Conscia Divorum operum, Domus hospita Divum.
Da facilem, da Sancta Parens ad littora cursum
Thracia ; da placidos reditus huc ad tua rursus
Limina, et Italiæ fer opem Regina jacenti.
Talia finierat, cum mox longinqua Truenti
Hostia prospectant, ubi se Samnitica jungunt
Littora Picenis, leva procul albicat Aulon.
Velaque rara vident niveas referentia nubes
Scindere iter liquidum : e vento contraria eodem
Littora, et oppositos serpendo inquirere portus.

F. Baptistæ Mantuani Carmelitæ, Theologi, Poetæ, etc. Operum ejus
tom. primo in Poemata Angelariorum, etc., lib. sexto.
Vide Martorelli, tom. I. p. 515.

Historia Lauretana Hieronymi Angelitæ.
(Page 132.)

ID quod a Domino factum est, et est mirabile in oculis nostris, ut
scilicet, cubiculum idem illud, quo Virgo in parens unica in lucem
edita, educata, in quo ab Angelo salutata, quod fuerat olim in paternis
Domibus, Nazareæ Civitatis Galilææ, nunc in agro hoc Rachanatensi
ex omni natione delecto, miro modo transvectum super æquora, con-
sideat. Cujus rem seriem, et si priscorum morem imitari Rachanatenses,
tenui quo datum est eo tempore, Artificis penicillo, id novo cubiculi
pariete coloribus exprimendam curassent primum. Mox ejus cubiculi
antistes (diminute quidem) annotasset in tabella, nunc vetustate pene

I I

et carie consumpta, cujus exemplum impressoribus traditum, formis excusum, passim circumfertur, etc.

Vide Martorelli, tom. I. pp. 517, 518.

Text of the Relation attributed to the Blessed Peter Compagnoni, Bishop of Macerata.

(Page 139.)

TRA gli altri luoghi della Cristianita, che sogliono essere da Pellegrini con grande religione visitati, è molto principale e di singolare venerazione la Santa Casa di Loreto nella Marca di Ancona ne confini del territorio della città di Recanati, la quale è la medesima camera, dove la santissima Vergine Maria Madre di Dio, e Signora nostra nacque, e fù annunziata dal Angelo Gabriele, et dove si incarnò il Verbo Divino nel suo Virginal ventre, e dove abitò la maggior parte della sua santissima vita : e questo si sa per diverse informazioni autentiche scritte sopra ciò con molta diligenza. Il modo come questa santa Camera fù miracolosamente trasportata in questo luogo, fù questo. Considerando li santi Apostoli dopo l'Ascensione di Cristo Redentor Nostro, quanto era la dignità, e santità di questa Beata Casa, li parve cosa giusta dedicarla al culto Divino, e cosi la consecrarono per un Tempio, o Cappella, dove l'Apostolo S. Pietro, e gli altri Apostoli alcuna volta celebrarono, e poi li successori loro fecero il medesimo : et il Populo Cristiano, che in quelle parti si trovava, concorreva con gran divozione a questo santo luogo a Divini officii, che in essa si celebravano, et quanto più cresceva il Populo Cristiano, tanto più cresceva la divozione di questo santo luogo et il desiderio, e fervore, con che da lontan paese venivano a visitarlo, e onorarlo. Questo durò per longo tempo infino a tanto, che succedendo da poi per li peccati nostri le perfidie della setta Maomettana, ed altri diversi errori, eresie, guerre, e dissensioni, che abbondavano nel Mondo, et specialmente nelle parti di Oriente, mancando il fervore, e devozione, che prima era, ed essendo pericolo, che questa Santa Casa venisse ad essere profanata, volse l'Onnipotente Dio riservarla, ordinando che per ministero degli Angioli fosse trasferita alle parti di Dalmazia, o Schiavonia presso una città, che si chiama *Fiume*. Questo fù ed avvenne nel tempo del imperatore Astolfo* e di Papa Niccolò IV. Nel anno del Signore 1291 e non sapendo gli abitatori di quelle Terre vicine d'onde, ne come quel sacro tesoro fosse venuto nel loro Paese, ne anche che causa fosse, volse Iddio, che si fosse verificato per rivelazione fatta al Paroco Alessandro, al

* Adolfo.

quale una notte apparve la SS. Vergine, e li manifestò il mistero di Santissima Casa, ottenendoli sanità d'un infermità, che pativa questo Rettore. Poi con molta allegrezza detto sacerdote notificò alli Popoli di quella Provincia, ed al Vice Rè loro, chiamato Nicolò Francesco Frangipane quello gli era avvenuto, e questo Principe ordinò, che alcuni andassero a Nazareth per meglio informarsi della verità, e tra loro andò questo medesimo Paroco Alessandro portando la misure della Santa Cappella, le quali trovarono poi, che pareggiavano col luogo, che restò vuoto in Nazareth donde fù levata, ed informati di ogni cosa tornarono al loro Paese, dove diedero piena informazione della verità conosciuta, e questa fù la causa, che tanto più crescesse la divozione, e venerazione di quella Santa Cappella, massime con li molti, e grandi miracoli, che si degnò fare Iddio Nostro Signore, in testimonio di questa verità. Ma questo li durò pochi anni; imperciochè o per mancar la divozione o per divino giudizio, nel anno 1294 o 1295 fu loro tolto questo prezioso tesoro, e per il medesimo ordine, e ministero Angelico, fu trasferita in Italia, nella Marca d'Ancona prima in una selva di Loreto, dalla quale pigliò il nome, che ancora tiene, di poi ad un monticello di là discoto un miglio, che era di due Fratelli di Recanati, e finalmente per gli inconvenienti, che nell' una, e nell' altra parte successero, fù per il medesimo ordine e ministero collocata nella via publica, che và da Recanati al porto; dove al presente si ritrova, e tutto questo si sa per tradizioni antiche di testimoni degni di fede, li quali di mano in mano tutto, ciò hanno testificato; ne accade dubitar punto di questa verità ricevuta, ed accettata dal consenso di tutti: e massime essendo confermata con tanti e sì stupendi miracoli, e col continuo universale concorso da tutte le parti della Cristianita, che vengano a visitarla.

O Beatissima Cappella picciola sì, e povera agli occhi carnali, ma alli spirituali piu ricca, e preziosa che li Palazzi, e Tempio de Salomone.

O degnissima Camera, dove fù riposto il maggior Tesoro, che mai nel Mondo fù ne sara trovato.

O sacratissime Mura alle quali tante volte si appoggiarono le membre Santissime del Figliuolo, e della Madre. O felice camino bastante ad infiammore li cuori degl'Uomini, che contemplino come piu volte fù fatto fuoco per le mani Verginali, e dove più volte si riscaldarono le tenere membra del fanciullo Gesù.

O Pietre, e Mattoni più preziose, che le Perle Orientali, le quali tante volte foste percosse dal suono delle parole, con le quali il Figliolo parlava alla Madre, ed essa graziosamente li rispondeva.

O Santuario Divino, dove piamente se crede, che tante orazioni del Figliolo si mandavano al suo celestiale Padre, e dove tanti sospiri, e gemiti, e pietose lagrime cosi della Madre come del Figliolo furono sparse per la salute de'peccatori.

V. *Teatro Istorico della Santa Casa*, Martorelli, tom. I. p. 503.

Text of the Letter attributed to the Magistrates of Recanati.
(Page 140.)

In Dei nomine. Amen.

PRIORES communitatis Recanati communione * tibi factâ Magnifico Alexandro Q. Antonii de Servandis oratori nostro dilecto, et honorando civi nostro. Postquam Romam perveneris cum salute, loqueris cum Magnifico nostro honorando agente, et simul quam primum ibis nomine istius civitatis antè suam Beatitudinem, repraesentando Ei nostras litteras testimoniales, quae tibi datae fuerunt à nobis, et factis debitis reverentiis, humiliter Ipsius pedes deosculando, et dando Ei notitiam quomodo diebus praeteritis Sancta Domus a situ nemoris miraculose translata fuit ad collem Magnificorum Simeonis et Stephani Rinaldis de Antiquis, nostrorum honorandorum civium, et deindè pete gratiam ab Ipsa, quod dictus collis, et situs pertinent et debeatur nostro publico, ut possit ibi aedificare propter commoditatem populi devoti, qui quotidiè venit ad visitandam illam, et quod data bona possint impendi in beneficium fabricae; tantò magis quod inter dictos fratres non est concordia, secundum attestationes tibi datas, et praesentabis illud ampliùs quod tibi ore significatum est, ut talem gratiam obtineas. Operaberis tamen totum cum intercessione D. cardinalis nostri benevoli, quòd jam tibi datae fuerunt litterae credulitatis, et negotiaberis ità ut fratres praefati non sint informati de hoc negotio; et Deus mittat et remittat te salvum. Recanati, 9 Septembre 1295.

FRANCISCUS PANTA, *Cancellarius*.

Vide *Summa Aurea de B. V. Maria*, tom. II. 803.

Text of the Letter attributed to Paul della Selva.
(Page 141.)

REX ob satisfaciendum tuæ piæ curiositati, quæ mihi commisit narrationem magni miraculi de Translatione Virgineæ Domus facta per Angelos ad oram Italiæ in Piceni Provincia in Territorio Recanati inter

* Legit Montanus : *commissione*.

flumina Aspidis, seu Muscionis, et Potentie, res ita successit, prout sepius
ego audivi a viris fide dignis ipsius Recanati, scilicet a Francisco Petro
Canonico Recanatensi, et Uguccione Clerico exemplari, et etiam ab
eximiis legum Doctoribus Cisco de Cischis, et Francisco Percivallino de
Recanato, qui omnes cum aliis multis popularibus, cum quibus habui
discursum, vivebant tempore miraculi, quod quoque in publicis Codicibus
attentè legi. Anno ab Incarnato Domino Jesu MCCLXXXXIV. die Sabbati x.
decembris, *dum medium silentium tenerent omnia, et nox in suo cursu
medium iter haberet, lux de Cœlo circumfulsit* oculos multorum commo-
rantium prope littus maris Adriatici, et dulcisona canentium armonia
somnolentos, et pigros traxit ad videndum prodigium, et rem supra
naturam. Viderunt igitur, et conspexerunt Domum circumfusam magnis
splendoribus ab Angelis sustentatam, et per aerem deportatam. Steterunt
villici, et pastores, et obstupuerunt admirantes rem tam grandem, et proni
ceciderunt, et adoraverunt eam, expectantes videre finem, et exitum adeo
stupendum; interim sacra illa Domus ab Angelis portata in medio magni
nemoris posita fuit, et ipsimet arbores se inclinantes adorabant Reginam
celorum, et usque nunc conspiciuntur proni, et recurvati, quasi *exultantes
ligna silvarum.* In hoc loco fama extat fuisse templum dicatum cuidam
false deitati lauris multis recinctum, et ideo locus hic Lauretum usque
nunc vocatur. Interim vix mane facto rustici nuncii velociter perrexerunt
Recanatum, et narraverunt que facta sunt, et omnis populus ad nemus
Laureti iter arripuit, et vidit que audivit. Aliqui ergo de nobilibus, et alii
de populo partim obstupefacti mutescebant, partim non credebant miraculum,
meliores pro letitia lugentes cum Profeta dixerunt: *Invenimus eam
in campis silve; et non fecit taliter omni nationi:* et colentes illam
sanctam Domunculam, et devotè intrantes, simulacrum ligneum dive
Virginis MARIE sanctum Filium amplexantis adoraverunt. Igitur
redierunt Recanatum, quod magna letitia impleverunt, unde populus
sepe sepius ibat, et redibat circumfluens ad adorationem illius sancte
Domuncule, et Beata MARIA continua prodigia, et miracula faciebat.
Fama tam magni miraculi ad viciniores, et longinquiores partes por-
rexit, et omnes currebant ad silvam lauriferam, que populata fuit variis
habituris ligneis, ut peregrini devoti hospitium haberent. Dum hec
fierent, quia semper infernalis leo *circuit querens quem devoret,* predones
et impii ab isto moti sacram illam silvam latrociniis, et homicidiis
fedabant, ita ut devotio multorum tepesceret timore latronum. Post
menses octo novo miraculo fuit confirmatum novum prodigium. Sacra
enim Domuncula reliquit silvam profanatam, et in medio collis duorum
nobilium fratrum comitis Stephani, et Simonis Rainaldi Antiqui de
Recanato collocata fuit ministerio Angelorum. Interim crescebat devotio
fidelium, et magnis donis, et muneribus augebatur sacra Domuncula, et

nobiles, et devoti fratres custodiebant, sed declinaverunt post avaritiam, acceperunt munera, et perverterunt judicium, et statim facta est contentio inter eos, quis eorum videretur esse major. Discessit ergo sacra Domus post quatuor menses a colle duorum fratrum, et tertio miraculo Angeli asportaverunt eam in situ novo distante quantum est jactus lapidis in media via publica, per quam itur Recanato ad littus maris, et ibi etiam hodie video existentem, et propriis oculis cerno continuas gratias poscentibus facientem.

Quamquam vero celestia prodigia autenticabant hoc tugurium pro Domo Matris Dei, ubi *Verbum Caro factum est*, attamen ad veritatem inveniendam, facto prius generali parlamento Recanati, ubi intervenerunt proceres totius provincie, fuit decretatum transmittere sexdecim illustriores viros ad uniformandas mensuras ipsius sancte Domus tam in vestigiis Tersacti, quam Nazareth, ubi prius fuit edificata, et per longum tempus extitit.

Que decretata fuere, facta sunt, nam ex numero sexdecim, Legati fuerunt pro Recanato scilicet Quarterii Sancte Marie, Politus comitis Martii de Politis. Quarterii Sancte Flaviani Marchio juvenis comes Matheus comitis Simonis Rainaldi de Antiquis. Quarterii Sancti Angeli preclarus Legum Doctor Cicottus Monaldutii de Monaldutiis, qui cum aliis colleghis abierunt, viserunt, redierunt, et omnia esse conformia tam ratione mensure, quam testium ab ipsis auditorum in illis partibus asseruerunt.

Hec pauca, o Rex, libenter accipe in testimonium Domus miraculose, et meo erga te observantie, et ut certus sis huc pervenisse tuam pecuniam in eleemosinam transmissam, certiorem facio illam recepisse, et tu in celis recipies mercedem. In Nomine Patris, et Filii, et Spiritus Sancti, Amen. Apud Sanctam Domum anno Domini MCCLXXXXVII., die octava Junii.

PAULUS SERVUS JESU CHRISTI.

POPULI PRIORES CIVITATIS RECANATI.

Omnibus notum facimus, et attestamur omnia narrata esse vera, et concordare cum nostris annalibus, et scripturis publicis, in quorum testimonium, et fidem has nostro sigillo mandavimus sugellari, et subscribi a nostro publico Imperiali auctoritate Notario, et Magistro nostrum Actorum hac die XII. Junii anno a Circumcisione Domini Nostri Jesu Christi MCCLXXXXVII.*

FRANCISCUS JACOBI, *Magister Actorum.*

* Vide Martorelli, tom. I. p. 500.

Inscription on the Tomb of Cardinal Cajetan.

(Having omitted to call attention to this monument in Part VII., we may mention here that it is on the south side of the Choir, and that the bronze figure of this celebrated Cardinal is by Antonio Calcagni.)

HIC HABITABO, QUONIAM ELEGI EAM.

NICOLAUS Gaetanus cardinalis Sermoneta, gentilis Papæ Bonifacii VIII., cùm sub id tempus quo ille pontificatum iniit sanctam hanc Domum hic tandem divinitùs consedisse, et multa se à Deo Opt. Max. Beatæ Virginis Deiparæ precibus obtinuisse meminisset, sperans ejusdem opem morienti non defuturam, monumentum hoc marmoreum vivens et incolumis sibi faciendum curavit, atque in eo, ubi mortalitatem exuisset, corpus suum recondi voluit, an. agens LIV. Obiit annos natus ferme LX., an. Sal. hum. MDLXXXV. mense maio.

Torsell. *Hist. Lauret.* lib. V. cap. 7.

Donation of Gualfiero.
(Page 237.)

CONCESSIO quam fecit Gualferius filius q. Ugoni Firman. Ecclesiæ. In nomine Domini Dei salvatoris nostri Jesu Christi. Amen.

Anni sunt millesimo sexagesimo secundo, et infra mense martio pro indictione quintadecima. Firmo.

Quoniam profiteor me ego Gualferio filio q. Ugoni hodierna die cogitante me, etc.... Do vendo dono trado atque concedo in ipso episcopatu Firmano et tibi Domino Ulderico Episcopo vel a posteris successoribus usque in perpetuum possidendam rem juris mei quæ mihi advenit de jure parentum aut de meo conquisito, idest medietatem de ipso castello de Laccio cum portis et carvonarie et cum introitu et exitu suo quantum ad ipsam medietatem pertinet vel pertinere videtur et cum medietate de ipso castello.... Cum omni ædificio quantum ad ipsam medietatem pertinet et pertinere debet, et in fundo *Umbremano* et in fundo *Passeriano* quæ est infra ministerio di S. Elpidio magiore ubicumque mihi pertinet, et medietatem de ipso castello de Loreto cum partis et carvonarie et cum clusimine et cum introitu et exitu suo quantum ad ipsum castellum de Loreto pertinet et quantumque mihi pertinet.

Et habet fines : da Capo via quæ venit de Asula et vadit ad Montem Causarum et pergit in flumine Clenti et in Collemardo et pergit in Eta morta et vadit in sancto Elpidio majore et per ipsam viam quæ vadit in Tenna, et quomodo pergit sub montem *sancto Savino* et vadit in leto vivo et pergit in Eta et vadit in sancto Elpidio et pergit de *Tonquenna* et vadit in trivio de Cuti, et pergit in trivio de *Brasciano*, a pede fino pelago maris.

Ab uno latere medio rigo de Asula qui pergit in mare, ab alio lato rigo de Brasciano quomodo pergit in mare.

Catalani, ad annum 1062, p. 325

Donation of the Countess Gaeta.
(Page 237.)

ACTIUS qui et Azo et Actiolinus ac semel etiam Massius dictus est, anno MLXXXIX. ut diximus pontificatum auspicatus est...

E multis donationibus quae ecclesiae Firmanae, Actio sedente, factae sunt, unam et alteram commemorare satis est. "Gaeta comitissa, Bambonis filia, et Ugonis comitis vidua, consentiente Gozone filio in cujus mandurio erat, donavit in Ecclesia S. Mariae, ac Azoni venerabili Pontifici medietatem de curte Paradiso et *Umbremano*, et universam suam proprietatem, excepta Curte de Loreto. Fines erant mare, flumina Aso et Potentia. Exaratae sunt tabulae anno MXCIV, quas vero mox asseram in sequentem annum respiciunt...

Catalani, ad annum 1089, p. 128.

Donation of the Bishop of Humana to the Camalduli.
(Page 238.)

IN Dei nomine : Anni sunt ab incarnatione Domini N. J. C. MCLXXXXIII, die intrante Januar. indict. XII, domno Celestino papa sedente in sede Beati Petri apostoli, et regnante Henrigo imperatore Fredericis imperatoris filio anno ejus imperii III.

Nos quidem Jordanus Humanensis ecclesiae episcopus, una cum voluntate et consensu canonicorum meorum q. praeordinati sunt in nostra ecclesia intuitu pietatis ... et religionis et pro redemptione nostrorum peccatorum necnon et predecessorum ... tradimus et cedimus et per transactum concedimus in perpetuum in eremo sanctae crucis fontis Avellanae, et tibi domno Marco venerabili priori et toti vestro conventui et vestris successoribus, et per manus domni Rainerii q. est praepositus et rector ecclesiae S. Mariae de Recaneto, quae est edificata in fundo Rasenano, q. Antiniano vocatur, idemque damus et concedimus ipsam ecclesiam S. Mariae qua exitu in fundo Laureti, totam cum omnibus suis dotibus et pertinentiis, et cum libris et calicis et campanis et paramentis et cum cellis et cum circuitu et parochianis cum terris et vineis et olivis et ficis et salicis et cum molendinis et aquis aequimolis cum pratis et pascuis et herbis et cum omnibus suis pertinentiis et cum omnibus suis actionibus et rationibus quae ad ipsam ecclesiam pertinent vel pertinere debent de jure vel usu. Ita a die presenti tu ... una cum tuis successoribus habeatis teneatis possideatis usufruatis praedictam ecclesiam cum omnibus suis possessionibus et pertinentiis et in perpetuum possidendo tenendo et exfructuando et quidquid vobis placuerit faciatis.

Et ego Jordanus Humanensis episcopus una cum canonicis meis promittimus per nos et per nostros successores vobis domno Marco priori et toto vestro conventui et omnibus vestris successoribus ipsam dationem et concessionem semper firmam et ratam habere et tenere et nunquam retractare et nullam quaestionem vobis facere, sed semper stare et defensare et bonam facere et auctorizare vobis promittimus per me et meos successores contra omnes personas hominum. Quod si defendere noluerimus aut non potuerimus aut hanc concessionis chartam irritare, corrumpere vel falsare voluerimus, vel si dolo malo ingenio cuncta quae superius leguntur non observaverimus, tum obligo me Jordanus episcopus una cum canonicis meis meosque successores vobis supradicto priori vestrisque successoribus pene nomine libras lucenses c, et post pena data et soluta cartula ista donationis, cessionis et concessionis semper firma permaneat sicut superius legitur.

Dominus Jordanus, Humanensis ecclesiae episcopus hanc cartulam fieri precepit.

Matthaeus archidiaconus in hac cartula consensit.

Marcus archipresbiter in hac cartula consensit.

Sanguineus canonicus in hac cartula consensit.

Goffredus canonicus in hac cartula consensit.

Nicolaus canonicus in hac cartula consensit.

Rainaldus canonicus in hac cartula consensit.

Domnus Angelus plebanus Gardeti in hac cartula consensit.

Petrus Stefani de hac cessione et concessione fuit investitor et testis.

Acto Stefonis (sic) Becti. Acto postere ab ipso episcopo et a canonicis rogati fuerunt testes.

Ego Acto notarius precepto ipsius episcopi et rogatu et ab ipsis canonicis hanc cartulam scripsi.

Annales Camaldulenses, tom. IX.; *Summa aurea de B. V. Maria*, tom. II. 785.

Decretum.

(Page 200.)

ETSI altitudinem divitiarum Sapientiæ et Providentiæ Numinis Æterni, cujus judicia sunt incomprehensibilia, et viæ investigabiles, nos homines infirmi et lutea vasa portantes nec cernere nec intelligere quidem possumus, attamen opera excelsa et mirabilia, quæ præ oculis nostris Deus patravit in hac terra peregrinationis, si ea devoto et humili intuitu animadvertamus, non solum admiratione, verum etiam grati animi sensu afficimur in Auctorem Supremum, ac Ipsum quantum in nobis est, Ejusque opera mirifica summis laudibus extollere nitimur. Inter hæc, si mentis aciem convertamus ad mysticam Arcam fœderis, quæ intra parietes hujus augustissimi Templi Lauretani asservatur et colitur, quisnam obsistere poterit, si nos maxima admiratione et pari devotione commoti fateamur, ac gestientes exclamemus, quod Deus non fecit taliter omni nationi, qualiter Italicæ Genti, ac præsertim Picentibus, quum in Agro Recinetensi, hodie Loreto, divinitus sex abhinc sæculis apparuerit sacra Domus Nazarethica, quæ altissimorum mysteriorum memoria commendatur, et quotidiana mortalium frequentia ac religione celebratur?

Quamobrem nos considerantes et animo volventes quæ in Ecclesia Catholica gesta fuerunt, hodieque amplius geruntur ad majorem Dei gloriam et salutem animarum procurandam per institutionem plurium piorum conventuum Christifidelium, qui enixe incumbunt devotioni erga beatissimam Virginem Mariam Genitricem Dei et Matrem nostram amantissimam sub variis titulis gloriosis Eidem rite adtributis; Nos ipsi pro viribus nostris consilium cepimus magis magisque venerationem et cultum adaugendi erga ipsam Deiparam in hac sua sacratissima Domo Lauretana.

Igitur ut consilium nostrum, Deo favente, ac eadem Virgine opitulante perficiatur: ut idem cultus, qui jam universalis dici potest, in dies magis extendatur et cumuletur, Nos per hasce litteras instituimus atque erigimus pium Comitatum, seu piam unionem, aut melius Congregationem Universalem Sanctæ Domus Lauretanæ, eamque canonice erectam et institutam declaramus, cui quilibet de populo Christiano huc certatim affluentes proprium nomen dare possint tamquam devotionis tesseram ob mysteria, quæ in prælaudato habitaculo cœlesti completa fuerunt. Et revera Regina Virginum in eo fuit ab Angelo salutata Mater Salvatoris mundi, ibique *Verbum Caro factum est.* Ibi vixit cum ejus purissimo Sponso Josepho et cum vera vita Jesu, qui ex materno domicilio dictus fuit Nazarenus.

Hinc proponimus Exercitia (vulgo *Pratiche*) observanda a novis Congregatis, quo bonis spiritualibus fruantur. Ut vero indulgentiis jam adnexis uberiores fructus et favores spirituales accedant, nostrum erit humillime ab Apostolica Sede postulare, ut amplioribus facultatibus donemur ad opus.

Praeterea hortamur cunctos Christifideles tam Laureti degentes quam advenas, ut alacri ac devoto animo dent propria nomina in apposito Cathalogo, qui patebit cura RR. PP. Capuccinorum huic Almae Domui inservientium.

Denique omnibus innotescat quatenus confirmatio Moderatoris Generalis novae Congregationis reservatur nobis et successoribus nostris. Hodie vero declaramus ac dicimus Moderatorem Generalem Reverendum Patrem Petrum Mariam à Màlacha Sacerdotem ejusdem Ordinis S. Francisci MM. Capuccinorum.

Haec omnia decrevimus atque decernimus auctoritate nostra ordinaria, fidentes maxime in auxilio divino, et in speciali patrocinio Immaculatae Virginis, suique Sponsi Beati Josephi.

Datum Laureti die 27 Maii 1883.

✠ Thomas Episcopus Lauretanus et Recinetensis.

QUID QUÆRIS ORDINEM FACTI, UBI TOTA RATIO FACIENDI EST VOLUNTAS ET POTENTIA FACIENTIS ?—*S. Augustin.*

Quis enim cognovit sensum Domini aut quis consiliarius ejus fuit ? —*S. Paul. ad Rom.* xi. 34.

Juxta voluntatem suam facit, tam in virtutibus cœli quam in habitatoribus terræ: et non est qui resistat manui ejus, et dicat ei : Quare fecisti ?—*Daniel* iv. 32.

Tu vero, O Diva Thaumaturga, hostibus tuis spontaneam cæcitatis larvam detrahe, ut veritatis radios aspiciant, et tua nobiscum admiranda suscipiant, resipiscant, teque tuumque Filium, in hac sacra Lauretana Domo unice colant, adorent, venerentur. Amen. (Glavanich.)

THE END.

www.ingramcontent.com/pod-product-compliance
Lightning Source LLC
Chambersburg PA
CBHW030628030726
47497CB00006B/1693